THE ART OF INSUBORDINATION

HOW TO DISSENT & DEFY EFFECTIVELY

TODD B. KASHDAN, PhD

AVERY
an imprint of Penguin Random House
New York

an imprint of Penguin Random House LLC
penguinrandomhouse.com

Library of Congress Cataloging-in-Publication Data

Names: Kashdan, Todd B., author.
Title: The art of insubordination: how to dissent and defy effectively / by Todd B. Kashdan, PhD
Description: New York: Avery, [2021] | Includes bibliographical references.
Identifiers: LCCN 2021017338 (print) | LCCN 2021017339 (ebook) | ISBN 9780593420881 (hardcover) | ISBN 9780593420898 (ebook)
Subjects: LCSH: Conformity. | Dissenters. | Creative thinking. | Diffusion of innovations. | Persuasion (Psychology). | Interpersonal communication.
Classification: LCC HM1246 .K38 2021 (print) | LCC HM1246 (ebook) | DDC 303.3/2—dc23
LC record available at https://lccn.loc.gov/2021017338
LC ebook record available at https://lccn.loc.gov/2021017339

Printed in the United States of America
1st Printing

Book design by Silverglass Studio

To my three daughters, Raven, Chloe, and Violet.

My hope is you are empowered to rebel against every norm, rule, order, and authority figure that warrants insubordination, and you live life on your own terms.

One of my life ambitions is to ensure this happens.

Contents

Preface: Is This Book for You?

This book is for anyone who believes that at least some elements of conventional wisdom and practice require urgent improvement. It's for anyone who yearns to see more justice in the world. More freedom. More financial stability. More purpose. More community. More *humanity.* It's for anyone who understands the value of nonconformity and recognizes that we desperately need freethinkers willing to disrupt unhelpful norms for the sake of progress. (Oh, yeah, and it's also a book for people who don't take themselves *too* seriously and think it's okay to laugh, cuss, and have a little fun while changing the world.)

PART I
IN PRAISE OF INSUBORDINATION

CHAPTER 1

The Critical Importance of Cartwheeling in the Library

Despite what you learned in high school, Charles Darwin didn't invent the theory of evolution. Okay, maybe he did, but he didn't do it alone. In the preface to *On the Origin of Species by Means of Natural Selection*, the awkwardly titled book that would change the world, Darwin listed thirty men who previously mustered the courage to question intellectual and religious orthodoxies about nature.

These characters paid a steep price for their boldness. Have you heard of Abu Uthman Amr ibn Bahr al-Kinani al-Fuqaimi al-Basri (nicknamed Al-Jahiz)? Good luck finding a refrigerator magnet of him. Muslim scholars refer to Al-Jahiz as "the father of the theory of evolution," and for good reason: he arrived at the notion of "survival of the fittest" a thousand years before Darwin, in the year 860. Al-Jahiz wondered why certain animals imported from Africa and Asia to what is now Iraq easily adapted to their new environment whereas others caught illnesses and perished. His reward for this biological discovery was arrest and banishment from his native land. And he was lucky. The chief Muslim ruler of Baghdad got downright medieval on the wealthy patron funding Al-Jahiz's research. Military officials imprisoned Al-Jahiz's patron and executed him inside an iron maiden (a spike-laden metal coffin that impaled victims when the doors closed).

You'd think scientists would take a hint and keep their strange and dangerous theories to themselves. About seven hundred years later, in the 1500s, a French scientist named Bernard Palissy dared question the Catholic Church's proclamation that the Earth was only a few thousand years old. Noting that tides and winds required long periods of time to visibly alter the landscape, Palissy argued that our planet was much older than a few thousand years (how much older he refused to say). Palissy also proposed that an elephant thousands of years ago would not be the same as an elephant today. This concept of species transformation across generations was heresy. His reward: several arrests, a spate of flogging, and destruction of his books. Oh, and they burned him at the stake.

Others on Darwin's list received better treatment—the authorities spared them death or ostracism—but nobody would characterize their lives as rainbows and gumdrops. They were denounced as infidels. Monitored by the police. Disowned by their families. Censored. Physically assaulted. Threatened with death. All for doubting Biblical claims that animals and humans were *really* created in six days, that God was *really* the only force responsible for their evolution, and that humans were *really* the zenith of God's achievements (a rung lower than angels). Questioning orthodox beliefs made you an outsider, a threat, a heretic deserving of torture and death.

I use Darwin's predecessors as an example here to highlight the price that many, if not most, dissenters, deviants, revolutionaries, rebels, and outliers pay for the sake of progress. Sometimes progress happens by happy accident, but more often a courageous person defies social norms. Somebody noticed that the existing orthodoxy in some small or large way was unhealthy, stagnant, or even dangerous, and championed a countervailing idea. And some member of the majority decided to give new ideas a fair reception instead of the middle finger. More often than not, dissent yields progress. Outlaw dissent, and you slow the speed of cultural evolution.

Darwin's predecessors matter because they inspire a question: why did he succeed while they failed? Yes, Darwin received hate mail and anonymous nineteenth-century trolls called him a heathen, but his ideas found a big audience. The greatest European scientists of the nineteenth century elected him a Fellow of The Royal Society, the oldest scientific academy in existence; and awarded him the prestigious Royal Medal for his research explaining the formation of coral reefs. Popular readers loved his book of travel adventures, snazzily titled *Narrative of the Surveying Voyages of His Majesty's Ships* Adventure *and* Beagle, *between the Years 1826 and 1836.* In a world without the Travel Channel and *National Geographic*, Darwin's book sparked imagination and enlivened many a dinner table conversation. If highway billboard signs existed, which they didn't, his face would have adorned them selling sneakers and chocolate milk. So why was his insubordination so much more effective than those of other, like-minded thinkers around the world and across the centuries?

A full answer to this question would fill many books, requiring an extensive historical analysis of both Darwin and his predecessors. But we can raise some interesting possibilities by turning to social psychology. In recent decades, researchers studying a number of topics—emotion, self-regulation, creativity, persuasion, minority influence, intergroup conflict, political psychology, group dynamics—revealed how we might differ and disagree successfully. Science has also helped us understand how members of the majority can become receptive to dissenters, increasing the odds that the valuable but subversive ideas of insubordinates will take root.

Darwin lacked the benefit of this knowledge, but he intuitively followed a number of successful insubordination strategies. We know, for instance, that dissenters boost the odds of convincing others if they take a careful measure of society's prejudices and calibrate their speech and actions accordingly. Darwin understood how provocative it was to suggest life stemmed from something other than the divine spark of God. His own grandfather, Erasmus Darwin, saw the Vatican ban his books for articulating a theory of evolution. In order to preserve his mental health, the younger Darwin sketched out his theory of evolution and then waited not two, not five, not ten, but fifteen years before publishing it. Only at that point, after another controversial work, *Vestiges of the Natural History of Creation*, became an international sensation, did he believe society was finally ready—or as ready as it would ever be—to digest ideas as controversial as his. "In my opinion," he wrote, *Vestiges* "has done excellent service, in removing prejudice . . . preparing the ground for the reception of analogous views."

Psychologists emphasize how important it is for principled rebels to communicate in ways that help overcome listeners' emotional resistance. Darwin contemplated how to strengthen his argument. He wrote in an accessible, jargon-free style comprehensible to everyday readers, not just scientists. He relied on analogies as illustrations. Victorian readers delighted in Darwin's vivid descriptions of "hairless dogs" and "pigeons with feathered feet." They learned about the mingling of ant slaves with masters, what happened when young chickens lost their fear of dogs and cats (it wasn't pretty), and the engineering feats of bees. Besides entertaining his readers, Darwin engaged them as participants by using phrases such as "we can see," "we can understand," and "we ought to find." He asked for reader commitment by posing questions such as, "What now are we to say to these several facts?" An interactive video game it was not, but by the standards of the time, it was compelling.

Researchers studying successful dissent have found that allies play a critical role in the promotion of unconventional ideas. Here Darwin truly shined. A year before he published *Origin of Species*, he received a manuscript from Alfred Russel Wallace outlining a competing theory of evolution. Having delayed publication of his book, Darwin feared that Wallace alone would receive credit for discovering evolution. To stake his own claim, Darwin allowed friends to take charge and set up a presentation at an upcoming public meeting. The meeting featured Wallace's manuscript and a time-stamped letter showing that Darwin arrived at his conclusions first. Neither Darwin nor Wallace were present, but Darwin's four-man infantry of fellow scientists—Charles Lyell, Joseph Dalton Hooker, Asa Gray, and Thomas Henry Huxley (the latter known as "Darwin's bulldog")—fought valiantly on his behalf, lending their own credibility to his theory. Darwin was an unimpressive orator. His friends, though, were skilled enough to debate critics and win over experts and laypeople.

Darwin deployed specific strategies for successfully selling his theory to the mainstream and radically changing how people today think about the origins of human behavior. These strategies, coupled with later research, can help non-conformists in our midst become more resilient, persuasive, and effective at mobilizing others. I know because over the past decade I've conducted, collaborated on, and synthesized studies that explore how people with fresh ideas can become courageous. I've designed practical strategies for championing ideas others regard as outlandish, threatening, or just plain weird. I've taught these strategies to corporate executives, government intelligence officers, global financial leaders, and other prominent people around the world. These interventions work, and published studies provide the scientific evidence explaining why. With a bit of extra effort, we can all succeed more in our efforts to help members of the disbelieving majority overcome their internal resistance and give change a chance, whether our ideas are minor refinements of conventional wisdom or revolutionary departures, like Darwin's were.

Of course, the success or failure of a subversive idea hinges on more than its merits. We humans are tribal creatures who frequently sacrifice sound reasoning to bolster our group affiliations, whether with political parties, sports teams, religions, genders, racial groups, countries of origin, or musical genres. Tribal thinking leads us to exact a "novelty penalty" on unorthodox thinkers, particularly if we perceive them as "others" or outsiders. To prepare the way for more successful insubordination, my colleagues and I created research-based strategies to help people think more flexibly when confronted by unfamiliar—and thus potentially distressing—ideas. These strategies boost tolerance and civil discourse, creating environments where non-conformists can flourish and members of the majority can extract more value from divergent thinking.

Principled rebels are more relevant now than at any time in recent memory. Notables include Malala Yousafzai (who risked her life advocating for girls' education in Pakistan), Peter Neufeld and Barry Scheck (who helped exonerate over 375 wrongly convicted prisoners in the United States), and Alexey Navalny (who served time in prison and faced multiple assassination attempts just for protecting citizen votes from Vladimir Putin's interference). Each of them is speaking out and demanding change, as are countless lesser known activists. But many of us are not resisting successfully. Nor is society greeting our resistance in healthy ways.

In 2020, a picture circulated on the Internet showing an elderly woman standing at a rally and holding a sign that read, "I can't believe we still have to protest this shit." Many of us can sympathize with that sentiment. But as slow as change can be, and as bleak as the world might sometimes seem, we're not at all doomed to see our controversial ideas ignored, repudiated, or banned. By learning to practice and respond to dissent more effectively, we can overcome fear and mistrust, replace commonly accepted ideas with something superior, and build better functioning teams, organizations, and societies.

The Art of Insubordination is what Darwin's thirty unlucky predecessors wish they had read before embarking on their lonely quests. I wrote this practical handbook to teach readers how to increase their odds of success as dissenters, non-conformists, rebels, or as I'll often refer to them, insubordinates. I also wrote it to help readers prepare the ground for other insubordinates everywhere to succeed, whether we happen to agree with what they propose or not. As important and valid as non-conformist ideas might be, insubordinates can't expect the world to welcome them with open arms. If you're going to rage against the "man" or the "machine," you must think ahead and protect yourself with some psychological armor and weaponry. And you must prepare yourself and others to receive new ideas more effectively rather than reject them out of hand, as we so often do.

The Art of Insubordination can be viewed as a cookbook filled with recipes for reaping the benefits of a neglected asset in life and the workplace. Recipes for permitting dissent and embracing it when present. Recipes for effectively expressing unpopular, important ideas and how to best champion them. Recipes for managing the discomfort when trying to rebel or when interacting with a rebel. The chapters ahead provide powerful "recipe steps" for introducing novelty and baking change into the system. In Part I, I prepare you to rebel by helping you understand why most of us resist new ideas, and why society so desperately needs the rebels in our midst. Part II of the cookbook—the heart of the book—offers tactics for furthering new and unusual ideas. You'll learn how to communicate more persuasively, attract valuable allies, persevere in the face of resistance, and conduct yourself responsibly once your ideas go mainstream. Part III of the cookbook advises how you can build a society that is more receptive to challenging ideas and that can make the most of the opportunities they represent. I'll reveal how to better engage the outrageous as an individual, how to extract wisdom from non-conformists in team environments, and how to raise a generation of insubordinate kids in your capacity as a parent or educator. Insubordination matters. I want to jar you into looking at the world a little differently, challenging others more carefully and deliberately, and lowering your guard when others might challenge your own beliefs and assumptions.

Skeptics might accuse me of indulging an overly romantic view of insubordination. The Cambridge Dictionary, after all, defines insubordination as "the refusal to obey someone who is in a higher position than you and who has the authority to tell you what to do." Lots of people do that, sometimes in ways that don't benefit society or even hurt it. *Principled* insubordination is a brand of deviance intended to improve society with a minimal amount of secondary harm. Principled insubordinates seek to build momentum for worthy and important ideas. At some point, they consciously decide to take that first, uncomfortable step away from the security of the herd, not for their own benefit (or at least not exclusively), but for humanity's. I want more of us to take that step, and I want society to refrain from punishing us.

Defining Rebellion

Not all insubordination is created equal. In writing this book, I've sought to sniff out people who are rebellious for the wrong reasons. Because they are impulsive. Because they don't like anyone telling them what to

do. Because they want attention. I hope to draw attention to rebels with integrity and ethical standards. "Principled insubordination" is my name for a rebellious bent on contributing to society, and we can think of it as a simple equation:

$$\text{Principled Insubordination} = \frac{\text{Deviance} \times (\text{Authenticity} + \text{Contribution})}{\text{Social Pressure}}$$

If you're not a math nerd, don't worry, we're going to unpack this. **DEVIANCE** is the most important element defining principled insubordination, which is why I've positioned it as a multiplier.

Bear in mind, we're talking about a particular kind of deviance here, one that you consciously take on. Successful rebellions don't come from a place of ignorance, duress, compulsion, or randomness. There's nothing impressive about being different merely because you are not paying attention to existing standards of behavior (ignorance), you are forced to disagree (duress), you can't resist the temptation of disagreeing (compulsion or a lack of self-control), or you give little thought to what you do on any given day.

If you consciously choose to rebel, your motivation matters. I include **AUTHENTICITY** in the definition to ensure that the principled insubordinate's actions arise from deeply held convictions as opposed to superficial preferences. Principled insubordinates act from the heart. They don't simply deliver what others want from them, nor do they imitate others who came before them. They're secure and powerful in their own uniqueness and individuality. Given how easy it is for audiences to sniff out insincerity, you *must* be authentic if your stand against authority is to have a fighting chance of succeeding.

I include **CONTRIBUTION** in the formula to ensure that principled insubordinates intend to create social value. As I envision it, principled insubordination is an act of kindness and caring. Those who perform it don't question authority from a place of disdain (feeling one is above the norm), spite (wanting to upset the mainstream or powerful minority for the hell of it), or self-interest (such as the financial benefit of crime). They question authority because they want to give back in some way. Contribution is what distinguishes insubordination with a cause from its cynical, destructive, superficial cousins. It entails careful consideration of collateral damage that might arise from questioning and attacking social orthodoxy.

Another critically important element of contribution is remaining respectful and open to those who might disagree. Contribution is not the province of white supremacists or cop killers. Yes, they're insubordinates, but their ideas are inherently hateful and intolerant, and history shows they don't lead society anywhere good. You've probably met people across the political spectrum and members of various religions who harbor principled views. These individuals might be well-intentioned on some level, but if their views are ultimately intolerant and close-minded, they're not principled insubordinates as I think of them.

Let's not forget the all-important denominator in our formula, **SOCIAL PRESSURE.** Insubordination means little without stakes. The real test of your principles is if you hold on to them when the deck is stacked against you. Acts of rebellion begin with a single, uncomfortable step away from the safety and security of the herd. Take Charles Darwin's story to heart, and don't underestimate the risks of making your ideas visible to the outside world. You become fair game for misrepresentation, criticism, scorn, and even hatred—an unpleasant consequence of principled insubordination as I'm defining it.

Even better, I'd like society to reward and encourage principled insubordination, like my mom and grandmother did for me. As a twelve-year-old, I asked my rabbi why Jews are allowed to eat shrimp but not tuna fish. Did God really have so little to worry about that he/she spent time devising painfully specific dietary rules? This learned man turned me away without even entertaining my legitimate if provocatively posed question (Jews can't eat shrimp—I purposely reversed shrimp and tuna fish to demonstrate that regardless of which food is deemed blasphemous the rule is absurd). On the drive home, my mom kept her gaze fixed on the road and said to me, "Keep questioning the rules until you get good answers."

She died the following year but my grandmother, who became my caretaker, also relished insubordination. As one of the first women to work on Wall Street, she acknowledged that although authority figures often possess wisdom, we should judge them by what they do, not what they say. People defer easily to the powerful, she argued. We should celebrate the brave renegades who stand up to authority figures in their teams, organizations, and social groups. And we should endeavor to manifest that bravery ourselves.

I've written this book in homage to my mother and grandmother. I've written it to encourage people who deserve to be heard but who are struggling and perhaps even giving up. As I see it, it isn't only our continued progress that is at stake, but also, quite frankly, our sanity. If nobody deviated in principled ways from society's prescribed script, civilized life would be less interesting and inspiring, in addition to being less just, safe, and prosperous. It would be less fun—and funny.

I opened with a story of a dead white male who rustled the branches of convention and succeeded. Here's one about an undead white female. One evening during my freshman year in college, some friends and I were sitting in the library studying. At one point, as I struggled to stay focused, a beautiful blond woman appeared. No, she wasn't walking idly through the stacks in search of a book. She was turning cartwheels and barreling right at us. When she had come close enough, she stopped and made eye contact with me. "Give me that textbook you're studying," she said, gesturing with her hand. Bewildered, I handed it over. She opened to a random page and scribbled something down. "Here you go. When you get to this chapter, give me a call." Before I could respond, she cartwheeled away.

I was flabbergasted. In this one, small act of principled insubordination, this woman broke many of the established, gender-based rules of dating. On the one hand, society has long taught women to hide their physical selves, suppress their sexual desires, and wait passively for men to approach them. On the other, society applauds men for confidently seeking out willing partners. This woman didn't merely ask me out; she did it in her own unique way. She *owned* that library study space, gifting me a story that I continue to ponder to this day. Imagine a society without people like her who experiment with unconventional ideas and practices, even in relatively minor ways, because existing social scripts seem stifling. How often would we experience emotions like curiosity, inspiration, awe, admiration, elevation, and elation without such daring and imaginative souls?

I called this woman a few weeks later. We went out on a date but never started a relationship. A year went by. I transferred to another college. During orientation week, I walked across the main quad and there she was again—this incredible cartwheeling woman. I walked up to her, tapped her on the shoulder, and asked if she would think it weird if she happened to be studying in the library and someone performed gymnastics around her, only to say nothing other than "call me." She smiled and said something to the effect of "I can think of no other way of asking a boy out." We went out again and dated for over a year. She was the first woman I ever loved.

If you have an exceptional idea or if you occupy an outsider position of any kind, I urge you to speak up and make yourself heard. Don't wait. Don't ask permission from the powers that be. Do it now. Make your mark. Educate and enlighten the rest of us. Change the world. Listen to others who seek to do the same. But for heaven's sake, do what Darwin did. Be smart about it.

RECIPE STEPS

1. *Be deliberate and disciplined.* Famous rebels like Charles Darwin deployed specific strategies for selling their theories to mainstream audiences, and so can you.
2. *Know the difference between reckless and principled insubordination.* If you're contributing to society and taking action from a place of authenticity, consider your rebellion principled.
3. *Don't take rebels for granted.* Principled rebellion is vital for improving society. It's also part of what makes your life and the lives of those around you rich, fun, and fulfilling.

CHAPTER 2

The Strange Things We Do to Be Liked

How we're wired to fit in

As any kid versed in playground ball will tell you, there's a simple way and a less simple way to shoot a basketball from the free-throw line. The simple way is to shoot it underhand. You stand fifteen feet away from the basket. Nobody guards you (the other players stand still, waiting for you to shoot). You rock the rock (as pro players call a basketball) back and forth between your legs and release it so that the ball arcs upward toward the hoop. It's not pretty, but it f*#$ing *works*. One of the National Basketball Association's greatest players of all time, Hall of Famer Rick Barry, shot free throws in this way, sinking an incredible 90 percent of his attempts over the course of a ten-year NBA career. During his last two seasons combined, he took 322 free throws and missed only nineteen, an incredible 94.1 percent success rate. By comparison, today's greatest basketball player, LeBron James, missed 132 overhand shots in a single season, a 73.1 percent success rate.

The less simple (and according to multiple sports scientists, less effective) way to shoot a free throw is to do it overhand. You grasp the ball with two hands and raise it to eye level, with one hand supporting the ball and the other steadying it from above. Gazing intently at the basket, you flick the wrist of the hand supporting the ball so that the ball flies toward the basket. Your hands work together, but they bear varying amounts of weight and perform different tasks. You rely primarily on the shooting hand to push the ball with considerable strength while simultaneously using the non-shooting hand as a guide. For an optimal trajectory, as your wrist snaps with the ball gently rolling off the fingers, the basketball should arc upward between 45 to 52 degrees. If you get the basketball to spin backward, the speed and energy lessens upon contact with the rim—allowing for a softer shot that might bounce off the backboard and drop. I could go on, but you get the picture. Break down the mechanics of a free throw, and it becomes an overwhelming physics experiment. No surprise, then, that many otherwise amazing players suck at it. Hall of Famer Wilt Chamberlain made only 51.1 percent of the free throws he attempted during his career. Hall of Famer Shaquille O'Neal, just 52.7 percent.

Given the great success Rick Barry had shooting underhand free throws, you'd think a solid chunk of pro and college players would try that method, especially those who, despite endless hours of practice, remain piss-poor at shooting overhand. You'd be wrong. In thirty-five years, not a single NBA team has reached out to Rick Barry for foul-shooting advice. In college basketball, only two players shoot the simple, underhand way, and one of them is Rick Barry's son. The basketball world perceives underhand shooting as "girly" and a "granny shot," so players are too self-conscious to do it. Former NBA great Shaquille O'Neal, notorious for his poor free-throw shooting, proclaimed that he'd "rather shoot zero percent than shoot underhanded. Too cool for that." Another epically bad free-throw shooter, Andre Drummond, refused to adopt the granny shot in no uncertain terms. "Let me make this clear," he said. "I'm not shooting free throws underhand."

To his credit, Wilt Chamberlain did try underhand for a spell during the 1962 season, about ten years into his career. It went astonishingly well. He averaged a league record 50.4 points per game that season and improved his free-throw shooting percentage from an abysmal 38 percent to a not stellar but respectable 61 percent. In one memorable game, he scored an astronomical one hundred points, hitting twenty-eight of thirty-two free-throw shots. But rather than stick with shooting free throws the simple way, he returned to shooting overhand. His free-throw shooting declined once again. Why would he possibly have gone back to what didn't work? "I felt silly, like a sissy, shooting underhanded," he explained in his autobiography. "I know I was wrong. I know some of the best foul shooters in history shot that way. Even now, the best foul shooter in the NBA, Rick Barry, shoots underhanded. I just couldn't do it."

Think about that for a minute. Professional basketball players are paid enormous sums to score points and win games. Wilt sacrificed points, in the process failing teammates and disappointing fans, just to avoid looking foolish. Thousands of professional and college players since have done the same. The average player in the National Basketball Association shoots at about 75 percent, college players at about 69 percent. Not bad, but not Rick Barry-awesome. And these averages haven't improved in decades. As talented as they might be, these players lacked the cojones to buck the norm and undertake a simple act of principled insubordination that would improve their performance.

We shouldn't beat up on basketball players. Brave acts of nonconformity are tragically rare. We know the names of great mavericks and renegades like Nelson Mandela, Susan B. Anthony, Harriet Tubman, Leonardo da Vinci, Martha Graham, and Jesus, not just because of their successes, but because they were among the relatively few of their generation to reject conventional thinking and pursue progress.

In recent decades, social psychologists and scholars in other disciplines have chronicled just how powerful our tendency to conform really is. Scientists delved into the specific emotional dynamics that cause us to perform stupid, self-destructive acts for the sake of being liked. Before we examine how we can break with convention more effectively, we must take a closer look at why we struggle to muster the courage to buck convention, and why it's an uphill battle to convince others to question outdated, undesirable norms and practices.

THE BIG IDEA

To disobey effectively, it helps to know our enemy: the overriding human motivation to fit in, stick to the herd, accept conventional wisdom, and "go along to get along."

THE VIRTUES OF "OLD SCHOOL"

This enemy might be more pervasive than you think. In fact, it might sweep along the *last* person you ever thought would fall victim to it: you. Other people act like lemmings who would run over a cliff if that were accepted belief and practice. Not you. You read. You question. You critique. You analyze. You challenge. You take risks. You think *differently*.

I used to see the world this way, until I came across research by the University of Arkansas's Scott Eidelman and the University of Kansas's Chris Crandall about how we make decisions about the value of ideas or practices. In one study, researchers told different groups of participants that acupuncture had been around for 250, 500, 1,000, or 2,000 years, respectively. When participants thought acupuncture had existed for a longer period of time, they felt more confident that acupuncture was "a good technique" and "ought to be used to relieve pain and restore health." Participants thought they had conducted a rational analysis of the benefits of acupuncture. In truth, participants made judgments based primarily on how long-standing or widely accepted the practice was. Acupuncture's appeal jumped by 18 percent if participants learned that it was ancient, with no information given about whether it worked. As skilled in critical thinking as we might think ourselves, humans have a general preference for the entrenched status quo.

In another study, researchers told one group of participants that a painting was created a century ago, another group that it was merely five years old. Participants who thought the art older judged it as higher quality and more pleasant. In yet another study, United States citizens were more inclined to support the use of violent enhanced interrogation techniques on terror suspects in the Middle East if they learned such techniques had been a standard military practice for forty years as opposed to a new practice. This finding held for both liberals and conservatives.

We rationalize the existing state of affairs when we feel an undesirable situation is "psychologically real." Consider the strange mental shift in voters from the moment a candidate wins a presidential election to the inauguration ceremony—honoring day one of the presidency. In a remarkable longitudinal study, Dr. Kristin Laurin at the University of British Columbia found that even Americans who disliked and did not vote for the president held increasingly more positive attitudes about him. The power of "psychological realness" extends beyond elections. Something strange happened once the 1954 U.S. Supreme Court ruled racial segregation unconstitutional. Even students at an all-Black college "unambiguously opposed to segregation" felt increasingly negative attitudes about the existence of all-Black colleges *after*, compared to just a few weeks before, the legally binding decision. Dr. Laurin proposed "that it is this sense of realness—the recognition that a state of affairs is an immediate part of their lives—that drives people to rationalize." Feeling the "psychological realness" and inevitable consequences of the current state of affairs pushes us to swap out resisting for a new trifecta of coping behaviors: conforming, rationalizing, and legitimizing.

THE BIG IDEA

People blindly assume that the prevailing system is better. Next time you want to convince someone of an idea or approach, remind them of its long, storied history.

WHY MOST PEOPLE DON'T LAUNCH REVOLUTIONS

It's one thing to harbor a bias for established wisdom when it comes to subjects like acupuncture, art, or torture that don't directly impact our lives all that much. But our motivation to conform is so powerful that it prompts us to accept established systems or regimes that do affect us, and indeed, that oppress us. As a presidential candidate in 2015, Donald Trump expressed disdain for Mexican immigrants, saying, "When Mexico sends its people, they're not sending their best. They're sending people that have a lot of problems . . . They're bringing drugs. They're bringing crime. They're rapists." You'd think Hispanic Americans hearing that would be appalled (especially since 76 percent of Hispanics are Mexican), but they weren't. Over a quarter of them agreed with Trump's statement.

A survey of 6,637 randomly selected adults in America found that 33 percent of Black people reported being treated no worse than Whites by the criminal justice system. This sounds reasonable—until you consider that America's criminal justice system has a long, sordid history of discrimination against Black people, and that it stands today as perhaps the clearest modern example of institutionalized racism. According to forty years of nonpartisan data from the

U.S. Department of Justice, Black adults are almost six times more likely to be imprisoned than Whites. Despite representing only 13 percent of the population, Black people account for more than 33 percent of state and federal prisoners. And yet, 41 percent of Black people polled in 2001 said they are treated identically to White people, or that Whites are the ones treated unfairly. Surveys fielded since have produced similar findings.

If you're tempted to disparage Black and Hispanic people for dismissing a system that oppresses them, do me a favor and pay close attention to the psychological biases discussed here. We all tend to support systems in which we function, even if those systems harm us. Since its inception, the discipline of psychology has struggled to explain this tendency. Professors John Jost of New York University and Harvard's Mahzarin Banaji have led the way by propounding a theory of system justification. As they've observed, people feel internally conflicted when the systems of which they're a part treat them indifferently or oppressively. People will go to bizarre lengths to rationalize and protect a social system that harms them. Disadvantaged people often do just as much (or more) to affirm a system's validity than those who occupy privileged positions within the same system.

As Dr. Chuma Owuamalam at the University of Nottingham explained, rejecting an entire system is a big deal, a step that often goes too far even for the most disadvantaged people existing within it. "The alternative to accepting a social system is to reject it," Owuamalam wrote. "In most cases, such a rejection is likely to be regarded as being unrealistic because it implies a revolution and anarchy that could invoke much greater uncertainty and threat than the alternative of dealing with dissonance. Hence, people who are invested in their group identities and interests may choose to explore all options before considering the revolutionary role of system rejection."

Citizens with ties to Mexico, targeted in Donald Trump's comments, want to believe that home in the United States is a place where they feel safe, secure, and a sense of dignity. Once you have family, friends, and perhaps a job, leaving the United States is not a simple, realistic option. A strong dependency on the system leads numerical minorities in a society to respect the status quo and even accept principles, norms, and rules that oppress or harm them.

Over the past quarter century, psychologists have produced a large body of research supporting system justification theory, shedding light on our tendency to uphold and support oppressive systems. It turns out that a slew of rational and nonrational impulses lead to our continued loyalty to standard, long-standing practices when better alternatives might exist. For the sake of brevity, I've teased out from the literature some key mechanisms that induce us to conform much of the time.

THE BIG IDEA

Four psychological "boosters" fuel voluntary conformity on our part.

1. We Feel Reassured by the Status Quo's Familiarity

   We like to believe we retain personal control over our lives. We want to feel a sense of agency, deciding what happens to us as opposed to existing as pawns pushed and pulled by outside forces. Hurricanes, terrorist attacks, and other crises shake our confidence in a predictable, stable world. Even in "normal" life, so much lies beyond our influence. When your fellow passenger on a packed flight starts coughing violently while eating a pungent peanut butter and raw onion sandwich, there's not much you can do. Mother Nature, bad highway drivers, your next-door neighbor's membership in the douchebag hall of fame, mistakes you've made in the past, *anything* that's happened in the past—you can't control any of this.

Deprived of control, we tend to take comfort in the familiar, well-understood parts of our lives because they offer a sense of stability and security. Hence we show relatively little resistance to existing systems such as governments, religions, and corporations, even those that might oppress us. In one study, researchers prompted a group of participants to feel temporarily disempowered by asking them to reflect on a particular incident in the past when they lacked control. Another group of participants received instructions to imagine a future where uncontrollable incidents happen—they, too, came to feel temporarily disempowered. Researchers then gauged participants' willingness to defend the existing society and its accomplishments or argue that the system was flawed and required an overhaul. Compared with a control group, participants who felt a loss in personal control were more willing to defend the existing society and its accomplishments. Researchers noted a 20 percent increased willingness to defend the establishment.

In the search for a coherent, sensible system, we often accept harmful consequences rather than wade through feelings of uncertainty. When we feel impotent, we don't just support leaders who promise law and order. We try to surround ourselves with people who uphold the system against critical detractors. We seek to affirm our fundamental belief that the world is progressing just fine and that we thus need not remove authority figures nor challenge existing norms.

2. In the Face of Systemic Threats, We Salute

On September 10, 2001, President George W. Bush held a job approval rating of 51 percent, with 38 percent of Americans saying they disapproved of the way he was handling his job. Just two weeks later, in the wake of the 9/11 attacks, Bush's job approval rose to 90 percent, the highest level of presidential support recorded since Gallup began tracking data in the 1930s. It remained high for a full two years before tumbling back to where it had been. Conservatives extended an already high level of support for a conservative president, while liberals showed an appreciation for policies that ran counter to their own value system.

Events that jeopardize the survival of a group on which we depend tend to motivate a defensive reaction. Our initial impulse is to protect what we care about, especially if the perpetrator of the attack is an outsider. Few elements are more effective at bringing people together than a common nemesis. We become upset at the outsider. We share our dismay with other group members. And we support the powers that be inside the system. Rallying behind a system under siege feels like a worthy cause. Even if we feel ambivalent, there's a time and a place to criticize, and this isn't it. Now we're in Proud Defender mode. Love it or leave it, baby.

Authorities and organizations often intentionally evoke symbolic links to powerful, dominant belief systems as a means of sustaining legitimacy. They know people swept by patriotic fervor will easily forget that the system they are justifying is the same one that has been depriving and harming them. The presence of threats to the system and our identity-based reactions to them goes a long way toward explaining why human beings favor the status quo, including the very organizations that compromise our well-being.

3. We Feel Dependent on the Status Quo

If you've served any time in prison you know the chances of survival go way up if you're affiliated with a gang. Stand next to a pack of people wearing the right colors or bearing the right tattoos, and other potentially murderous prisoners will identify you with the gang. You'll enjoy enough protection to walk fearlessly through the dining halls and outdoor yards. You might even lie in bed at night untouched instead of suffering at the hands of another inmate. By joining that gang, you've entered into a dependent relationship with the group and will feel hesitant to voice concerns about its rules, hierarchy, and leadership. The gang is keeping you alive and safe. Your fellow gang members might treat you like crap, but it's better than getting killed or raped. And over time, that gang becomes part of your identity. You're no longer just a person. You're a member.

The deal with the devil we strike in prison doesn't differ all that much from those we strike with other existing hierarchies in our lives. We rally behind the status quo because the group of which we're a part satisfies our basic needs to feel understood, validated, and competent. Because we identify with the group, we no longer have to think for ourselves all the time: knowing what high-ranking members of the group prefer makes it easy to select what to wear, what music to listen to, what beliefs to hold, what politicians to support, and so on. Our sense of belonging comforts us because we know that our fellow group members will show us favoritism over outsiders when we need it.

As research has found, people are willing to sacrifice material payoffs to feel connected with powerful authority figures. Individuals who are poor, who lack education, and who live in crime-ridden neighborhoods will vote against their own self-interests and fight against economic redistribution if they identify strongly with the nation and its power. Perceiving the country as a direct extension of their own identity, they willingly forgo their own self-interest because their attachment to the country serves other needs, providing a sense of security, safety, and belonging as well as a stable sense of meaning. You remind yourself that this is *your* country, and it's far better than living in countries you view as inferior. You can justify corruption as a few bad characters in a system that, if operated as intended, would be the best imaginable. What could be more American than feeling discontent while plastering on a goofy smile?

Researchers find that conformity intensifies as people become more dependent on a system. In Malaysia, the authorities regularly mistreat the country's Chinese minorities. Because members of this minority are successful economically, the Malaysian government reserves college scholarships for Malays only, not Chinese. Thanks to government-mandated quotas, colleges only allocate a small number of slots to Chinese citizens. Government loans exist for buying houses and starting businesses, but many are reserved for Malays, not the Chinese minority. If you are Chinese and fortunate enough to secure a loan, expect to pay a premium rate.

You'd expect the Chinese minority to be pretty pissed off. Not so. In one study, Dr. Owuamalam had Chinese adults in Malaysia reflect on their government-sponsored disadvantages. He found that members of this minority articulated strong support for the existing government. Why? Although the Chinese received inferior treatment, they depended on the government for transportation, health care, and everyday survival. It's not easy to defend mistreatment handed down from the existing system. Chinese minorities in the study had to work harder cognitively than Malays did when asked to write down supportive comments about the Malaysian government. But as mentally draining as it is to be oppressed in Malaysia, the Chinese minority maintained strong support for the government.

None of this means oppressed people *like* being part of the system. Of course they don't. It's not easy for a woman to accept that even in 2021, the business world is still dealing with misogyny—high-level positions are dominated by men, giving male friends an edge when finalizing leadership succession plans. And yet, for all its sordid injustices, America still offers more autonomy, financial opportunities, and safety for women than most other countries. Human beings often do what they can with the world as it is rather than complicating their lives in a possibly unsuccessful quest to produce the world they'd like to live in.

People often end up expressing appreciation and fondness when forced to operate within a social system, defending the benefits while ignoring the pain. In one Canadian study, researchers told participants that the government was tightening immigration policies and they wouldn't be able to leave the country. When people believed the system was inescapable, they reconsidered Canada's endemic sexism. Instead of regarding sexism as a systemic problem, Canadian citizens attributed it to biological differences between men and women. Believing there was no escape from Canada, they shifted from criticizing to legitimatizing an unfair status quo. Researchers obtained similar results in a separate experiment when they told college students they would have difficulty transferring to another institution. College students who thought their university was inescapable showed less interest and desire to help a student-led group that criticized and offered suggestions to the administration for improving the university. Students who felt empowered to transfer anytime showed stronger support for the student-led group.

Restricting people's movements didn't lead to their greater scrutiny of authorities or the system oppressing them. Instead, individuals defended the legitimacy of the powerful, higher-status, decision-making figures in their lives. Even worse, those reluctant to acknowledge problems with the existing system also held stronger negative attitudes about dissenters who stood up and criticized the system. When we regard an existing social hierarchy as problematic and unchanging, and we happen to be positioned on a lower rung with little power and influence, we exhibit a status quo bias. Oddly, we support policies that perpetuate existing inequalities. It happens when we deal with big problems, such as people experiencing economic disadvantages in society. It happens when we deal with smaller problems, such as when we feel unable to leave an unsatisfying friendship or romance.

4. You Hold Out Hope for Better Days Ahead

Hope is powerful. A conservative college student can matriculate for another semester, despite repeated prejudice in the classroom, as long as they see signs of progress—such as the founding of a club for conservatives or a statement by the university newspaper that it will cover liberal and conservative viewpoints equally. A low-level military member deployed abroad can stifle moral disagreement with a superior's directives if they know the situation will eventually end. We can bide time within a crappy system if we believe our situation is temporary and that existing disadvantages are eroding.

When we feel hopeful, we won't merely tolerate the existing system, but accept, defend, justify, and protect it. Dr. Chuma Owuamalam's research shows what happens when a country starts to display signs of gender equality over a fifteen-year time span. As women make inroads in society, such as greater decision-making autonomy and greater representation in corporate boardrooms, women throw more support behind status quo beliefs that sex is irrelevant to opportunities and success. Feeling hopeful about upward mobility helps explain why women in the present support beliefs, policies, and politicians that appear antithetical to women's interests. Experiments produced similar findings. After learning their university suffered a dramatic drop in prestige, students didn't try to transfer nor did they pen op-eds denigrating the university. As long as students believed their university's reputation would improve over time and the value of a degree would rise again, they maintained high levels of trust and affection for their academic home.

If you think about it, there is nobility in being able to stick with the program in hopes of a better future. The hopeful defenders of oppressive systems possess true grit, a factor that often predicts educational, financial, and occupational success better than curiosity or intelligence does. But let's not get carried away in celebrating our capacity to endure a hurtful system.

Tell me, which of the following seven statements accurately describe you?

1. I've always felt that I could make of my life pretty much what I wanted to make of it.
2. Once I make up my mind to do something, I stay with it until the job is completely done.
3. When things don't go the way I want them to, that just makes me work even harder.
4. It is not always easy, but I manage to find a way to do the things I really need to get done.
5. In the past, even when things got *really* tough, I never lost sight of my goals.
6. I do not let my personal feelings get in the way of doing a job.
7. Hard work has really helped me to get ahead in life.

If many of these items describe you, you're probably congratulating yourself for grittiness. But despite appearances, these questions capture not grit, but something called *John Henryism.* Coined by Dr. Sherman James, John Henryism denotes the tendency of disadvantaged racial minorities to work too hard in ways that bring short-term success but that create long-term health problems. In the old folk tale, John Henry was the strongest man for hundreds of miles. Competing against a steam-powered drill in a race to break rocks for a railroad tunnel, he emerged victorious but then died from exhaustion. John Henry stands as a legend for superhuman single-mindedness. He persevered at his short-term goal with unwavering commitment, unrelenting vitality, and the circumvention of emotional and physical impediments. Yet his story serves as a parable for the potential costs of working as hard as possible to gain social approval and success when operating within a dysfunctional system.

Scientists followed 3,126 young adults (in their twenties) for twenty-five years. They discovered that young adults who displayed extreme perseverance suffered physically, just like John Henry himself. Higher blood pressure. Higher risk for cardiovascular disease. Twenty-five years later, they were still suffering. Slower mental speed. Poorer memory. Inferior executive functioning (a lack of attentional control, planning, and mental flexibility). The physiological and psychological toll of persevering through hardship is particularly pronounced in people from disadvantaged backgrounds. They're told they just need to buckle down, work harder, and the future will reward them. Sure, hope has its benefits. Let's just remember the potential costs that come with believing that oppression will subside and everything will turn out okay.

OPEN YOUR MIND TO CHANGE

Reading about how primed the oppressed are to conform to unjust and flawed systems might feel odd in a book celebrating insubordination. Am I blaming victims for not being more enlightened? Hell, no! I'm detailing psychological reality. Defending oppressive social arrangements makes sense if, as a member of a disadvantaged group, you feel psychologically vulnerable. It's difficult to embrace an aspirational vision of the future when you're coping with imminent dangers, when you find it impractical to escape a group, and when you hold out hope for the promise of a better future. As we've seen, during times of uncertainty, all of us tend to glom on to conventional wisdom.

THE BIG IDEA

It's human nature to defer toward long-standing, widely accepted practices and beliefs. The would-be insubordinates among us must acknowledge this reality so that they can deal with it and ultimately overcome it. The rest of us must, too, so that we can overcome our internal resistance to change and support progress.

It's f*#$ing hard to be different, to dissent, to deviate from traditional thinking. Fitting in offers a short-term respite from the turmoil of being the target of animosity and rejection. If you're suffering in an unjust system, sometimes you just want a break from thinking about it. But sticking by the system is ultimately unworkable, as it will compromise your well-being over the long term by making change impossible.

Let's all become more aware of our tendency to conform, opening our minds to the prospect of change. This cookbook provides psychological recipes for the rebels and renegades among us, those who have found a mission worth fighting for. I've also written it for the rest of us who are less inclined to resist but still seek a better life than the one we're living. As we'll see, non-conformists can get more people onboard if they make small tweaks in their behavior. And the rest of us can adopt tactics to help us glean the most benefit from non-conformists and their brave interventions. But before we get to all that, let's set the stage just a little more. We acknowledge the strange things we do to be liked, and some key psychological mechanisms underlying and influencing our behavior. Now let's examine why principled insubordination is necessary. Let's unpack why renegades *rock*.

RECIPE STEPS

1. *Point out the cost of inaction.* Adults rarely (if ever) switch brands of soap, yogurt, and cable providers, even when they don't like them. Non-partisan voters overwhelmingly vote for the incumbent in political elections. By sticking with undesirable goods, services, and decisions, we allow negative events to dominate daily life when healthier, more meaningful alternatives exist. Next time you want to convince someone of an idea or approach, remind them that doing nothing when problems exist harms your well-being.
2. *Know the four psychological boosters.* Gaining insight into the mechanisms that fuel voluntary conformity on our part will help you to resist conformity pressures. What pulls for conformity and legitimization of a corrupt state of affairs include a lack of personal control, threats to the system, dependence on the system, and hope of upward social mobility.
3. *Acknowledge your status quo bias.* It's human nature to defer to long-standing, widely accepted practices and beliefs. Would-be insubordinates among us must acknowledge this bias so that they can deal with it and ultimately overcome it.

CHAPTER 3

Renegades Rock

Why principled rebellion matters so much

In American history, institutionalized racism was always a Southern thang. The Northerners were righteous warriors fighting for freedom and equality. That's the stereotype, right? A feisty young teacher named Elizabeth Jennings would beg to differ. Institutionalized racism was a Northern thang, too. She had the cuts and bruises to prove it. As well as $225.

The date was July 16, 1854. The place, New York City. Jennings headed to church, where she played the organ. It was too far to walk, so she hailed one of those newfangled, eco-friendly, biofueled vehicles known as a horse-drawn streetcar. No sooner did she get on than the conductor reminded her of three pertinent facts: (1) she was a Black person; (2) according to New York City's transport system policy, any White passenger who was a racist hater could have a Black person thrown off the streetcar; and (3) if a White patron asked, the conductor would enforce rule two. Jennings received no respect, no gentle plea, only a barked order from the conductor: if anyone here objects to your presence, you can get the f%$# off and walk.

Jennings could have nodded her head, sat down, and enjoyed the ride. But she was having none of it. It was one too many times that someone told her what she could or could not do because of the color of her skin. She lit into him, "I am a respectable person, born and raised in New York, and I have never been insulted before while going to church!" Not to mention, in her humble opinion, "you are a good for nothing impudent fellow, who insults genteel people on their way to church."

The conductor wasn't used to Black people talking back. Because at the time, they tended to keep quiet. He grabbed Jennings and, with the help of a nearby police officer, physically dragged her off the streetcar and onto the road. They tried to rip her off the platform steps, but she held her own. As a result of the struggle, her dress became soiled and her body cut and bruised. When additional police arrived, they didn't help her. They arrested her.

The only lawyer who agreed to represent Jennings during her court appearance was a sprightly twenty-one-year-old White dude named Chester Arthur (who would later go on to become the twenty-first President of the United States). In the view of one expert, Chester sported "both the bushiest and boldest mustache of any president." Chester did his thing. Not only did Jennings not pay a fine or serve jail time; she sued the transit service. The court granted Jennings $225—quite a princely sum back in the day, about as much as a civil servant made in a year. But that's not all. News of the incident spread. Black folk in the city were *pissed.* Others stood up against the transit service's racist policy. The following year, in response to another court case, the transit authority installed a racially neutral policy giving Black people equal access to their choice of public transportation and seat selection.

It's time to set the record straight. Although segregation in the South only ended during the second half of the twentieth century, the Northern states weren't exactly paragons of virtue. The government of New York State abolished slavery in 1827, almost three decades before Jennings's tangle on the streetcar. And yet New York retained racist laws, regulations, and policies for decades after abolishing slavery. It took brave souls like Elizabeth Jennings to challenge the powers that be and show society a new and better way. Over a hundred years before Rosa Parks allegedly pioneered the tactic of civil disobedience by refusing to sit in the back of an Alabama bus, Elizabeth Jennings was already doing it.

Nobody placed Jennings on a U.S. postage stamp or mentioned her in history textbooks. Elementary schools don't teach kids her story. But forgotten acts of insubordination like hers make a big difference. We need rabble-rousers in society as well as in our organizations and teams. As we'll see in this chapter, the very presence of non-conformists pushes us forward, even when we disagree with them, and even if their proposed solutions are wrong. Creating space for principled insubordination enables an upward spiral to take root, affirming that nothing is ever "finished" and that we should always strive for improvement. Principled insubordination makes individuals more rational, and groups more creative and productive.

That's not to say that having principled insubordinates in our midst is easy. Quite the contrary. As Bill Clinton told an audience in 2016: "America has come so far. We're less racist, sexist, homophobic and anti-specific religions than we used to be. We have one remaining bigotry: We don't want to be around anyone who disagrees with us." His audience laughed. It's no laughing matter. Humanity today continues to struggle with injustice, and we face existential challenges, from global warming to nuclear weapons to global pandemics. If we want to survive, we better up our game, and fast. That means seeking out brave souls—unsung heroes like Elizabeth Jennings and famous ones like Rosa Parks—to point out problems, provide their best ideas, and rally others to do the same.

THE BIG IDEA

To nurture bravery, we must improve at not just tolerating people who disagree with us, but welcoming and fostering them.

DISSENT EQUALS PROGRESS

The power of principled insubordination becomes obvious in situations when non-conformists have taken down unjust systems like segregation. Less obvious are the multitude of ways a non-conformist's spirit fuels incremental progress across society, making daily life more efficient, productive, prosperous, safer, and just plain better.

I hate to be a downer, but we desperately need more progress. Although we do have *The Simpsons*, self-cleaning fish tanks, and an ability to 3D-print a fully functional acoustic guitar, other important dimensions of daily life either totally suck, largely suck despite some recent improvement, or only moderately suck but could still be better. Doctors might not bore holes in people's skulls any longer, drain blood from bodies, or give poisonous mercury and arsenic elixirs as a wellness treatment (I'll save the Egyptian dung ointments for the endnotes). Still, at least 44,000 patients die each year in the United States from avoidable medical errors. Astronomy has improved since the days when humans thought they resided at the center of the universe. Still, scientists in 2019 discovered they had been somewhat off when estimating the universe's age—like, by more than a billion years. Our educational system is better than it was in Elizabeth Jennings's day, when virtually no Black people attended school and only about half of White kids aged five through nineteen did. Still, as of 2019, 22 percent of American citizens failed to name a single branch of the U.S. government; only 39 percent could name all three. Not to mention, school-based physical education affords students a mere sixteen minutes of bodily movement per class, with "a few jumping jacks before a halfhearted game of softball." Will 960 seconds of exercise prevent kids from growing into morbidly obese adults? C'mon, people!

The way to do better, in these areas and practically any other, is to actively recruit people like Elizabeth Jennings. More frequently than you imagine, diverse perspectives lead in turn to refreshingly counterintuitive ideas and highly workable solutions.

Consider the issue of how to prevent or stop mass shootings. One of the most popular solutions advocated around the country is to allow teachers and other employees to carry weapons. That way, teachers can fight back when an active shooter menaces their classrooms—they don't have to wait for law enforcement.

In the wake of a 2013 attack on a heavily secured Washington Navy Yard building that killed a dozen people and injured eight, the Federal Law Enforcement Training Centers convened a panel of experts to proffer their opinions. The panel's goal: Generate new solutions to prevent future tragedies and, specifically, to keep the body count in every workplace targeted by active shooters to one victim or fewer. Instead of inviting the usual collection of bureaucrats, the Centers brought in a collection of outsiders, including a forensic psychologist, a psychiatrist, a surgeon, an architect, a Navy SEAL, and frontline responders who had experience with mass shootings.

The forensic psychologist offered up the creative but seemingly odd idea of training kids in schools to head straight for the girls' bathroom. "Nearly every shooter is male," he said, "and if you watch the video footage, they always walk past the girls' room." The Navy SEAL had a completely different idea. "I would grab a fire extinguisher," he said, describing what he'd do in an active shooter situation. Other panelists assumed he would advise using the fire extinguisher to hit the shooter in the head and take him down, but that wasn't it. "I'd spray it to create a smoke screen and plus the chemicals remove oxygen from the air making it harder for shooters to breathe and easier to take down." Remarkable for their simplicity and pragmatism, these ideas required mental leaps that only non-conformists—in this case, outsiders—were likely to make.

Of course, these tactics might not work. But it's not like arming teachers is such a great idea, either. When researchers asked 15,000 law enforcement professionals for solutions to gun violence, 86 percent believed that legally arming citizens would reduce the death count. In truth, when highly trained New York City police officers participate in gunfights, shooters miss the target 82 percent of the time. When only police fire the bullets, they still miss the target 70 percent of the time. Each bullet could inadvertently kill or wound an innocent person. Shouldn't we let the poetry teachers out there stick to rhyme and meter?

In this instance as in countless others, conventional wisdom is flawed. Room for improvement exists. Maybe girls' bathrooms and fire extinguishers would work better than having poetry teachers play *Call of Duty* in real life, but maybe not. But one truth seems clear: unleashing more non-conformity will probably allow us to find other potentially helpful solutions nobody has thought of or had the ovaries (or cojones) to put forth.

As evidence shows, groups of people perform better when we encourage principled insubordination. In 2012, Google began a much-publicized research initiative called Project Aristotle, seeking to identify what distinguished top performing teams. Frequently voted one of the greatest places to work, Google wanted to know why only a few teams fulfill their promise and produce higher quality work than any individual could do. After two years, researchers had their answer: psychological safety. Exceptional teams created conditions that encouraged team members to participate without fear of ridicule, chastisement, intellectual theft, a hit to their career, and so on. The media loved it. The *New York Times* published a front-page story, "What Google Learned from Its Quest to Build the Perfect Team." As of June 2019, 10,600 articles and videos have covered Project Aristotle's results. Organizations have undertaken a "safe place" revolution in the hope of boosting motivation, learning, performance, and innovation.

And yet, Google missed half the story. A year after Project Aristotle ended, two psychologists dissected fifty-one studies on the importance of psychological safety to team performance. The result: psychological safety often didn't correlate with performance. Sometimes teams that spent hefty sums training and hiring with psychological safety in mind did fantastically. Other times, they tanked. One factor *does* determine whether psychological safety works or not, and that's principled insubordination. Group members want to feel psychologically safe. But as research has shown, psychological safety reliably translates into superior performance only when sufficient minority viewpoints exist, and we permit and embrace them when present. You might tolerate minority dissent but this says nothing about whether its stimulation exerts influence on other group members. As emphasized by organizational psychologists Drs. Katherine Klein and David Harrison, "It is not sufficient for a group member to improve on another's solution; he or she must also win others' approval of the improved solution as the next best course of group action." Too many people fail to capitalize on the stimulation of principled insubordination. Teams need psychological safety *and* a welcoming of constructive dissent and deviance before they can consistently be open-minded to divergent thinking, make more informed, high-quality decisions, and be innovative.

If principled insubordination is so important, how exactly does it work? Here are three of the best explanations set forth by psychologists:

Reason 1: Principled Insubordination Neutralizes Our Cognitive Biases

As smart as we humans are, we struggle to form rational judgments. When confronted with information that threatens closely held beliefs, we respond automatically and defensively, dismissing perspectives that clash with our worldview. One big reason: cognitive biases. Our capacious *sapiens* brains possess limited processing power. We can only pay attention to a limited amount of stimuli at any given time. To make do in a world of infinite information, our brains take cognitive shortcuts, causing us to default to biases.

We also feel motivated to experience certain emotions and beliefs and prefer to avoid others. We want to be right. We want to be liked. We seek to validate our identities. We care about certain people, objects, sports teams, and ideas because of what they say about us. We defend what we care deeply about against detractors. Our sense of reality becomes biased and skewed.

To date, psychologists have identified about a hundred cognitive biases to which we fall prey, divided into three categories. The first category of biases relates to our need to feel like we belong to an in-group. We *love* in-groups. Thanks to our evolutionary experience, our brains tell us it's better to mistakenly avoid a kind, compassionate, altruistic stranger than to mistakenly approach a dangerous one. So, we pledge fidelity to all sorts of in-groups, including those based on race, gender, nationality, social status, political beliefs—even vegetarianism. We treat members of our in-group better than we do outsiders, hold them to different moral standards, interact with them more, evaluate their ideas and proposals more favorably. Most important for our purposes, we tend to associate unfamiliar ideas with the unfamiliar people who promote them, thus becoming resistant to changing our beliefs.

The second category of biases has to do with what scientists call "motivated reasoning," a jargon-y way of saying that we tend to evaluate evidence not in a perfectly objective way but based on what we hope to conclude. When we hear of information that confirms what we already think we know, we accept it more readily than information that doesn't. We tend to avoid information that doesn't conform to our beliefs. Thus, we tend to surround ourselves with like-minded people who say like-minded things. We delude ourselves into thinking that our perspective alone is the very embodiment of fairness and truth. Deluded approaches to acquiring and processing information interfere with our ability to recognize and accept alternative ideas that might serve us better.

The third category of biases relate to what scientists call "motivated certainty." As political psychologists Cory Clark and Bo Winegard note, motivated reasoning concerns "the substance of a belief, [whereas] motivated certainty refers to the 'momentum' of that belief." Simply put, we humans tend to feel overconfident in our positions and fail to see the costs of adopting them. We think we're *so* smart—or at least correct. For instance, we might believe immigrants should be able to cross borders freely and live wherever they want, that any human being can decide on their gender for whatever reason at any time, and that genetics fails to explain differences between men and women. In a dream world, such positions cost us nothing to hold. In the real world, holding a position comes with costs. We invest money, attention, and emotion into our ideas and their implementation, becoming increasingly motivated to feel certain about our beliefs. Weirdly, we become more motivated—and feel even more confident in our beliefs—as uncertainty increases. Our grasp on reality slips away, without our even realizing it.

Ten Biases That Eff Up Our Thinking

1. **Confirmation bias**—We tend to prefer information that matches our existing beliefs.
2. **Familiarity bias**—We prefer what or who is already known.
3. **Naïve realism**—We tend to believe that we perceive the world objectively, as it is, and that people who disagree with us are uninformed, irrational, or biased.
4. **Illusion of knowledge**—We think we know what other people are thinking.
5. **Fundamental attribution error**—We attribute others' mistakes and failings to their identity, but when we screw up, we conveniently blame it on circumstances and bad luck.
6. **Self-consistency bias**—We tend to think that our attitudes, beliefs, and behaviors are always stable, when in fact they change.
7. **Projection bias**—We think others tend to share our preferences, beliefs, and behavior more than they actually do.
8. **Authority bias**—We like ideas better when voiced by someone powerful or prestigious.
9. **Stereotyping bias**—When we observe a tendency in one member of a group, we assume that some or all fellow group members share it.
10. **Bias blind spot**—We think we can easily spot biases in others even as we fail to recognize our own.

If biases abound, if they skew and imprison our thinking, we're pretty much doomed to stupidity, right? Not necessarily. A tribe of heroic bias bashers live among us. They're called non-conformists. Bring in someone like Elizabeth Jennings who thinks differently and isn't afraid to let you know it, and we'll better see our own biases and correct for them. We'll become more curious about the world instead of remaining locked in and intellectually sterile.

Dr. Stefan Schulz-Hardt conducted an experiment exploring how best to obliterate cognitive biases in German business managers. Schulz-Hardt homed in on confirmation bias (defined in the sidebar on page 46). He created small groups and tasked them with choosing between investment opportunities in one of two countries. To make their selections, groups had to weigh fourteen different factors, including country tax levels, economic growth, environmental legislation, and the like. Groups could access up to a dozen articles written by economic experts familiar with both countries. Half of these articles pointed to one of the countries as an ideal investment, while half argued the opposite.

Do groups seek out information that confirms their initial investment choice and ignore the rest? What happens to deliberations after seeding groups with dissenters, as opposed to a bunch of like-minded? Schulz-Hardt found that groups of managers seeded with dissenting views were *twice as likely* to request articles that conflicted with the group's initial decision than homogeneous, ideologically similar groups were. If you want to override the tendency to think in more extremely polarized or prejudiced ways, inject a little good old-fashioned dissent.

Of course, dissent in a group setting doesn't come without cost. Groups with dissenters experienced twice as much controversy in their conversations (batting around alternative viewpoints) compared with homogeneous groups. Positivity, cohesion, and decision-making all took a hit. In the absence of dissent, homogeneous groups fell prey to strong confirmation biases, primarily seeking information that justified their premature conclusions while ignoring highly useful information that conflicted with group momentum. Although the homogeneous, dissent-free groups sought only half of the available information to make investing decisions, they felt an alarmingly high level of confidence compared to the broader thinking, questioning attitude of groups with dissenters. Studies of hospitals, courts of law, Broadway musical productions, and social movements observed similar findings. Inject dissent, and you find that confidence decreases and the number of arguments increase—a relatively small price to pay for improved group problem-solving and creativity.

THE BIG IDEA

Something special happens when you have even one dissenter in your midst. You don't robotically default to assuming the dissenter is right. Instead, you feel motivated to contemplate an issue carefully and consider that the dissenter might have good reason for upholding a contrary position.

Exposed to a dissenter's viewpoint, you become more apt to review information that supports positions contrary to your own. You open yourself to testing reality and raise questions about your own positions. Instead of remaining beholden to motivated reasoning and confidence, you become more critical minded and balanced. You start thinking less like a partisan and more like a disinterested scientist pursuing the truth. Overall, the presence of a dissenter prompts group members to abandon low-effort mental shortcuts and switch to elaborate, deep information processing. The Big Three categories of cognitive bias are *toast*.

Reason 2: Principled Insubordination Boosts Creativity

Here's a question: what factor best predicts whether elementary school children will receive recognition as innovative creators fifty years later? It's not whether they like to build weird things out of Play-Doh.

It's not their levels of curiosity or intelligence. It's whether they're "comfortable being a 'minority of one.'" In research published by Dr. Mark Runco and colleagues at the University of Georgia, sixty-year-old adults achieved more lifetime creative accomplishments if as kids they expressed comfort being a minority voice. They published books and plays, built profitable businesses, earned public acclaim, and exerted a greater influence on others. True, these young insubordinates suffered emotionally from their tendency to challenge the status quo, experiencing broken friendships, persecution, and so on. But as a group, they blossomed into creative trendsetters far more than their conformist peers.

Other research has found that exposure to principled insubordination enhances creative decision-making by stimulating divergent thinking. In one study, researchers took certain work teams and randomly selected one person for training in principled insubordination. Over a ten-week period, the group engaged in a variety of creative tasks, such as creating new products and navigating morally questionable business situations. Colleagues in these teams produced more original product ideas (as objectively rated by outside experts) than did members of other teams that lacked a trained insubordinate. Conversations in these teams were contentious at times, with some of the rebels feeling isolated and under strain. "It wasn't easy," one rebel reported. Another said, "Much of the time another group member and I were at each other's throats." But team members ultimately acknowledged the rebels' contributions. Rebels received higher performance ratings from peers than others. Initially, they slowed down the group and interfered with group cohesion. Over time, the presence of principled insubordinates helped clarify each person's role and thus amplified performance and creativity.

Many of us think of ourselves as tolerant people who appreciate the value of difference, dissent, and deviance. Throw a rebel or two in the mix, however, and we become irritated as tension erupts and group cohesion frays. For our own good, we need to push through that irritation and embrace insubordination.

THE BIG IDEA

Creativity isn't an innate gift. It's a way of thinking. Regularly interacting with those who hold non-conformist views pulls us into a creative mindset. With rebels openly airing alternate and unpopular views, groups become better than the sum of their parts.

Reason 3: Insubordination Breeds Even More Insubordination

As we saw in chapter 2, the pressures for conformity are wicked strong. But principled insubordination holds some persuasive power of its own. Drop a rebel into a group, go away for a period of time, and you're liable to find more rebels than you started with. We know this because of one of my favorite pieces of research, an experiment led by Dr. Charlan Nemeth. Wondering what made some people defy authority and group pressure, Dr. Nemeth and her colleagues instructed study participants to view twenty blue-tinted slides and state aloud the color. Tested alone, participants judged 100 percent of slides to be blue. Researchers then tested participants in groups of four, with each grouping seeded by an actor whose role was simple: dissent from the majority. When it was their turn, the actor stated quite confidently that the blue slides were green. Faced with the objective reality that blue slides were clearly blue, and the dissenter was obviously mistaken, participants ignored the dissenter and judged a full 100 percent of the slides to be blue.

Here's where it gets interesting. The experimenter brought each person to a private room as part of a new four-person group. You couldn't see the three new members, but there was a microphone for group communications. Participants received another set of slides to view, all of which were red. Now, when asked what color they saw, for each slide the three other group members spoke the same word into the microphone: "Orange." The conditions were ripe for conformity. The researchers wanted to know, what would participants do? Participants who did not witness any dissent in the first part of the study showed a reluctance to challenge error-filled judgments by the majority. Only 29.6 percent of the time would they timidly eek out the word "Red?" However, participants witnessing an actor's dissent in the first part of the study were transformed—bravely blurting the correct answer, "Red, obviously!," 76.1 percent of the time. And get this: *The transformation occurred even though in the first part of the study the majority was right and the dissenters gave wrong-headed answers. Even though participants didn't publicly agree with the dissenters in the first part of the study.* Think about that. Acts of insubordinates influenced people who initially ignored them. Somehow, exposure to an act of insubordination altered people's way of seeing the world.

THE BIG IDEA

Acts of insubordination don't usually win over members of the majority right away. Instead, they sow seeds of doubt, and these mature over time into new perspectives.

Dr. Robert Cialdini, one of the world's foremost experts on persuasion, found that opponents of the status quo often initially fail to change other people's attitudes and perceptions. Follow up weeks and months later, however, and you witness modifications in how others think and behave. Initially shocking, insubordination over time ultimately has a much more profound impact, changing how people regard themselves, others, and the world.

MAKE OPENNESS YOUR DEFAULT

In presenting this research on the benefits of insubordination, I hope to inspire you in two ways. First, I want you to behave more rebelliously. To think differently. To speak up. To take action. I also want to inspire you to look upon deviants you encounter with a more open mind, especially when you disagree with them. As I like to say after a whiskey or two, insubordination is a portal to the adjacent possible. It allows us access to new possibilities that, because of biases, inexperience, or a lack of wisdom, we wouldn't cultivate on our own. As we've seen, principled insubordination enables social changes both large and small. You don't have to agree with every non-conformist out there. Just hear them out. Instead of sticking with your existing opinions when confronted with a novel perspective, do something radical and make *openness* your default.

The openness of non-rebels matters because, as scientists have documented, lone rebels don't get very far on their own. Researchers wanted to see what it would take to get a group of people to change an established social norm. They set up an experiment in which they assigned 194 participants to groups of twenty to thirty people, showed groups the headshot of a stranger, and had groups decide on what name to give that stranger. Researchers fostered conversations within the groups about the name choice. Unbeknownst to participants, a certain number of them were rebels assigned the task of overturning whatever name the group was on the verge of agreeing on by offering alternate suggestions. The researchers discovered that if more than 25 percent of a group were rebels, the group eventually decided on the alternate name. If fewer than 20 percent of a group were rebels, this minority had no impact on the final selection. One or two brave rebels like Elizabeth Jennings might trigger a change in a particular policy, but it takes a solid block of about a quarter of a population espousing a minority position to transform a group's beliefs or behavior.

I'll show later how you can shine as part of that 25 percent by becoming more receptive to non-conformists around you and making the most of their wacky ideas. But first, let's examine how you rebels out there can win over more people so you break clear of that 25 percent threshold and effect change. A good part of it comes down to how you talk. You can have the best, most earth-shattering ideas out there, but if you don't know what you're doing as a communicator, you won't get far. Scientists have produced intriguing insights into how underdogs can best present their ideas to win over doubters. If you have an unpopular idea you think might serve the cause of progress, please do me a favor. Hit pause on that YouTube video, stop checking your Instagram, and pay close attention. The world needs you.

RECIPE STEPS

1. *Bring dissenters into your teams.* Exposed to a dissenter's viewpoint, you open yourself to testing reality and raising questions about your own viewpoints. With a single rebel airing alternate and unpopular views, a group reduces its confirmation bias and motivated reasoning and increases its creative output.
2. *Be patient.* Principled insubordinates often initially fail to change other people's attitudes. But over time insubordination

ultimately has a much more profound impact, changing how people regard themselves, others, and the world.

3. *Make openness your default*. You don't have to agree with every non-conformist out there. Just hear them out instead of sticking with your existing opinions.

PART II

THE NON-CONFORMIST'S COOKBOOK

CHAPTER 4

Talk Persuasively

How to win over an audience of skeptical conformists

What I'd like you to pay close attention to is a little something called Fugazi. Fuga—*what*? No, it's not a $150,000 Italian sports car brand, nor is it a curse word levied by a fist-shaking Italian grandma. It is, according to Urban Dictionary, a slang word originating among military veterans for a "fucked up" situation, so I guess an Italian grandma could use it. But the Fugazi you need to know about is a four-man punk rock band, probably the most influential musical artist of the past thirty years.

That's a bold claim. What about Nirvana? Or Jay-Z? Yeah, influential acts, but consider this: Fugazi directly influenced Nirvana as well as Jay-Z, Pearl Jam, Rage Against the Machine, the Red Hot Chili Peppers, Lorde, Blink-182, Kesha, the Foo Fighters, Billie Eilish (thanks to the musical tastes of her older brother). All of them are huge Fugazi fans. When you consider that numerous musicians influenced by Fugazi are big influencers themselves, you realize today's musical landscape would have looked radically different were it not for this uniquely named band.

According to one music journalist, Fugazi, drawing on an array of reggae, funk, and jazz artists, established itself "as a channel through which to vent the confusion, rage, and anxiety bred by hostility to the absurd security of conformist culture." Unlike giants such as the Beatles, Led Zeppelin, U2, or Garth Brooks, who became money-making machines, Fugazi stood for artistic integrity, bold political activism, anti-consumerism, anti-corporatism, and a do-it-yourself (DIY) mentality. Its enemies were self-importance, showmanship, and "selling out." More than any rock or pop band of the late 1980s and 1990s, Fugazi stripped away the puffery and elevated its audience to active participants rather than fawning worshippers.

These guys were hard-core artists with a soul. No matter how popular they became, Fugazi only charged fans five dollars to attend concerts, and ten dollars for a record, tape, or CD. To keep costs low, the band said f%$@ it to roadies, booking agents, distributors, accountants, and other money-grubbing professionals whose services musicians feel compelled to buy. Members of Fugazi recorded their own albums. They slept in fans' living rooms. They just didn't care about becoming rock stars. Remembering how much it sucked being a teenager barred from attending shows, they refused to play shows that weren't open to all ages. They embraced a general ethic of inclusion, welcoming everyone as fans including women (whom they didn't objectify sexually) and people of color (whom they didn't treat as "others"). A great deal of popular music today stands up to injustices of one sort or another, whether misogyny, homophobia, violence, economic inequality, materialism, unethical government intrusion—you name it. That very gesture is a Fugazi thing.

Fugazi declined to play in bars because band members didn't want the musical experience muddied by intoxication. They spurned mainstream magazines that published alcohol and tobacco company advertisements targeting impressionable teenage readers. To maintain creative control, they declined million-dollar offers from major labels.

They skipped music videos because the oversexualized content splattered on the likes of MTV repulsed them. To minimize transactional relationships with fans, they didn't sell T-shirts, stickers, or buttons at shows. Fugazi's priorities were clear: music first, fans second. The band always—*always*—supported the little guy over big business.

People assume that artistic integrity and commercial success are mutually exclusive. Fugazi smashed that assumption. The band sold more than three million records during its seventeen-year existence. As of this writing, over 1.5 million monthly listeners stream its music, even though the band has been on "hiatus" since 2003. On a deeper level, Fugazi succeeded where so many musical artists failed: its members shifted cultural norms, creating a movement of grassroots, DIY, socially conscious musical artistry. The band expanded the circle of moral concern in music, which is why famous musicians like Kurt Cobain and Eddie Vedder invoked the names of Fugazi band members in interviews, hoping the integrity would rub off.

What was the secret to Fugazi's success as principled insubordinates? One answer is sheer determination. Between 1987 and 2003, Fugazi played more than a thousand live shows, amounting to one live show roughly one out of every five days for seventeen years straight! That is serious visibility. But there is a second, more important answer. Fugazi became influential because its members mastered what we might call the "underdog's guide to influence." Like Charles Darwin, they had an uncanny knack for getting their points across in ways that won over members of the majority, including music industry power brokers and fans who never before identified with the punk rock community.

Scientists have established that people with minority status (a designation that by definition applies to rebels) instigate change more readily if they're consistent in what they say, without being overly rigid. Fugazi checked that one off. The band lived by an ethos called "straight edge" that translated into a ban on drugs, drinking, smoking, meat eating, and nonconsensual sex. While band members espoused these values for themselves, they never pushed them on fans. On stage, in interviews, and during face-to-face conversations, members of Fugazi clarified that theirs was simply one approach to living, not the only way. They refused to cast judgment on others who chose differently, nor did they expect fans to copy or obey them. Because fans didn't view Fugazi as preachers, they were more inclined to listen to Fugazi's opinions and adopt "straight edge" lifestyle habits for themselves.

Scientists have arrived at a number of fascinating insights that inform how those with minority opinions most effectively persuade others. These insights come baked into several psychological theories, including Conversion Theory, Conflict Elaboration Theory, the Context/Comparison Model, the Source-Context-Elaboration Model, and the Elaboration Likelihood Model. Cutting through this sea of academic jargon, I've arrived at certain governing principles rebels can use to maximize their persuasive potential. Disregard these principles, and you all but ensure your failure. Pursue them, like Fugazi and other principled insubordinates have, and you're in a much better position to gain a hearing.

Asked "Who is you favorite band?," my answer remains the same since the age of thirteen: Fugazi. Quizzical looks follow, and then I rattle off details about them before playing their greatest album, *Repeater.* I listen to them when working out, on long car rides, or for a jolt of vitality. My three daughters know Fugazi. Past Father's Day gifts include a flask with the band name inscribed, hand-drawn bookmarks of album covers, and a ceramic mug with lyrics. When I first moved to the suburbs of Washington, D.C., I met lead singer Ian MacKaye at a local church concert where 100% of the proceeds went to clean needles and contraception for streetwalkers. After finishing this chapter, make sure to appreciate Fugazi's cathartic fusion of musical sounds, not just their cultural contributions. Give these beloved songs a chance (one from each album): "Waiting Room," "Repeater," "Reclamation," "23 Beats Off," "Bed for the Scraping," and "Break."

THE BIG IDEA

There are *five essential principles* rebels can use to maximize the persuasive potential of their message.

PRINCIPLE 1: WORK IT FROM THE INSIDE

Rebels take note: audiences will more likely listen if they view you as a member of their in-group rather than as an outsider. We know this in part thanks to studies such as one conducted at the University of Arizona in the mid-1990s. Legalized gay marriage seemed unfathomable then. Government officials adopted the infamous "don't ask, don't tell" policy that allowed gays to serve in the military so long as they hid their sexual identities. In this social milieu, researchers asked students supportive of gay rights to read an article called "The Case Against Gays in the Military." Some students learned that the Student Association of the University of Arizona authored the article—in other words, it reflected a mainstream opinion within the student community. A second group learned that a small, radical, conservative organization from the University of Arizona wrote it—in other words, a minority within their University of Arizona tribe. A third group learned that a radical group of outsiders from another college penned the article.

Students objecting to the anti-gay article (perceiving it as contrary to their core beliefs) had more than twice as many positive thoughts about the arguments if they thought a mainstream member of their

University of Arizona tribe wrote it. However, students spent more time systematically processing the article's message and retained more information if they thought minorities from their tribe wrote it. Minorities have special persuasive powers, if and only if they articulate how a common identity exists between themselves and their audience.

The mechanisms underlying this phenomenon are pretty interesting. When someone in an in-group thinks differently from the rest, that dissenter elicits a spark of curiosity in the majority. Two questions pop into audience members' heads: "Why does this person think differently from the rest of us?" and "What information does this person have that I don't?" In the short term, deviance might unsettle the group, causing tension or conflict. But it fuels innovation by bringing attention to new ideas, unresolved problems, or a broader list of options. Group members listen carefully to acquire knowledge and wisdom. They reassess their existing beliefs, behaviors, and policies to determine which have become outdated and unworkable. Because the deviant, as an insider, possesses credibility that an outsider doesn't, they can better catalyze change.

THE BIG IDEA

When you take time to first establish common bonds with an audience, and in particular to support group norms and a positive group identity, you gain what social scientists refer to as "idiosyncrasy credits." You rack up cultural capital, if you will. When proposing innovative ideas, you can "spend" this cultural capital in return for support from fellow group members.

If you're politically conservative trying to convince conservative friends to embrace gun safety legislation, remind them of your shared conservative beliefs and track record of voting for Republicans. *Then* make your pitch. Sidewalk preachers usually fail to persuade listeners because they don't or can't establish a common, "insider" bond; their message gets lost before anyone even hears it. You can and should do better.

PRINCIPLE 2: SPARK THEIR CURIOSITY, NOT THEIR FEAR

You can be the smartest person in the world with the best idea, but if you frighten the crap out of people and alienate them, they won't pay you a lick of attention. Dr. Ignaz Semmelweis can attest to that. Back in 1847, before medical science knew much about germs, Semmelweis argued that handwashing prevents human sickness. Conventional wisdom at the time held that diseases spawn from imbalances in the relative amounts of blood, phlegm, black bile, and yellow bile, also known as the "four humours." Dr. Semmelweis had data that said otherwise. While working in Vienna General Hospital's First Obstetrical Clinic, he noticed that mothers in a maternity clinic died far more frequently than in a second clinic. Dr. Semmelweis autopsied every dead mother to find the answer. It turns out that small particles of organic matter from corpses festered inside the mother's bodies, contaminating them. Back then, the same doctors who delivered babies conducted autopsies. The doctors' unwashed hands spread diseased remnants from cadavers onto new mothers. The solution: wash hands with chlorine before delivering babies.

These doctors tried it, and the death rate plummeted to nearly zero. Incredible! Even more incredibly, and tragically, nobody listened. It would be another century before the medical profession adopted handwashing as standard protocol. Highly educated, authoritative doctors had a hard time believing that their unclean hands were deadly. But Dr. Semmelweis also didn't do himself any favors. He made no attempt to reconcile his findings with the four-humours theory of disease. And he went out of his way to attack doctors who rejected his thesis, devoting a full sixty-four pages of one of his publications to attack a single obstetrician from Prague who questioned his results.

Dr. Semmelweis assumed that data and strong arguments suffice to persuade the mistaken establishment. They don't. You must also go out of your way to present your message in a nonthreatening way, regardless of how irate you feel. It's really, really hard to argue from the position of a minority, since members of the majority scrutinize your arguments far more closely than those from majority members. When strongly identified members of a group view your message as a personal threat, even if your arguments are unassailable, many of them will stick even more intensely with the opinions and practices of elite, popular members of the group. In general, your window of influence shrinks when emotions such as fear, embarrassment, and guilt dominate over a sense of wonder and curiosity.

THE BIG IDEA

As a principled insubordinate, adopt a conciliatory approach and friendly tone. Don't shame, blame, or maim status quo enthusiasts. View exponents of orthodoxy as your future allies.

PRINCIPLE 3: PROJECT AN AURA OF OBJECTIVITY

Whether we're in the majority or not, all of us come across more persuasively when we make statements that appear objective and verifiable. Why do you think there's so much science in this book? Creative experiments have confirmed that principled insubordinates in particular stand a better shot at influencing the mainstream when objectively verifiable facts exist.

In one study, researchers asked participants to pretend they were college admission officers tasked with evaluating new applications. Everyone received identical information about the applicants. Half of the admission officers learned that the decision to accept or reject was objective, based on hard data. Researchers told the other half that the decision was subjective, with a wide range of information requiring interpretation. Admission officers made their initial admission decisions privately before considering input from others in the group (one of many best practices to avoid groupthink).

Here's the twist: researchers asked each officer to solicit a second opinion from another admission officer of their choice. They could seek a second opinion from an officer who agreed or disagreed with their viewpoint. When college admission officers thought decisions were subjective, they intentionally surrounded themselves with like-minded thinkers. If they believed admission decisions were objective, they sought out dissent, disagreement, and alternative perspectives that would offer a semblance of protection against biases.

As these results suggest, when a contention seems objectively based, we tend to open our minds to it, seeking out opportunities to grow, and entertaining opinions that deviate from our own. When it's subjective, we close down. It's not hard to understand why. When we hear a contention has evidence behind it, we feel motivated to learn more so as to avoid appearing unintelligent, irresponsible, or lazy, adopting what we might call a "prevention" or "defensive" mindset. We might also seek to learn about contradictory evidence because we aspire to get to the best answer, instead of merely seeking to minimize mistakes or errors—what scientists call a "promotion mindset."

THE BIG IDEA

As a rebel, you'll be far more likely to attract a receptive audience if listeners possess a promotion mindset. Support a promotion mindset in your listeners by clearly identifying when you're providing evidence-based knowledge, and when you're just stating an opinion. Go heavy on the objective knowledge and spin out for listeners how instead of holding on to mainstream ideas long past their expiration date, they might benefit from learning about a new, better way.

PRINCIPLE 4: PROJECT COURAGEOUS SELF-SACRIFICE

In prior chapters, we reflected on the serious risks rebels run in breaking with the status quo. Think back to the sorry fates of Darwin's unfortunate predecessors, or the sense of shame that prompted Wilt Chamberlain to end his short experiment with underhand free throw shooting. The life of a rebel can truly suck. But there's a plus side: when attempting to convince people that their ideas have merit, rebels can turn the psychological toll they suffer and the social dangers they face to their advantage.

THE BIG IDEA

We tend to find others more credible if they come across as heroic risk-takers. Rebels can alter perceptions by engaging in so-called courage-signaling, in which the personal sacrifices and costs for standing out from the crowd are made visible.

In experiments with criminal trial juries, researchers found that people in the minority who seem palpably uncomfortable speaking out but do so anyway can exert more influence. When a small number of jury members dissent and prevent a unanimous verdict, ridicule spewed by members of the majority boomerangs back to the dissenters' advantage. Other members of the majority observe dissenters being (unfairly or excessively) disparaged, respect their courage, spend more time contemplating their views, and show a greater willingness to adopt their views.

One caveat: if the majority builds strong, compelling, evidence-based arguments, jury members find mainstream and dissenting views to be equally persuasive. But if majority jurors present flimsy arguments, the seemingly outmatched, impotent dissenters become increasingly persuasive. Why? Because jury members regard dissenters as more committed, sincere, and credible.

One more caveat: few people care about the difficulty of mustering the courage to speak if they perceive a dissenter as a naysaying asshole. So, don't be a naysaying asshole! As a dissenter, when the majority has a good point, show solidarity with them. That way, you'll build up niceness "credits" you can spend during some future argument, when you vehemently disagree.

Exposure to ridicule isn't the only basis for bravery in others' minds. Researchers found that audiences tend to view dissenters as more trustworthy if they pay a clear financial cost for expressing unconventional ideas. Audiences are surprised—in a good way—by a readiness to sacrifice and are then more receptive to implementing the dissenter's proposal. Conversely, when members of a dissenting minority have palpable conflicts of interest, they lose credibility. Whistleblowers who might otherwise seem trustworthy lose traction if they stand to profit from, say, a lucrative book deal. Members of the majority understand this and will often seek to discredit critics by looking for anything smacking of hidden profits.

As a rebel, highlight the sacrifices you're making (without going overboard, as that will backfire). Show your psychological vulnerability when speaking out. Say it aloud: "I feel seriously uncomfortable disagreeing." Let people know that you lost sleep wondering whether to speak. If your viewpoints gain traction, avoid gloating or seeming elated and continue highlighting the very real sacrifices you are making. People understand how scary it is to publicly interrogate the status quo. Increase your own persuasive powers by candidly evoking the difficult journey you have undertaken.

PRINCIPLE 5: BE FLEXIBLY CONSISTENT

In 1994, Duke University's Dr. Wendy Wood and her colleagues used a powerful statistical tool to synthesize 143 experiments that examined the capacity of minorities to exert influence (yes, we've been studying this for some time!). The single best thing a minority could do was: present a consistent message over time. If a minority caved and showed signs of inconsistency—or worse, hypocrisy—she lost. The existence of stable, consistent messages over time is the greatest predictor of whether principled insubordination successfully shifts others' beliefs.

To affect change, you must come across as—and ideally, actually *be*—a true believer. When change is challenging, audiences look for reasons not to engage, including times when rebels hedged on their positions, showing a lack of conviction. But when audiences perceive a rebel as the living embodiment of a cause, they can't help but be impressed. Tying back to Principle 4, consistency means that rebels will likely incur social costs and persecution because of the deep commitment they feel to their cause. And yet, as we saw earlier, true believers can't just ram their ideas down others' throats, lest they alienate their audience and spark fear (Principle 2). The answer is *flexible* consistency.

THE BIG IDEA

Some issues might be so important to you that you'll be willing to die for them. Others, not so much. Know the difference and stick by it.

When pursuing important goals, consistency is vital. Rebels must stubbornly cling to their positions, and they must convey a united front as a group—even a single defection compromises their credibility. On issues that seem less important to you, try to bend. Be willing to concede a point (research shows that small concessions encourage others to reciprocate generously). Show genuine concern for members of the old guard. Empathize with the effort and sacrifices required on their part to change. Leave opponents feeling great about their interactions with you. Show them respect. You'll find, as researchers have, that such efforts on your part will inure others to your perspective, allowing them to admire all the more your consistent advocacy.

CHANGE CAN HAPPEN—IF YOU LET IT

As we've seen in this chapter, rebels don't need to flail helplessly when trying to bring others around to their point of view. A new body of scientific evidence shows us how to increase the odds that our principled ideas will sway proponents of the status quo: Present ourselves as insiders. Spark curiosity as opposed to fear. Convey what elements of what you believe in are objectively true. Evoke an impression of courageous self-sacrifice. Behave in ways that are flexibly consistent. None of this is particularly hard to do. We just have to take a bit of time when presenting our idea to think about our audience, empathize with their fears and needs, and tweak our presentations accordingly. Fugazi did it, and so can you!

Applying insights from the science of principled insubordination doesn't guarantee success. You might diligently deploy these techniques and still not obtain your intended outcomes. Don't despair: your impact may be greater than you think. Lasting change is slow, frequently bubbling below the surface as others contemplate whatever you said or presented. Confronted with new ideas, a few members of the establishment will throw caution to the wind and leave their existing ideas behind. Many more will publicly stick with the status quo while privately experiencing seeds of doubt. It's psychologically difficult to change our identities, especially if a long paper trail of public proclamations exists that documents what we believe, like, and dislike. The first reaction to a new idea will usually be neither positive nor negative, but rather ambivalent—a mixture of resistance and intrigue, confusion and sadness, hope and disappointment.

Such ambivalence isn't a bad thing. Members of the majority will naturally feel uncertain and want to resolve that uncertainty by contemplating the costs and benefits of changing course. If as a rebel you instill just enough uncertainty, audiences might feel impelled to give your idea a fair shot, if only to avoid regretting their failure to do so later. Over time, ambivalence resolves, and opinions and behavior change—scientists call this the "sleeper effect." Researchers found that ambivalence toward unexpected messages from atypical minority sources is an early harbinger of change. Ambivalent people update their beliefs upon downloading sufficient enough knowledge to determine whether an idea is a good one or not. Thanks to the advocacy of minorities, individuals, groups, and societies can gain that knowledge, revising and improving in turn.

As a rebel, you want change *now.* I get that, but it won't usually happen that way. When it does happen, however, the change tends to be lasting. Because members of the majority hold power, they can often compel people to *comply* with their ideas. But they struggle with converting people on a deep level. Rebels *can* convert members of the majority. Initially, rebels might simply succeed in dislodging some of the conceptual frameworks that underlie majority thinking. Later, as members of the majority scrutinize dissenting positions, they come to agree more. Evidence mounts, and the rebels seem more credible, their formulations more influential. Behavior starts to change, subtly at first, then more overtly.

Research has confirmed that members of an in-group minority can influence a group to change their position not just when their message is heard, but later, when the message is fully internalized. After hearing activists advocate the banning of animal experimentation, we might not sign up for their late-night Molotov cocktail throwing event at a perfume company's laboratory. But we listen. And we think. Soon, we start boycotting perfume. We publicly denounce television shows and websites that promote perfumes through paid advertisements. We vote for politicians who seek an end to animal testing. Change happens, imperceptibly but inexorably.

As a rebel, you must stay strong. Individual results vary, and race, sex, gender, and visible personality features factor into how your expressions of principled insubordination are interpreted by others. Don't expect to be liked. Play the long game. Aim for evolution, not revolution. And make the five principles your bible. Mainstream thinking does evolve. With each act of principled insubordination that takes hold, we move closer to a better world. As a rebel, it's your calling and privilege to be the agent of that change. Embrace that mission.

And here's some good news: you don't need to do it alone. To enhance your chances of success, you can enlist others to get in the trenches with you and fight. As we'll see in the next chapter, certain strategies can enhance your ability to win over key allies. New scientific research on how to optimize social relationships for effective disobedience offers helpful answers for well-intentioned, principled people seeking to topple misguided mainstream thinking.

RECIPE STEPS

1. *Devote energy to establishing common bonds with fellow group members, supporting group norms, and adding to the positive group identity.* You gain what social scientists refer to as "idiosyncrasy credits." You can "spend" this cultural capital on social support and a fair hearing.
2. *Signal your courage.* Principled insubordinates can alter perceptions by publicizing the personal sacrifices they made in bucking the system. Of course, don't go overboard, as that will backfire.
3. *Don't expect to dazzle everyone right away with your non-conformist idea.* Initial reactions to a new idea are usually neither positive nor negative, but ambivalent. If as a rebel you instill enough uncertainty about conventional wisdom, your audience might feel impelled to give your idea a fair shot.

CHAPTER 5

Attract People Who've Got Your Back

How to off-load some of the pressure while defying the status quo

It's bright and early on a summer morning, and you're about to embark on a three-day hiking trip. You're new to hiking, and frankly, any form of exercise that doesn't involve walking from the couch to the fridge and back again. Physical exertion just isn't your thing. But your doctor said to bring down that stratospheric cholesterol, so now, reluctantly, you're getting in shape. You've got new hiking boots, UV-resistant clothing, and a backpack loaded with thirty pounds of food and three different kinds of bug spray. You're ready. Or are you? Reaching the trailhead, you're chagrined to find it's located at the base of a pretty big-ass hill—as in, a *mountain*. How will you ever carry a thirty-pound pack up that beast, and then keep going for another three days?

We can't work on the physical fitness portion of that dilemma—this isn't that kind of book. But I can share knowledge that might make difficult tasks of any kind—including daring acts of principled insubordination—much easier motivationally. In a fascinating bit of research, Dr. Dennis Proffitt at the University of Virginia escorted people to the bottom of a hill in preparation for a hike. Dr. Dennis

Proffitt and his team found that participants in their study greatly overestimated the steepness and difficulty of the climb before them. Although the hill only rose at a 10-degree angle, they pegged the rise at 30 degrees. Researchers then asked people to approach the hill wearing a backpack loaded with weights. The hill seemed even steeper. When out-of-shape people approached the hill, they viewed that very same 10-degree ascent as steeper still.

Such misperception owes to a subtle budgeting decision on the brain's part. To survive, our bodies evolved to conserve the expenditure of metabolic energy. When confronted with a task, our brains calculate how much energy we'd use up by performing that action, and how much we'd use up by pursuing reasonable alternatives. Judging the height of the hill to be greater is our brain's way of nudging us to prioritize options that will leave us less enervated. In effect, *laziness* is our species' secret survival mechanism (for bosses out there, maybe not-so-secret).

There is another, quite fascinating dimension of this laziness. Proffitt had participants stare up at that hill in the company of a trustworthy friend. Incredibly, these participants judged the same hill to be 13 percent less steep, and they expended less energy mounting it than people who viewed the hill without a friend. The physical challenge seemed easier. The mere presence of a trusted friend shifted visual perceptions of reality, leaving participants more confident they could surmount this physical obstacle. This isn't some bizarre experimental result. Other research found that men in the company of friends exposed to a bearded terrorist pointing a gun at them perceived the terrorist as smaller in stature, less muscular, and less worrisome than men standing alone.

Friends are essential helpmates when we face trials and tribulations. This, too, has to do with how our brains are wired; we have a tendency to leech off our friends so as to sustain our laziness. It's not especially heroic, but we base decisions about how to invest physical and mental resources with reference to a "social baseline"—our perceived proximity to trusted, reliable social relationships. Confronted by a task, we run a quick mental scan to determine whether we can access helpful social resources. If so, we get a performance boost. Our brains interpret the presence of an ally as an extra pair of hands and set of lobes to help carry the load when taking on mental, physical, and social challenges. Whew—we can relax a little! Our allies are literally encoded as part of the "self" in our brains. We assume our buddies will shoulder part of the load, cueing our brains to scale back and conserve metabolic energy. We literally, not metaphorically, borrow the resources of close, trustworthy allies as our own.

Just like climbing a hill or confronting someone who physically threatens you, bucking the system and trying to persuade people to accept a new idea sucks up a shit-ton of mental juice. With trusted allies by our side, we off-load some of the pressure in preparing to defy the status quo. One of our friends will remind us about the importance of opening with points that others in the room can agree upon. Somebody will offer us a reassuring smile or nod of encouragement while we're talking. Another somebody will help us counter an unforeseen objection raised by a skeptic. With allies, we need not remember everything. We need not say everything right. We need not be the master of all trades. The question for would-be rebels, then, is how best to seek out and retain allies who are most likely to help us. Science points us to three basic principles.

THE BIG IDEA

You don't need to change the world on your own. Enlist trusted allies to support you through the tough times.

PRINCIPLE I: MAKE THE MOST OF YOUR SOCIAL CAPITAL

If you're a rebel seeking allies, you want to be discerning about whom you select, albeit in a counterintuitive way. You might presume it's to your advantage as an outsider to seek out people based on how much influence, power, wealth, or access to privileged information they possess. Yes, the rich and powerful can be very nice friends to have. If you're going to hatch a plan to win the majority over to your beliefs, it's more pleasant to do so on your ally's two-hundred-foot, jacuzzi–equipped, super-yacht moored in the Galápagos (not that I would know). But science suggests you'd do better seeking out allies who'll enhance your intellectual or emotional capabilities. Will a person contribute insight and wisdom, boost your ability to pose better questions, help you solve problems, or expand your sense of self? Then they're a great candidate to recruit as an ally, irrespective of how much money or power they possess. If you're rebelling against the status quo, it's essential to expand the self by entering into close relationships with other people. Evidence-based self-improvement books are great for self-expansion. Same with documentaries (especially *The Imposter*, *Spellbound*, and *Searching for Sugar Man*). But the quickest, most effective way to stretch and strengthen the self is through relationships.

Such advice in turn means rebels should seek out people who are *different* than they are to become trusted allies. If someone eats the same foods, reads the same books, listens to the same music, and circulates in the same social set as you, they'll likely think the same. You'll feel validated, but you won't enhance your capabilities. You know that old slogan "great minds think alike"? No, they don't. Great minds (in alliances) think differently.

THE BIG IDEA

Seek out people who complement you. Partners who are interesting, challenging, and a source of enlightenment. You want people who'll blow your mind—in a good way—on account of their ability to introduce you to new ideas and perspectives.

Also, seek out allies who can expand your emotional reach. Dr. Elaine Cheung advanced the concept of "emotionships," or the presence of specific people who help you manage particular emotions. The more allies you count who can help address different emotional needs, the greater your life satisfaction and, potentially, your effectiveness as a rebel. Along those same lines, look for allies who can serve as what the University of Michigan's Dr. Kim Cameron calls "net positive energizers." Some people leave you charged up after you spend time around them. Others sap your energy to the point that you want to curl up into a ball and avoid the human species (while consuming copious amounts of whiskey). You want the energizers by your side as you're taking on power-hungry authority figures, not the Debbie Downers. Net positive energizers show interest in you, build relationships with you, follow through on commitments, are alert to new possibilities, and are curious in the face of disagreements. They encourage you to experiment, take risks, and innovate. Net positive energizers are Red Bull for personal growth—yours.

The Emotionships Test

Do you have people in your life to help you regulate important emotions you might experience? Who in your social network will reliably:

- *cheer you up?*
- *boost your energy supply?*
- *soothe your nerves until you feel calm?*
- *bring out your playful side?*
- *commiserate with you during sad days?*
- *fight oppression by your side?*
- *make you laugh?*
- *join you in deep, intellectual exchanges?*

Hopefully, you know people who can support you in each of these ways. While you alone can initiate a rebellion, a diverse group of friends with particular emotional skills and tendencies can help you become far more effective.

Is Your Friend a Net Positive Energizer?

Are they mentally and physically engaged when socializing? Energizers don't just go through the motions of being engaged. They show genuine interest in other people and what interests them.

Do they prioritize relationship development? Energizers care about people and don't treat them as a means to an end.

Do they follow through on commitments? There's no better way to deflate someone's balloon than to promise something and flake on it. Energizers wouldn't dream of doing that.

Do they look for possibilities? Or just identify constraints? Energizers aren't perpetual critics who'll shit on your brilliant idea. They're "yes-*and*" people.

When disagreement arises, do they show curiosity? Or defensiveness? Energizers don't have to win every argument. *Hmm,* they think, *maybe I don't know everything.* And when they stick by their guns, they don't antagonize their opponents.

Do they use their knowledge and skills appropriately? Instead of rushing to find a solution or dominating a conversation to demonstrate their intellect, energizers are content to let ideas unfold via collaboration.

Do they take a one-size-fits-all approach? Or do they individualize?
Rather than demand that others accept their approach, energizers draw people into conversations and projects, finding opportunities for them to contribute. Rather than assume what someone needs during difficult times, they ask whether someone would prefer a supportive ear or a helping hand. They query how they might tailor a conversation for people with particular personalities and preferences, so that they can tap others' potential.

Seeking out people who can expand us isn't easy. Trying to start a relationship, romantic or otherwise, that offers the potential for self-expansion is risky. In my very first research study, I conducted an experiment to determine when, if ever, people select dissimilar over similar partners. Using a mock dating site, my colleagues and I split study participants into two groups. Some believed they were looking at profiles of people who shared the same interests and values. Others believed they were looking at people with a completely different personality and interest profile. Get this: If we told participants that an attractive person liked their profile and wanted to meet them, participants strongly preferred dissimilar people. If we failed to provide information as to whether an attractive person liked them, they strongly preferred people who were like them. We humans crave inclusion even more than self-expansion and exploration (more on that in a moment). If in "shopping" for a relationship we doubt people will accept us, we're liable to throw aside growth opportunities and settle for someone similar. If we don't harbor such doubts, or if we happen to feel comfortable with ourselves, we seek out a partner who will help us learn and grow.

Rejection stings harder and longer when we judge the people who snub us as attractive and interesting. And we might be more or less socially anxious by temperament, taking it personally if others react negatively to our appeals. Social anxiety is perfectly normal, especially during the initial phases of forming relationships. If you're a rebel seeking allies, wait to see if your fears of rejection dissipate before approaching a desirable potential ally. Or muster up the courage and make your approach despite your fears. Don't overthink it—just do it. (I'll offer more ideas about how you can work through anxiety in the next chapter.) To prepare, spend a few minutes reminding yourself why self-expansion will benefit you.

Research shows that contemplating the value of growth opportunities offers a motivational push, even during initial, uncertain interactions with strangers. Helpful alliances begin with a willingness to swallow your pride, take a risk, and approach the right people to join your mission.

FORGET SNOBBERY—GO FOR GROWTH!

Unlike status-oriented people, people who orient themselves toward growth view social interactions with strangers as an exciting challenge and an opportunity to broaden their horizons. Stay alert for opportunities to learn from people who have stories different from yours and who have acquired a different body of knowledge. Each time you gain exposure to a new person or idea, you can develop and expand yourself as a person. You have a choice. Instead of trying desperately to impress everyone with your existing intelligence and wisdom, intentionally seek out ways to expand and grow. You will become stronger and wiser. People will find you far more likable and attractive.

PRINCIPLE 2: PERSEVERE TOGETHER THROUGH HARD TIMES

Once you've identified potential allies, you've got to build strong, meaningful relationships with them. The best way is by confronting painful challenges together. Doctors Michael Argyle and Monika Henderson sifted through scientific studies on interpersonal relationships to distill six fundamental features of friendship. Good friends (1) are there when their partners require emotional support; (2) volunteer help in times of need; (3) stand up for partners in their absence; (4) trust and confide in their partner; (5) strive to make partners happy in their presence; and (6) share triumphs and successes. Break these rules, and friendships disintegrate. But notice that the first four rules aren't about happiness. They're about suspending judgment, compassion, and being available when someone is in pain—abilities that come in handy when you encounter shared challenges together. The last two also relate to the tackling of shared challenges. When you're under strain, it's nice having someone around who cares about your happiness. Once you've vanquished adversaries, it's also nice having someone with whom to share the glory.

Additional research has found that social animals are hardwired to connect through pain. If we're in a friendship, your pain is my pain. The same regions of the brain light up when we feel pain as when our friends do. Sharing pain serves as a strategy for bringing people together. Most people think we should establish trust with others first and only then expose our perceived flaws, insecurities, failings, and pain. This line of reasoning is actually backward. Doctors Patrick McKnight, Simone McKnight, Lisa Alexander, and I found that trust emerges as we *share* adversity with others. When we feel uncertain about whether we'll achieve a goal that's important to us, and we think we must rely on someone, we come to trust in others. Vulnerability first, trust second.

Pain offers a shortcut to forming mutually beneficial relationships by speeding up the establishment of intimacy. In one study, researchers found that strangers enduring a gauntlet of painful tasks together felt a greater connection to one another than those collaborating on painless tasks. The comrades-in-pain also tended to cooperate more with one another. Other experiments found that members of groups enduring painful activities tended to make more eye contact with one another, and help, encourage, and comfort one another more than members of groups that didn't endure pain together. We see these dynamics unfolding outside the laboratory all the time. Men and women going through the Navy SEALs super-intense, twenty-four-week, Basic Underwater Demolition/SEAL training (or BUD/S) bond so intensely that they show up decades later for weddings, births, and funerals. Likewise, business organizations with emotion-laden leadership development programs inadvertently facilitate long-term friendships.

THE BIG IDEA

If you wish to enlist allies to your cause, don't shrink from tackling difficult challenges and sharing painful moments together. To the extent you can, run headlong into moments of shared adversity. It's not easy making yourself vulnerable around others but doing so leaves us feeling more connected and courageous.

As philosopher Alain de Botton wrote, "It's deeply poignant that we should expend so much effort on trying to look strong before the world when, all the while, it's really only ever the revelation of the somewhat embarrassing, sad, melancholy and anxious bits of us that renders us endearing to others and transforms strangers into friends."

PRINCIPLE 3: BALANCE CONFORMITY AND UNIQUENESS

Seeking a single ally is one thing. Building a whole team is a far more audacious undertaking. How can you integrate team members so everyone feels emboldened to contribute?

Social psychologist Dr. Marilynn Brewer argues that people define themselves by who they are as well as by their memberships in social groups. When we define ourselves as part of a social group, we seek to satisfy two conflicting psychological needs that crop up. First, we must feel that we fit in and belong. Second, we want to feel that we aren't expendable, carbon copies of other group members. We want to know that we possess a distinct set of life experiences, a distinct personality. We want to be ourselves, contributing our unique perspectives, experiences, and strengths. As great as it might be to feel a sense of camaraderie, we never want to lose sight of who we are, what we think, and what we care about in a group.

If you seek to motivate a team of allies to break with the status quo, help them as individuals to balance these competing needs. On one hand, help them to feel like they belong. Reassure them that it is commonplace to worry about whether they fit in or whether their position in the group is secure (too many people hide and conceal their insecurities). You might even whip out some facts: 34 percent of Americans are somewhat or very dissatisfied with their social lives. Two out of five Americans say they have zero close friends. In a survey of 20,096 adults aged eighteen and older, more than half of the U.S. participants said nobody knows them well and really understands them! When researchers asked 148,045 adolescents from fifty-two countries how often they felt lonely, 10 percent said they felt this way most of the time or always during the past year. Confirm that when they worry about fitting in, they're not outliers. As this sinks in, they can resolve the dilemma of belonging to a group while being able to be themselves.

One sure way to provide a sense of belonging is to connect with group members around points of commonality. Look for experiences from your past and those of your allies that might create an immediate sense of connection. Build rapport by asking questions about the past that generate intimacy such as: "What did you do with your close friends in childhood?"; "What were your personal interests and obsessions as a kid?"; "What are some of the memorable things you were praised and punished for as a kid?"; "If you could relive one moment, what would it be and why?" Present-day commonalities can also give rise to a shared sense of belonging. Ask questions such as: "What does friendship mean to you?"; "If you knew that in one year you would die suddenly, what would you keep the same and what would you change about the way you are living?"; "What is your greatest failure that parlayed into something valuable?" And don't forget questions about the future: "What would you do if you won the lottery?" and "What is something you've dreamed of doing for a long time? Why haven't you done it?"

These questions spark conversations that introduce common ground and a sense of belonging. The goal here isn't to take turns mesmerizing each other with intriguing stories. Rather, the aim is to provide clarity that you both belong to the same tribe (and in some small way, share meaningful commonalties). To up your game further, draw freely on the following belongingness cues.

Eighteen Cues to Offer a Quick Sense of Belonging

1. Treat people better than they expect.
2. Be an exceptional listener by interrupting with curious comments, such as: And what else? Why do you think that happened? What would you have done differently?
3. After asking a question, actually listen to the answer.
4. Bring enthusiastic energy to a conversation.

5. Instead of asking how you can help, just do it.
6. Err toward smiling or laughing when someone tries to be funny.
7. Make a big deal of putting a phone away before locking into a conversation.
8. Ignore incoming texts and phone calls when with someone.
9. When talking, keep your head from swiveling when other people pass by.
10. Invent a moment to be silly with them (even if it's just a sound effect).
11. Highlight things you like about the person you are with.
12. Detail things the other person did that you liked.
13. If you thought of someone when doing something enjoyable or meaningful, tell that same person afterward.
14. Share knowledge that you think they would be interested in.
15. Tell jokes at no one's expense.
16. Be open-minded when they share something that is weird or unusual about themselves.
17. Reveal compelling insights such as what you crave, envy, regret, mourn, or dream.
18. Express whatever positive sentiments they brought out now and later.

Amidst the gush of inclusion and belonging, don't forget to help fellow allies satisfy their need for uniqueness. Help group members feel comfortable deviating from the group by explicitly welcoming them to do so. Affirm the value of deviance in groups. Remind them that dissenters protect the group from making ill-conceived plans, and that they improve the group's performance by introducing unique solutions and novel ideas. Don't just offer a welcome mat to dissenters. By actively probing what unique value each member brings to the group, you will normalize the power of dissent. Build into the culture a set of genuine questions for each group member: What do you believe, read, and think about that most people don't? How do your views, philosophies, and values differ from other people of the same sex, race, age, and political party?

Asking people to contemplate how they differ from the rest of the group prompts them to break out and do their own thing. Another strategy is to encourage small but noticeable gestures of deviance. Think of Silicon Valley CEOs heading to a Senate hearing in blue jeans and a cotton hoody rather than a suit and tie. Think of the female Harvard Business School professor who lectures in an expensive, well-tailored outfit with a single touch of defiance: red Converse sneakers. Encourage public expression of unusual personal preferences for music, books, and podcasts. Instill a culture in which people regularly seek out diversity of thought as an integral part of decision-making.

THE BIG IDEA

To bind a group of allies together, it pays to consider the psychological needs of individuals. By helping people develop a sense of belonging *and* their own uniqueness, we can help them flourish and thus sustain their interest in contributing as allies. Maintaining this balance is not a one-time effort. You have to keep at it, paying attention to changes in individual behavior, the group's norms, and the group's success or failure.

BOLDLY GO WHERE NO ONE HAS GONE BEFORE

Silver-haired readers of this book might remember that pivotal moment in television history when the *Starship Enterprise*'s dashing Captain Kirk and beautiful Lieutenant Uhura shared an on-screen kiss. The year was 1968, the show *Star Trek.* The actors involved—the White William Shatner and the Black Nichelle Nichols—crossed the racial divide, boldly going where no television show had gone before. Today most people wouldn't think twice about an interracial kiss. But back then, with the fires of the civil rights era burning, it was hugely provocative. Just a year earlier, the Supreme Court had ruled against sixteen Southern states in a case that questioned the legality of interracial marriages. The potential for a backlash against the show was real, especially in the South.

How did the two actors muster the courage to go through with the kiss? A number of Shatner's friends urged him on. Gene Roddenberry, *Star Trek*'s creator and producer, was also enthusiastic about the kiss. As a less established actress and a Black woman, Nichols had more to lose. Yet no less a figure than Martin Luther King, Jr., advised her to stay on the show and make out with Captain Kirk (who can resist a guy in a tight, futuristic uniform?). Here, at some length, is how she recalled the conversation:

> He said, "You cannot leave. Do you understand? It has been heavenly ordained . . . You have changed the face of television forever because this is not a black role, it is not a female role, anyone can fill that role. It can be filled by a woman of any color, a man of any color. It can be filled by another Klingon or alien . . . This is a unique role and a unique point in time that breathes the life of what we are marching for: equality. Beside, you're fourth in command," and I'm thinking nobody told me that, you know . . . "Besides, Nichelle, you have no idea the power of television. This man has shown us in the 23rd Century what started now, this man has created a reality, and because it's in the 23rd Century and you are the chief communications officer, fourth in command of a Starship going on a five-year mission where no man or woman has gone before, it means that what we are doing today is just the beginning of where we're going, just how far we're going. You cannot leave. Besides, *Star Trek* is the only show that my wife, Coretta, and I allow

our little children to stay up late and watch, and Nichelle, I can't go back and tell them this, because you are their hero."

Disrupting the status quo sucks up a great deal of psychic energy, not to mention other resources. It's so much easier when we have friends by our side, urging us on, supporting us, listening to our fears and concerns, sharing our pain. Not only do we achieve more—we find ourselves happier and more fulfilled because of these relationships. Still, as important as friends are for principled insubordinates, they only take us so far. Rebels also have to keep *themselves* in the game. How do you manage your own psychology knowing you face a long, arduous, uncertain path ahead? You develop some good old-fashioned resilience, that's how, using powerful techniques revealed by science.

RECIPE STEPS

1. *Get some allies to help you.* With people on your side who complement your skills, strengths, and viewpoints, you can enhance your capabilities and off-load some of the effort when defying the status quo.
2. *Build trust with your allies by making yourself vulnerable.* Trust emerges as we *share* adversity with others. If you wish to enlist allies to your cause, tackle difficult challenges and share painful moments together. Shared pain serves as social glue.
3. *When creating alliances, attend to the dual, opposing psychological needs of individuals in groups.* Help people feel certain that they belong in the group *and* also are valued for expressing their uniqueness. Clarify that deviating to make the group better (not conformity) is what characterizes an ideal group member. Regularly attend to both of these psychological needs and you will fire up people's motivation to express unique contributions.

CHAPTER 6

Build Mental Fortitude

How to handle the negative emotions and pangs of rejection when rebelling

We touched on how difficult it is to rebel, but if you want a sense of the sheer psychological strength required, you would do well to talk to Martha Goddard. Back in the 1970s, many police officers had no clue how to react when a rape survivor stepped forward to report a crime. Instead of providing survivors with a safe haven, police dismissed them and handled physical evidence so shoddily that they compromised criminal cases. In the course of investigations, officers would cut off survivors' shirts with scissors, contaminating the evidence. Investigators accidentally destroyed useful DNA samples from hair, sweat, and semen. After making a woman remove her shirt and underwear, police gave her a paper-bag gown to wear on the drive home in a police car—broadcasting the incident to onlookers in the survivor's neighborhood. Hospital emergency rooms were hardly better, treating survivors coldly. The situation was so bad that many women advised friends not to bother visiting a police station or hospital after they'd been raped because it would only cause more trauma.

As a frontline worker helping homeless teenagers, Goddard heard heartbreaking stories about the mistreatment of rape survivors in legal and medical settings. So she did something about it. As clinical psychologist Dr. Dean Kilpatrick, a rape victims' advocate at the time, told me, Goddard in 1976 "worked with law enforcement, prosecutors, and medical experts to develop a standardized rape kit that was designed to collect evidence in a standardized way that was mindful of the needs of rape victims." A comb to collect loose hair. Nail clippers to remove substances buried under fingernails. Swabs to smear orifices for foreign fluids. Plastic tubes for blood samples. Plenty of bags and plastic envelopes to store salvaged details from bodies and clothes. The advantage of a rape kit is "all the materials required for the collection of evidence are [at] hand prior to commencing the examination . . . the contents act as a prompt for inexperienced practitioners." As a 1978 *New York Times* article observed, the kits were "a powerful new weapon in the conviction of rapists in Illinois."

Powerful, but not universally welcomed. The men in charge shrugged. What business did she have telling *them* how to do their work? To convince police and health care workers to adopt rape kits, Goddard worked seven days a week visiting individual police precincts and hospitals. Goddard tried raising money to further spread the word and advocate on survivors' behalf, but nobody in Chicago would open their checkbooks. That is, except for the very last person you'd expect: *Playboy* founder Hugh Heffner. Say what you will about the Hef, but he forked over $10,000 through the Playboy Foundation, his company's nonprofit arm. He opened his office space, allowing Goddard's recruited volunteers to create a rape kit assembly line there. Regarding Heffner as an enemy, feminists were outraged. "I took a lot of flak from the women's movement—but too bad," Goddard said. "Boy, was I roasted for that. But I gotta tell you if it was *Penthouse* or *Hustler*, no. But *Playboy*? Please, give me a break."

Over time, Goddard's relentless pursuit of justice for female survivors of sexual abuse paid off. Some two dozen Chicago-area hospitals were using rape kits by the end of 1978. By 1980, health care workers were using them in thousands of hospitals across the country. A one-stop package for preserving DNA that officers, detectives, medical professionals, and prosecutors could use to produce a database matching individuals arrested for criminal activity with rape kit evidence. "Marty Goddard was a true pioneer in the anti-rape movement," Dr. Dean Kilpatrick said, as "the rape exam was transformed from something that many women described as nearly as bad as the rape itself to something that treated women humanely and gathered the evidence needed to identify suspects and support a criminal prosecution." Summing up the impact of Goddard's work, he noted, "Marty deserves incredible credit for having the courage, fortitude, and persistence to make this very important thing happen in the face of much opposition."

Rape remains extremely hard to prosecute in the United States, with fewer than a quarter of survivors reporting. But if Goddard hadn't stayed the course, fighting the good fight year after year, visiting all of those police stations and hospitals and knocking on Hugh Heffner's door, rape survivors would receive less justice than they do today. Bear in mind, Goddard operated in an era when terms like "date rape" and "marital rape" didn't yet exist, and when the behaviors they describe went unprosecuted. It was a time when police officers, prosecuting attorneys, and even judges defended rape by arguing that "there are many sexually frustrated men who do not have a nonviolent way of satisfying their sexual desires" and "women who are raped dress or behave in a seductive manner." Somehow, Goddard managed to persevere in this unsympathetic environment, fighting the good fight even when she felt tempted to give up or scale back her efforts. How do people like her do it? How can *you* stay in the game over the long term as a rebel, taking bold risks and persevering in the face of emotional distress caused by persecution, ostracism, loneliness, and unanticipated setbacks?

Virtually all mental health interventions developed in recent decades proceed on the assumption that the best way to respond to distress is to minimize it. If you're a rebel struggling in the face of adversity, you go to a therapist or undertake some other intervention in hopes of obtaining some kind of relief that allows you to function better. More recently, psychologists have argued that trying to reduce distress can cause *more* suffering. As they point out, distress is a human experience and not inherently bad. What's bad is the avoidance of and unwillingness to experience distress. When worried about an impending deadline, we procrastinate and scroll through social media. When sad or lonely, we comfort ourselves by gorging on food. When overcome by pangs of regret, we spend hours mulling over what might have been, failing to live in the present moment. Too often, our strategies for coping with distress, while possibly effective in the moment, distance us further from the life we want, causing us more distress over time.

How can you learn to withstand distress so that it doesn't drag you down? One powerful solution is to cultivate what scientists call "psychological flexibility." When bad shit goes down, the psychologically flexible person doesn't freak to the point of breakdown. Rather, she takes steps to quickly recover and make progress anew. She shifts promptly away from managing the pain she feels to driving assertively toward her goals. Sounds good, you say, but how the hell do I do that? Glad you asked.

THE BIG IDEA

To withstand distress better, cultivate your new secret weapon: psychological flexibility.

DIG THE DASHBOARD

A powerful tool you can use to become more psychologically flexible is—wait for it—the Psychological Flexibility Dashboard. Weaving together a number of evidence-based strategies, the Dashboard is a simple, four-step process of reflection that prepares you to deal effectively with the inevitable adversity you'll confront as a rebel. In the face of an emotionally intense situation, you can use the Dashboard to break down your experience of the situation, process overwhelming feelings of distress, short-circuit unhelpful ways of handling these feelings, and inspire yourself to take courageous action. Making sense of short-term hardship, you can turn back toward your larger purpose and pursue it with renewed vigor.

In summary form, the Dashboard looks like this:

(STEP 2) "What unwanted thoughts, feelings, memories, and bodily sensations am I experiencing?"	**(STEP 1) "What and who is important to me?"**
← ESCAPING PAIN	**HUNTING MEANING →**
(STEP 3) "What am I doing to reduce, avoid, or control unwanted mental content?"	**(STEP 4) "What am I doing or could be doing to chase my values?**

The essence of the Dashboard is a recognition of two basic directions toward which you can move when dealing with an emotionally challenging event. When moving in the direction of Hunting Meaning, you remind yourself of your purpose in dissenting, deviating, or defying the status quo. Maybe you're seeking social change. Maybe you want to feel a sense of autonomy or individuality. Maybe you're seeking to innovate. Whatever it is, you're pursuing goals that you find personally meaningful and important enough to merit a short-term sacrifice. When moving in the other direction to Escape Pain, you acknowledge the demanding strain put on you, and the sense of urgency to exert control over whatever negative thoughts and feelings appear. Each direction corresponds with two questions to ask yourself and, in turn, exercises to help improve your ability to self-regulate effectively. By sharpening your ability to think through these questions, you will become more flexible in the face of hardship. Psychological flexibility provides the seeds that produce resilience. Let's run through the four steps one by one.

Step I: "What and who is important to me?" (Remind Yourself of the Reason for Dissenting)

Clarity about your mission and its moral basis keeps you grounded, allowing you to absorb a higher level of pain than otherwise. If you know what you're trying to accomplish, harsh criticism by others won't matter so much, and you're more liable to confidently go your own way (as one fascinating study found, people with a greater sense of purpose reacted less to the number of "likes" received after posting selfies on social media). It's easier to defend a cause if you're clear on your mission, even when your body is disrupted by panic attack symptoms (rapid pounding heart rate, trembling or shaking, tightness in your throat, and so on) or when your mind tells you to fear being taunted or when there are reasonable worries about losing a job. Conversely, if you're rudderless or unanchored in your actions, ignorant of your core beliefs, you might find it harder to leverage your strengths, skills, and allies to meet the demands of a difficult situation.

To help yourself through hardship and inspire moral courage, ask yourself why you rebelled in the first place. Remind yourself of the beliefs that set your moral compass. Beliefs that prompted you to step up and dissent. "I got into fighting sexual abuse because I was sick of seeing women, especially children, go through all of that pain, with oftentimes no conviction of the culprit," Goddard clarified. She reflected on her desire for justice, her belief that survivors needed a voice, her desire to live in a country where women and men receive equal protection under the law. It was personal. "I knew I had to reveal that I had been sexually assaulted myself. I was sick of it being some big secret, and still am to this day. It was very painful to re-live my past, but it was so beneficial for so many rape victims." Making your own pain a springboard to help others can be personally healing and meaningful. She sought to make society better for other women. Armed with the underlying motivations behind her purpose, Goddard could steel herself in difficult moments by reflecting on what she was trying to accomplish in taking on the status quo.

Take out a blank sheet of paper and make lists of the following: (1) the people and things that are most important to you; (2) details about your current purpose in life (for Goddard, it was helping rape survivors receive dignified treatment and justice); and (3) the core values that underlie your purpose. Spend some time and really think about these lists. Write down as much as you can. Keep your answers nearby as a talisman to remind you of what you uncovered. A statement or manifesto in your wallet or on the wallpaper of your smartphone might work, something that evokes why principled insubordination is worth the pain. The following exercises will spur your thinking and help you populate the three lists.

Clarifying What and Who Is Important

1. **Who are the people you would most like to thank? Think hard about how they helped you, how they served as a role model, and what parts of your identity they reinforced.**

2. Who is the wisest person you know? Think hard about what is it that you admire and seek to emulate.
3. What do you think is your main purpose in life?
4. What makes you strong? Think about the stack of capacities that together allow you to obtain excellent results on a regular basis, whether when working, socializing, playing, or living. Everyone has a profile of strengths. Know yours. Own it.
5. If with a wave of a magic wand all of your insecurities disappeared, what would you be doing differently?
6. If you had unlimited money, what would you be doing differently?
7. Imagine you could achieve anything—what would it be and why?
8. At the end of your life, what do you want to be remembered for?

Value Trade-Offs to Know Yourself

1. Which of these would be most difficult for you to accept?

_____the death of a parent?
_____the death of a sibling?
_____the death of a spouse?

2. Which would you prefer to give up if you had to?

_____economic freedom
_____religious freedom
_____political freedom

3. Which would you least like to be?

_____a rifleman firing point-blank at the charging enemy
_____a bomber on a plane dropping napalm on an enemy village
_____publicly branded a coward by your own community

4. Which would you least like to be?

_____poor
_____sick
_____disfigured

5. Which would you prefer?

____a short, impactful life with a peaceful death

____a long, non-impactful life with a peaceful death

____a long, impactful life with a slow and painful death

6. Which would be the most painful way to spend the rest of your days?

____being unable to remember anything

____being unable to forget anything

____reliving only a single memory over and over again

7. Which type of romantic partner would bother you the most?

____one who spends frivolously

____one who interrupts constantly

____one who is very messy

8. How do you learn best?

____independent reading and study

____lectures

____discussions with others

9. Which is most important in a friendship?

____honesty

____generosity

____loyalty

10. How would you most like to spend a Saturday?

____alone on an activity you are passionate about

____with people you love, doing something you don't care about

____with acquaintances doing something novel and fun

11. Which do you respect most in others?

____intelligence

____kindness

____humor

12. If there were no negative effects, which of the following would you most want to give up?

____eating

____sleeping

____exercising

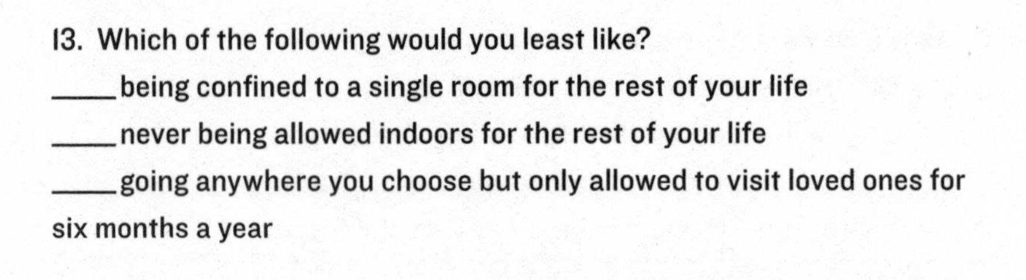
13. Which of the following would you least like?
____being confined to a single room for the rest of your life
____never being allowed indoors for the rest of your life
____going anywhere you choose but only allowed to visit loved ones for six months a year

Step 2: "What unwanted thoughts, feelings, memories, and bodily sensations am I experiencing?" (Get in Touch with Your Discomfort)

Now that you checked in with your motivations for dissenting, challenge yourself to register the unpleasant or negative emotions experienced. Make yourself aware of *why* you will benefit from mental fortitude. If you're Martha Goddard receiving angry messages from feminists upset about your affiliation with Hugh Hefner, you're probably feeling a gamut of emotions: shock, worry, fear, guilt, frustration, indignation, doubt, hopelessness, disappointment. Your mind might trail off into a whirlwind of self-defeating thoughts about yourself, your personality, the quality of your relationships with others, your future prospects, and so on. Physically, you might feel the signs and symptoms of distress—dry mouth, racing heart, shortness of breath, sweaty palms. As painful as all of this might be, chart the dimensions of your experience as fully as you can. As many discover, doing so can feel oddly liberating. The mental torture you've inflicted on yourself will come out in the open. When it does, your torture techniques lose some of their potency. Conversely, when we don't acknowledge the distress that arises from challenging conventional thinking, we become weaker and less effective.

The more specific you can be in describing your experience of adversity, the better. As my research has shown, it's difficult to identify and label the myriad of emotions experienced on a regular basis, but skillfulness at "emotion labeling" can prove extremely helpful. In one study, my colleagues and I asked participants to report intense negative experiences they had in daily life on a handheld computer. Those adept at labeling the specific emotions they felt consumed 40 percent less alcohol during a stress-induced drinking episode than participants who weren't. In other studies, we found that people who had been emotionally hurt by others and who were better at distinguishing their negative feelings were 20 percent (in one study) and 50 percent (in a second study) less likely to retaliate with verbal or physical aggression. In yet another study, people adept at describing their feelings over the course of two weeks were better able to handle experiences of rejection. They showed similar levels of brain region activation in areas linked to psychic and physical pain (the insula and anterior cingulate cortex) regardless of whether a stranger welcomed or rejected them in a video game. When you label your emotions effectively, you feel calmer in the face of stressful life events, and unwanted distressing mental content seems less bothersome. You become more capable of deciding what to do next.

As research suggests, training people to label their emotions more effectively increases resilience. In one study, researchers trained spider-fearing individuals to precisely label emotions they felt when observing a spider (e.g., "in front of me is an ugly spider and it is disgusting, nerve-wracking, and yet, intriguing"). Participants trained to precisely label emotions spent more time physically handling spiders and felt less flustered during the experience than others trained to distract themselves or generate positive thoughts. A week later, trained to describe their feelings proficiently, these participants could approach a stressful situation irrespective of the amount of disgust or fear they felt.

For rebels, emotion labeling has a number of specific benefits. First, labeled emotions become easier to manage. Felt emotions become manageable or harnessed into goal-directed energy. For instance, anger might make you speak with more volume, inflection, and confidence during a legal proceeding. For anxious people, labeling emotions makes events less scary. Second, the act of using words to describe what you feel conveys information about the situation and possible courses of action. Third, by improving the management of intense, distressing emotions, you become less likely to dedicate energy toward controlling emotions. Instead, you channel energy toward more meaningful life pursuits. My research team found that combat veterans who organize their lives around trying to manage their emotions experience less joy and meaning. Further, they contribute less effort toward and make less progress toward their most important goals. As you worry less about feeling worried, you have extra energy to dedicate to specific tasks related to your principled insubordination.

After conducting an inventory of the mental and physical toll of rebelling, do nothing more than describe your feelings. What words can you attach to them? Be precise as you can and repeat this practice whenever you encounter setbacks large or small. Refer to the list of emotions below. If you aren't clear on the precise meaning of some of these terms, look them up in a dictionary. The ability to label your emotions isn't an inborn talent. You can learn and master it. As you do, your ability to stay strong, focused, and effective will increase.

Notice how many words exist for describing the gradients of particular emotions such as anger (in bold), fear (underlined), and sadness (in italics). Expand your emotion vocabulary. Use greater precision in detailing the type of emotions you feel and their intensity.

A

Abandoned
Afraid
Aggravated
Agitated
Agony
Alarmed
Alienated
Angry
Anguish
Annoyed
Anxious
Apathetic
Appalled
Apprehensive
Ashamed
Astonished

B

Betrayed
Bitterness
Bored

C

Contempt

D

Defeated
Dejected
Depressed
Despair
Disappointed
Disgust
Disillusioned
Dismay
Dismissive
Displeased
Disrespected
Distracted
Dread

E

Embarrassed
Empty
Enraged
Envy
Exasperated
Exhausted

F

Fearful
Fragile
Frightful
Frustrated
Fury

G

Gloomy
Glum
Grief
Grouchy
Grumpy
Guilt

H

Hateful
Hesitant
Homesick
Hopeless
Horror
Hostile
Humiliated
Hurt
Hysteric

I

Indignant
Inferior
Insecure
Insulted
Irritated
Isolated

J

Jealous
Jittery

L

Loathing
Lonely

M

Mad
Melancholy
Misery
Mortified

N

Nauseated
Neglected
Nervous
Numb

O

Outraged
Overwhelmed

P

Panic
Perplexed
Pity
Powerless
Pressured

R

Rage
Regretful
Rejected
Remorseful
Resentful
Revulsion
Rushed

S

Sad
Scared
Scorn
Shame
Shock
Skeptical
Sorrow
Spite
Sympathy

T

Tense
Terror
Tired
Tormented

U

Uneasy
Unhappy

V

Vengeful
Victimized
Violated
Vulnerable

W

Withdrawn
Woe
Worried
Wrath

Step 3: "What am I doing to reduce, avoid, or control unwanted mental content?" (Get in Touch with Your Coping Mechanisms)

It's important to chart what you're currently doing to escape from the unpleasant thoughts, feelings, or sensations charted out in the previous step. Your go-to responses might not be helping you, and they could actually be hurting. Traditionally, people try to ignore unwanted thoughts. They suppress them, correct them, replace them with a positive affirmation, or seek out distractions. If Marty Goddard had tried to distract herself from her anxiety after pitching rape kits, she probably would have felt good for the two hours spent watching a movie or the ten minutes eating an ice cream sundae. Once she was reminded of the backlog of unsolved rape cases in Chicago, her distress might have returned. And then what??

Like many people, I respond to distress in a whole slew of unhelpful ways. I take medication, sometimes far too much. I drink too much booze. I distract myself, watching television mindlessly. I force myself to think of something else. I avoid social contact. I exercise excessively. I provoke verbal altercations with strangers and loved ones. I attack people relentlessly online, rarely for any decent reason. I bury myself in work. I hide away at home and withdraw from friends and family. I yell at my kids. I stop talking to my wife. I make excuses for not socializing, for saying no to things, for doing nothing. I play music or listen to podcasts throughout the day to avoid being alone with my thoughts.

Pull out a piece of paper and list (for yourself) your favorite coping mechanisms. How well are these working for you? Even if they ease your pain in the moment, do they cause problems for you afterward?

As an alternative to these and other common coping strategies, try "cognitive defusion." The name sounds pretentious but stick with me here. It's an approach uncovered by psychologists that you can easily perform at home without involving others, and has been shown to help you reduce the influence of unwanted thoughts and feelings. Cognitive defusion is a psychological exercise in which you create a mental space between yourself and the thoughts you're thinking. If you can create this space, it becomes easier to consider thoughts and feelings in a detached way, since you're no longer binding them to your identity. If our emotions and thoughts are like slices of pie, cognitive defusion has you switch from being the judge of a pie baking contest to a nonchalant audience member given a free taste—who notices the flaky crust that offsets the warm, soft apple filling, and the excess cinnamon that offers a tingling sensation on the tongue (hungry yet?). You don't get upset at the imperfections of the pie slices tasted. You're just observing. And the act of observing neutralizes the power of your emotions.

Dozens of techniques exist to help us separate ourselves from our thoughts and feelings. One powerful method is simply to treat thoughts and feelings like objects by externalizing them. Scientific studies have asked people to recall intensely distressing words about their identity (such as the words "fat," "ugly," "unattractive," "uninteresting," "unlovable," "friendless") and write them down on a piece of paper or say them aloud for thirty to sixty seconds. As participants view these ugly thoughts for what they are—just thoughts, not a reflection of reality—they regard them as less important and in turn become less distressed by them. The effect lasts as long as people keep practicing the technique. Even cooler, people find these thoughts to be less believable. When people write their ugly thoughts on paper, researchers ask them to rip the piece of paper into tiny, unreadable shreds and toss them into a garbage pail. Multiple studies have shown that the mere act of physicalizing unwanted thoughts and feelings and destroying them literally and metaphorically reduces their impact.

Here are a few other techniques you can use to neutralize thoughts and feelings by separating them from yourself and your identity:

1. *Treat your mind like a separate creature.* It's not as if we believe the mind is separate from the rest of us, but something psychologically powerful happens when you treat it as nothing more than an opinion generator. Get in the habit of using descriptive phrases when your mind produces ugly thoughts and feelings. Be playful or be serious. "Thank you, Mind, for being so unhelpful this morning." Ask questions such as, "Mind, what's your opinion on whether this section will be persuasive to readers?" Give feedback to what your mind produces with short phrases such as, "Good one, Mind" or "That's a new one" or "Way to go for the jugular!" This exercise will help you create distance between your thoughts and you, the thinker.
2. *Give the story a name.* You can label stories your mind generates that are getting old, trite, and appallingly boring. For instance, as a New Yorker, I speak rapidly, to the point where people often ask me to slow down. I'm a bit self-conscious about it. This is my "speed demon story." I have many moles, birthmarks, and brown spots on my body. For years, I felt insecure about it and never took off my shirt. This is my "chocolate chip story." Name it, play with it, and your negative thoughts will lose some of their sting.
3. *Go into detective mode.* When talking to ourselves, we rarely stop and ask: Who the hell is talking to us? And what is their sex, gender, race, age? When an ugly thought arises, go on a scavenger hunt and figure out the answers to these and other questions. What does the voice in your head sound like? Who is doing the talking? Where is the voice located? Is the voice

moving or changing? What will this voice come up with next? Show a level of curiosity about your thoughts, reminding yourself that you're not what shows up because a part of you notices what is happening. You can't be both the thing itself and the noticer of the thing (unless we are playing quantum physics games).

4. *Modify the thinking machine.* Your brain talks a lot. It rarely stops talking. You are better able to remain in the present moment, doing what you care about, if you change your relationship to the words. Alter the voice. Choose your favorite television character and imagine your mind speaking to you with their speaking pattern (I prefer Morty from *Rick and Morty*). Imagine your mind's thoughts appearing on a scrolling banner, just like the breaking news banner at the top of a newspaper website. Write your thoughts on index cards with artistic calligraphy (I prefer bubble letters). Envision leaves floating on a river. Put your ugly thoughts on a leaf and watch it float past. Do the same thing by putting your thoughts on clouds and notice as they blow by, slowly. As you experiment with how thoughts appear through your five senses, their influence on behavior lessens. When you normalize thoughts, they are less likely to pull you out of the present moment to ruminate instead of live.

Again, the point of cognitive defusion isn't to help you escape, avoid, or minimize negative thoughts and feelings. It's to let you experience negative thoughts so that you can behave courageously in the face of adversity. An extension of the immortal words of the renowned existential psychologist Rollo May in 1963, "Freedom is the individual's capacity to know that he is the determined one, to pause between stimulus and response and thus to throw his weight, however slight it may be, on the side of one particular response among several possible ones . . . I would define mental health as the capacity to be aware of the gap between stimulus and response, together with the capacity to use this gap constructively."

Step 4: "What am I doing or could be doing to chase my values?" (Gauge Your Opportunities)

Now that you've reconnected with your purpose, acknowledged your thoughts and emotions, and broken with unhelpful ways of processing them, there is one more step: invest in aspirational behavior that guides you toward meaningful living. Here you make that sharp turn and recommit to chasing a heroic version of yourself, even if it's psychologically difficult. You choose to contribute to a better society rather than tie yourself up in another attempt to escape pain. How will you deal with the onslaught of adversaries and detractors in the push for creating healthy, personally meaningful social change? What kind of person will you *really* be? Here is where you make that call—and start to live it.

Begin by noticing what you're already doing that, even in an emotionally intense situation, is bringing you satisfaction and fulfillment. For Goddard, it was the ability to retain decency amidst adversity. As she remarked, "I would say the most important strategy is don't name call. But along with that is, be nice, have a little class, and keep one foot in with the institutions and one foot out and then you can move any way you want. Left, right, up, down, backward, forward." For others, it might be asking for someone's perspective on an issue, acquiring new knowledge and wisdom, sharing knowledge to benefit other people, improving health by exercising, eating, and sleeping well, keeping a journal of lessons learned and exceptional moments, offering genuine apologies, or spending time connecting with friends and supporting each other's wins and losses.

When thinking about how you're chasing your values, be intentional. Don't rely on the kinds of superficial descriptions you've long used when introducing yourself to strangers. In fact, you might find it helpful to pause for a moment and separate out the real "you" in your mind from the public persona you cultivate. Pretend you're on a desert island with nobody serving as your audience. What music would you enjoy listening to, what books would you read, what movies would you watch, what topics of conversation would you find enthralling? How would you identify yourself to yourself if nobody else were listening?

Once you've thought about how you're already chasing your values, consider your current activities and how you might frame goals for intentionally spending your limited time in the days and weeks ahead. We might call these objectives "strivings." They capture what we're "trying" to do right now and plan to continue pursuing in the future. For example, we might adopt "trying to produce more persuasive arguments" as a striving, even if we don't necessarily succeed at it on a daily or weekly basis.

We can frame strivings broadly (for instance, "trying to transform my passions into a job") or more specifically ("trying to seek sources of financial support to transition into a full-time artist"). We can also construe strivings positively or negatively; they might convey something we're trying to obtain or keep, or something we're trying to avoid or prevent. For example, you might be trying to gain more attention from others, or perhaps you're trying to avoid calling attention to yourself.

Note that strivings are a pretty cool way of describing yourself that don't make use of personality adjectives such as "friendly," "intelligent," or "honest." For now, forget about personality adjectives. Focus just on defining the personal projects you're currently working on and would like to continue pursuing, jotting your ideas down in a notebook. Thinking carefully about what you value in everyday life, try to compose six strivings starting with the stem "I am trying to . . ." Don't mentally compare what you are striving for with what other people do. Keep returning to the idea of what you would like to pursue, even if nobody ever found out about your accomplishments. Just as carefully describing your exact feelings in a demanding situation can help you, you can benefit by breaking down your life into precise personal strivings.

From here, consider what it might feel like to embrace your pain and act in ways aligned with your core values. What do you want to do? What do you want to be about? You can accomplish a great deal in any situation when you switch from avoiding pain to hunting for a sense of meaning. Committing to positive behavior change can go far. In our research, my colleagues and I found that even adults suffering from severe social anxiety disorder enjoy practically the same sense of self-worth as healthy adults on days when they commit to positive behavior change or work toward personally meaningful strivings. A measure of their daily sense of meaning in life rose by 19 percent and they saw a 14 percent increase in how many times they experienced positive emotions. Meanwhile, their negative emotional experiences fell by 10 percent.

To ramp up your commitment to principled rebellion, share your plans with peers. Such tactics work with a wide range of personal goals we might have. In one study, a sample of 324 overweight, sedentary adults participated in a sixteen-week "Internet-mediated walking program." Participants who could post their goals, effort, and progress on an online discussion board were 13 percent better at sticking with the program than those without such access.

Whom you disclose your personal strivings to matters. If you really want to maximize performance toward personalized, mission-related goals, disclose this information to an audience that includes someone you respect, admire, and whose opinion matters. Sharing your mission plans with people you view as lower in status doesn't help, nor does recording your objectives in a secret black book with private notes and musings. As we'll see in the next chapter, we care about making a positive impression on others, and we worry about how others will think of us if we fail to meet our goals. Such concerns render us more likely to do the hard work of Hunting Meaning. Anxiety is energy, so find your carefully curated tribe and show your commitment by publicizing the plan. Our allies only benefit us if they know our commitments.

To Hunt Meaning effectively, we must prepare for obstructions, both internal and outside us. Think of the prison sentences levied on heroic liberators such as Martin Luther King, Jr., Nelson Mandela, Mahatma Gandhi, Emmeline Pankhurst, and Ahmet Altan (what a story, look him up!). Imagine how prison compromised their ability to deliver on their goals. At the beginning of each day, contemplate the efforts you'll make toward your strivings, but also anticipate disruption. I find the following meditation by Marcus Aurelius instructive:

> When you wake up in the morning, tell yourself: the people I deal with today will be meddling, ungrateful, arrogant, dishonest, jealous and surly. They are like this because they can't tell good from evil. But I have seen the beauty of good, and the ugliness of evil, and have recognized that the wrongdoer has a nature related to my own—not of the same blood and birth, but the same mind, and possessing a share of the divine. And so none of them can hurt me. No one can implicate me in ugliness. Nor can I feel angry at my relative, or hate him. We were born to work together like feet, hands and eyes, like the two rows of teeth, upper and lower. To obstruct each other is unnatural. To feel anger at someone, to turn your back on him: these are unnatural.

Don't stop at anticipating obstacles. *Plan* for them. Answer this question often: "What might get in the way of following through on today's intention to devote effort toward my strivings? And what will I try to do about it?" You want backup plans at your disposal, so make sure you envision the multiple paths available as you direct energy toward strivings. In short, hope for the best, but brace for the worst. Positivity alone won't help you build mental fortitude. You need to crack open a jar of psychological flexibility whup-ass. Above all, don't shrink from adversity. Do the hard work of realizing your full potential, using the four steps of the Psychological Flexibility Dashboard as a helpful set of tools.

REBEL *ANYWAY*

Rebels who are psychologically flexible possess an enviable ability to dissent despite pain. They suffer—and rebel anyway. To walk through the Dashboard is to reset yourself, turning away from merely escaping pain and toward the renewed pursuit of your goal. You engage in a variety of complicated tasks including a clarification of values ("What and who is important to me?"); a discovery of the unpleasant feelings and thoughts experienced ("What unwanted thoughts, feelings, memories, and bodily sensations show up?"); an analysis of your habitual reactions to those feelings and thoughts ("What am I doing to reduce, avoid, or control unwanted mental content?"); and an affirmation of aspirational solutions ("What am I doing or could be doing to chase my values?"). All along, take note of your experiences, planning how you might build the life you seek going forward. Working with a common language and set of questions, you sift through mental content to arrive at intentional, *workable* behaviors.

Use the Dashboard over time, and you really will become more psychologically flexible. You'll learn to break quickly from old patterns and prejudices and swap in new, healthier behaviors. You'll become more aware of the freedom of action you truly have, increasing the chance that you'll act on non-conformist ideas that occur to you. The key, as simple as it sounds, is to question. By opening up our assumptions to fresh analysis, we create a new potential for creativity and principled insubordination. The emotional hardships of pushing for a new, better way no longer seem as unsettling as sticking with status quo ideas, processes, and products.

Let's say you do manage to handle your distress and stay in the game long enough to defeat the establishment. You've won! But as you savor the glory of victory, you face a choice: How will you treat the members of the establishment who lost power and prominence? Will you extend your hand in partnership, treating your former enemy as a colleague, friend, or even ally? Or will you exclude them as you were once excluded, lording your newfound power over them?

Dealing with relationship transitions in group dynamics can prove just as difficult as remaining resilient during a hard fight. Although people often seek therapists to deal with distress, they seldom do so upon winning in the face of adversity. But we need help to adjust to winning in healthy ways, both as individuals and as groups, lest we compromise the very mission we as rebels have been advancing. As science reveals, wounds we inflict on others have a way of coming back at us. To rebel successfully, you must know how to win gracefully and inclusively, and you must challenge yourself to stay true to the humane values and intentions you nurtured all along. We've talked about the pain of fighting. Let's now turn to the responsibility that comes with winning, and how to exercise that responsibility admirably.

RECIPE STEPS

1. *To withstand distress better, cultivate your new secret weapon: "psychological flexibility."* A psychologically flexible person adapts their thoughts, feelings, and behaviors to a given situation, making sure their actions remain rooted in whatever it is that's important to them.
2. *Mobilize the Psychological Flexibility Dashboard.* By relying on four provocations, you can devise *workable* solutions to mentally distressing problems. First, remind yourself of the reason for dissenting. Second, get in touch with your discomfort. Third, get in touch with your coping mechanisms. Fourth, gauge your opportunities.
3. *Stick with it.* Building psychological flexibility using the Dashboard isn't easy, but it's worth the effort. Do the hard work of realizing your full potential.

CHAPTER 7

Win Responsibly

How to prevent moral hypocrisy if and when you become the new majority

Evo Morales, Bolivia's former president, knows what it's like to live in extreme poverty. Born into his country's marginalized Aboriginal community, Morales and his family lived in a traditional adobe farmhouse—just one small room served as kitchen, dining room, and bedroom. Four of Morales's six siblings died during infancy, and Morales's reward for surviving was childhood labor. At the age of five, he went to work as a llama shepherd to help his family afford their daily meals.

During the 1980s and 1990s, Morales dedicated himself to improving his community's plight, participating in a grassroots movement to legalize production of the coca plant, a vital crop for Aboriginal farmers and a fixture of traditional Bolivian culture. At the time, speaking up for Aborigine culture was risky. The U.S. government was fighting a "war on drugs," funneling money to Bolivia's entrenched elites to stop narcotics from reaching American soil. Instead of stopping drug trafficking and arresting drug dealers, corrupt Bolivian government officials cracked down on impoverished Aboriginal farmers, taking their coca leaves and extracting bribes. Officials also arrested farmers and subjected them to elaborate forms of torturous interrogations that included burning them with cigarettes, delivering electric shocks, injecting them with toxic substances, shooting their limbs, and keeping their heads submerged under water. Several arrested farmers died in custody. Morales himself was beaten, jailed, and on one occasion nearly killed after government forces left him in a remote area to die.

By the mid- to late 1990s, Morales was active in electoral politics, fighting for policies to improve the economic standing and power of marginalized members of society. In 2006, despite opposition from the U.S. government, he was elected president on a left-wing platform of poverty reduction, investment in education and hospitals, increases in minimum wage, higher taxes on the wealthy, and the extension of political rights to the Aboriginal population. Once in power, Morales made good on many of his promises, bringing widespread economic growth to his country. Taking back control of oil and gas production from foreign energy companies, he brought billions of dollars into government coffers that had formerly gone abroad. Salaries increased, unemployment fell by 50 percent, and literacy rates rose. Within four years of his election, the World Bank adjusted Bolivia's country classification from a "lower-income" economy, the lowest possible classification, to the next tier of "lower-middle income." This new designation translated into three to four times greater gross national income per capita, enabling the government to borrow money at lower interest rates and in turn lay the foundation for even more wealth creation. Between 2005 and 2018, Bolivia became Latin America's fastest growing economy.

But Morales's rule had a dark side. In the course of consolidating power, his government quashed dissent. In 2013, Morales issued a presidential decree allowing the government wide-ranging authority to disband civil society organizations. His government intimidated journalists and blacklisted dissenters. In 2011, when thousands of Bolivians protested Morales's plan to build a highway across a protected reserve of Amazon rainforest, police brutally attacked protesters with tear gas and rubber bullets. According to one account, "when the women marchers yelled their dissent, Morales's police bound their faces with duct tape to shut their mouths." The country's constitution mandated a two-term limit for presidents, but Morales clung to power for a third term and would have remained for a fourth had he not been forced out by elements of his military following allegations of electoral manipulation.

Many successful insubordinates underperform once they gain power, abandoning their values and failing to deliver on the good they promised to do. Vladimir Lenin led an uprising of workers with a vision of "peace, bread and land" for all Russian citizens. How did that work out? And then there was the French Revolution, which promised liberty, equality, and fraternity but devolved into a frightful period of head-chopping under Maximilien Robespierre. Perform an autopsy on successful revolutions large and small, and you will find that amidst the thrill of victory after long years of sacrifice, successful insubordinates often waste or taint the opportunity earned, struggling to catalyze and sustain healthy change. You might chalk this up to the extremism that insubordination often generates, especially after extended periods of repression by establishment forces. But that invites the question: what about human psychology helps fuel such fervor?

Our latent impulses toward tribalism go a long way toward explaining it. We share in our fellow group members' pride and joy, feeling empathy for them and responding to their needs, but we fail to behave similarly toward outsiders. We ignore when members of our group behave aggressively, violently, or exploitatively toward "the other," and we assign outsiders as our nemesis, defining our group in opposition to them. In difficult situations, it's handy to blame someone or something other than ourselves. All too often, these dynamics lead successful insubordinates to persecute members of the former majority, producing needless suffering. Insubordinates discount the fallen majority's potentially useful ideas, and lay the foundation for future conflict.

Researchers have uncovered several interlocking psychological factors that fuel tribal impulses among successful non-conformists, pushing them to behave destructively toward vanquished members of the former majority. As Martin Luther King, Jr., said, "We must either learn to live together as brothers or we are all going to perish together as fools."

THE BIG IDEA

With knowledge of how humans are tribal in nature, especially during transfers of power, we can behave more thoughtfully and rationally, neutralizing impulses to demonize those who once doubted or persecuted us.

THE REBEL'S DISCONTENT

When power shifts between majority and non-conformist members of a group, neither of these subgroups views the common group identity in the same way. Non-conformists often experience what I call the "rebel's discontent." They wish to abandon the group so as to distance themselves from those who previously rejected their views but who have now transitioned into champions of them. Former dissenters won primacy over the group, so why not stick around and enjoy it? In truth, it's not so easy. Wounds suffered when struggling as a persecuted underdog still burn. After so much pain, your own identity as a rebel is hardened, and it becomes hard to forgive those who previously disrespected and mistreated you. Why have anything to do with the former majority at all?

We can glimpse the rebel's discontent thanks to a set of cutting-edge experiments conducted by Dr. Radmila Prislin of San Diego State University. Imagine you're debating a controversial topic among a group of strangers. Initially, few people in the group take your position. As time passes, more people in the group agree with you. Or perhaps most people initially agree with you, and as time passes their support wanes and they adopt an opposing viewpoint. Now imagine that all of these other people are actors, and the whole debate is an experiment to see how you respond to shifts in your popularity and power. This is the gist of Prislin's research, which has turned up some surprising findings.

Shifts in power disrupt how both the new majority and the minority parties think about group identity. After a structural change in the group, people struggle to decipher what their membership signifies and why it matters. Understandably, defeated members of the former majority—I'll call them the ***Newly Powerless***—no longer see the group as an extension of their sense of self. Now that most group members disagree with them, the larger group seems undesirable and foreign. Members of former minorities—let's call them the ***Rebels Who Won***—experience their own kind of psychological confusion. They are disappointed and unimpressed at how long it took for the previous majority to finally come around to their views, and they rarely trust the former majority on account of its prior opposition (more on distrust in a moment). Harboring lingering grudges, Rebels Who Won regard the Newly Powerless as inferior. For these reasons, the Rebels Who Won want out. As Prislin provocatively noted in her experiments, "It is not those whose position remains disadvantaged (stable minority) who are eager to leave . . . it is those whose position within a group is improving (former minorities)" who are most likely to seek separation from the group.

THE BIG IDEA

In real-life settings, the loss of a common identity might lead Rebels Who Won to disregard the potentially valuable opinions of the Newly Powerless or to behave in ways that yield discord.

If you're a longtime rebel who has finally made good, stay alert to this dynamic and challenge yourself to discern all that you and members of the Newly Powerless might have in common. Pushing against your tribal impulses, reach out to your former adversaries and shore up a shared identity to the extent you can.

Although we might feel alienated from others in certain respects, we can almost always find nonideological identities that bind us thanks to common interests, life circumstances, or past experiences. We might, for example, share in common our identities as weight lifters, cigar aficionados, seafood lovers, people who grew up with divorced parents, survivors of the world's most dangerous amusement rides at Action Park (never heard of it? go watch a video of my childhood mecca!)—and the list goes on and on.

Take an inventory of your childhood, adolescence, and adulthood, noting the identities you have in common with people who seem to be locked in antagonism with you. Can you create new norms or rituals that include people whom you initially regarded as outside your tribe? Challenge yourself to set aside lingering antipathy or that sense of superiority you might feel toward members of the

Newly Powerless. As Martin Luther King, Jr., taught, "If we are to have peace on earth, our loyalties must become ecumenical rather than sectional. Our loyalties must transcend our race, our tribe, our class, and our nation, and this means we must develop a world perspective." You, too, must develop a grander "world perspective" toward the sects within your group, even if the relations between those sects remain raw.

THE REBEL'S NIGHTMARE

In 1969, after 268 years as a male-only school, Yale University admitted 588 women to join its class of 1973. A number of men didn't take it well. Sarah Birdsall, a student at the time, remembered the sophomore boys as friendly and supportive, but "the seniors were pretty horrible that first year. We girls had, after all, ruined their perfect fraternal experience. To them, girls existed for weekend fun." Yale administrators didn't go out of their way to make the women feel welcome. Yale failed to provide resources for women's sports teams, and when a woman signed onto the men's soccer team, staff told her to resign "for the good of the college." Her male teammates neglected to rise to the occasion. Instead, they announced their intention to forfeit any game in which a female athlete played.

It's no wonder Rebels Who Won fail to identify warmly with the Newly Powerless. When majority parties lose their power, they tend to behave badly. As research by Dr. Prislin and her colleagues documented, the Newly Powerless refuse aid to the group, expressing their hostility by taking advantage of the group when they can, and expecting hostility and a lack of helpfulness from Rebels Who Won. This reaction in turn engenders distrust and hostility in the Rebels Who Won. Recognizing that the Newly Powerless have become embittered and hostile (what we might call the "rebel's nightmare"), the

Rebels Who Won react defensively, spending far too much time searching for signs of disrespect and rejection, finding those signs, and battling them, all of which distracts from pursuing their own goals. At Yale, one female student wanted to work on the prestigious *Yale Daily News* but explained, "There really was a sense that women were not going to be considered for leadership positions. I was put off by that, and I guess the message was strong enough that it made me not want to put in the effort."

Antagonism begets antagonism. Aggression begets aggression. As another female student reflected, "The tragedy of all this is that I took on many of the male chauvinistic attitudes toward females . . . I didn't think females were worth spending time with. I picked that up from the institution, and I'm only now getting out of it." Basically, this female student (and probably many others) internalized the hostile attitudes of misogynistic Yale boys.

As a result of this dynamic, Rebels Who Won often wind up departing from the values they cherished while in the minority. Think back to Bolivian President Evo Morales, who literally used industrial-strength duct tape to shut the mouths of those who disagreed with his ideas and practices. Whereas previously they might have valued dissent, believing that all factions deserve a chance to speak and be heard, and that disagreements are healthy, now the Rebels Who Won have second thoughts. Suspicious of opponents' motives and fearing their aggression, Rebels Who Won become less interested in welcoming dissenting views, as they seem to detract from the restructured group's ability to solve problems and lock in progress. Instead of seeking out diverse viewpoints, the Rebels Who Won stifle debate.

In Prislin's research, the Newly Powerless became more tolerant of debate, whereas the Rebels Who Won increasingly interpreted disagreement as unwelcome and unhealthy, valuing cognitive diversity

50 percent less than they had before. The Rebels Who Won became rigid, tolerating the Newly Powerless's opinions in a frosty, disrespectful way. Rather than fostering debate, the Rebels Who Won felt there was only one way, their way. Revolt now seemed dangerous and unhelpful. In truth, dissenting ideas remain valuable no matter who is in charge (as discussed in chapter 3). By hardening their position and clamping down, the Rebels Who Won failed to reap the continuing benefits of dissent and, again, sowed the seeds for future discord.

THE BIG IDEA

If you as a successful rebel are gaining adherents and power, you would do well to provide assurances to everyone involved in the war of ideas—friends, foes, and neutral observers—that their opinions still count.

Reach across the divide to draw out former adversaries. Understand the pain that the Newly Powerless are nursing due to their loss in status and the reality that just being around you reminds them of this loss. Reflect on lingering traumas you might have suffered thanks to years of rejection as a marginalized minority. Rejection's sting might be damaging the quality of your attitudes and decisions today, coloring your view of former opponents. How might your emotions make matters worse, even if former opponents' mistrust and aggression remain palpable? Recall how *you* once felt as a member of the minority.

Most of all, resist the urge to pull away from the distrusted "other," even when they express hostility. As Prislin and her colleagues found, repeated interactions over time between the Rebels Who Won and the Newly Powerless brought a measure of reconciliation. Initially, relationships between these parties were awkward or tense. But after four or five interactions with their opponents, Rebels Who Won found it easier to spend time and collaborate with them. They could recognize more readily the common humanity and interests they shared with the Newly Powerless. Everyone became more attached to the group and willing to sacrifice for it. With time and effort, the old antagonisms faded, replaced by a new, fledgling spirit of cooperation.

THE REBEL'S BLINDNESS

At the peak of the French Revolution, during the Reign of Terror from September 1793 to July 1794, nearly 300,000 citizens were arrested, some 17,000 were executed, and thousands more died in prison. But get this: Maximilien Robespierre, a former judge who became the architect of the Terror, previously argued *against* judicial violence. Robespierre even resigned his judgeship after pressure to sentence a criminal to the death penalty. As late as 1791—just two years before the Reign of Terror—he argued, "The legislator who prefers death and atrocious penalties to the gentler means in his power outrages public feeling and weakens the moral sentiment among the people he governs; like a clumsy preceptor who, by the frequent use of cruel punishments, stupefies and degrades the soul of his student; he wears out and weakens the springs of government by wanting to wind them up too strongly." And yet, once in power, Robespierre spearheaded a law that allowed for the death penalty if the revolutionary government even *suspected* someone of dissenting against the newly established order. "There are only two parties in France: the people and its enemies," he said. "We must exterminate those miserable villains who are eternally conspiring against the rights of man. . . . [W]e must exterminate all our enemies."

We've seen that dissenters who take power regularly abandon their foundational beliefs about the benefits of diversity and dissent. But Robespierre's unparalleled and awful hypocrisy suggests another dynamic at play: a frightening inability of victorious insubordinates to remain self-aware. Indeed, Robespierre seemed blissfully ignorant of any contradiction with his former beliefs. In a 1793 speech, he proclaimed that constitutional regimes need only "protect the individual citizen against abuse of power by the government; but under a revolutionary regime the government has to defend itself against all the factions which attack it; and in this fight for life only good citizens deserve public protection, and the punishment of the people's enemies is death." Such words convey no clue of any deviation from his former beliefs. As one observer noted, hard-core ideologues strongly believe in their own justifications of violence. Indeed, "the atrocities only strengthen the utter certainty with which ideologues hold their convictions and impose their aim."

As Prislin and her colleagues found, hypocrisy creeps in almost immediately after a power shift within a group. In their experiments, the Rebels Who Won abused their power by creating rules that favored their in-group at the expense of the Newly Powerless. The Rebels Who Won implemented new rules that demoralized the Newly Powerless in an attempt to fortify the new status quo. As Prislin's work suggests, Rebels Who Won become unaware of their own hypocrisy out of a fear of losing hard-won power, status, and approval. Without knowing whether the Newly Powerless support the reformulated group, the Rebels Who Won believe their power is unstable. If they don't aggressively reinforce their power, they think, it will prove fleeting. This logic dominates, pushing aside other considerations, such as how consistent their present behavior is with long-standing values.

THE BIG IDEA

To prevent yourself from going astray as a victorious rebel, stay focused on the ways in which power compromises self-awareness.

Remind yourself frequently of your own established values. Setting aside your need to consolidate power, are your present actions truly consistent with your desired legacy? How would you like future generations to remember your accomplishments after gaining power? Are there ways to exercise power that are more humane, rational, and reasonable? Are you abiding by the golden rule of doing unto others as you would like done unto you? Are you going further, as the playwright George Bernard Shaw advised, and taking into account other people's unique needs and perspectives in determining your treatment of them? To help yourself remain compassionate, commit to two key principles of leadership: (1) block measures or rules that degrade or unfairly treat the minority; and (2) block measures that offer the majority extra privileges. You fought hard to level the playing field for your in-group. Now do your utmost to keep it leveled for the next generation of conformists and non-conformists alike.

THE QUESTIONS WE MUST ASK

I've referenced historical examples in this chapter, but the question of how victorious rebels come to treat minorities is an urgent contemporary issue. As I write this in 2021, historically oppressed minorities in the United States are on the verge of claiming unprecedented powers and perhaps even joining the establishment. American society is supporting gay rights as never before. Women and people of color are gaining unprecedented (albeit still imperfect) access to the levers of power in academia, business, and government. For the first time in American history, racial minorities are poised to become the numerical majority.

Although this shift in power remains incomplete, now is the time to raise difficult questions about the exercise of power and the responsibilities that it entails. Are the ascendant members of the new establishment poised to "win responsibly"? What can they do to ensure that they don't exercise the same repression imposed on them as disempowered minorities? Few people dare to pose such questions, fearing that others will accuse them of trivializing historical oppression. I do not downplay the need for justice and a shifting of power toward underrepresented minorities. But having immersed myself in the psychological research presented in this chapter, I wonder: What is the endgame of the fight against oppression? What, ultimately, do we hope to accomplish, and what kinds of actions and policies will get us there? Unless proponents of historically oppressed groups clarify their goals, their attitudes will likely shift upon gaining power, reinforcing the fortunes of their own tribes and diminishing the ideals of equality and justice for which they have long fought. Our country might be better off now, but worse off than it could be.

As traditionally underprivileged minorities gain power, they must take care to exercise restraint. Rather than simply hire, respect, or listen to people who look and think as they do, they should retain a healthy respect for difference and welcome in *everyone*, including those who might not pass the usual ideological tests that progressives cherish. Influence should stem from our intellect and wisdom, not our skin color, gender, socioeconomic background, sexuality, or any other perceived difference. Let's allow for a thriving discourse in which everyone's ideas are subject to critique on their merits, and in which skepticism and insubordination of all kinds are encouraged.

All of us, whether Rebels Who Won or the Newly Powerless, should carefully consider how we voice our skepticism. Across social media, righteous disagreement easily morphs into unbridled wrath, and our expressions of legitimate concerns can destroy a person's well-earned reputation, career, and livelihood within a single twenty-four-hour news cycle. Champions of historically oppressed minorities have been as guilty of such discursive recklessness as their opponents. In 2020, several students at Skidmore College circulated a petition with fifteen demands to increase racial justice, with number three being the immediate firing of Professor David Peterson, who had been teaching jewelry and metal classes at the college for thirty-one years. His classes were boycotted. He was harassed online with e-mails and social media postings claiming he was racist, sexist, and transphobic. On the door of his classroom, somebody posted a sign with the following statement:

> STOP: By entering this class you are crossing a campus-wide picket line and breaking the boycott against Professor David Peterson. David Peterson is notorious for the blatant sexism he treats his female students with, his outwardly transphobic treatment of trans students, and his general disregard for all students who are not white cis men . . . This is not a safe environment for marginalized students. By continuing to take this course you are enabling bigotted [sic] behavior on this campus

What did Professor Peterson do? He did not engage in racial discrimination, he did not use derogatory language, he did not hold offensive signs, he did not even express a point of view. What he did was quietly attend a rally with his wife, listening to speakers support local police officers. The president of the university contemplated terminating Professor Peterson and began a two-month investigation into student accusations. Professor Peterson was found innocent of all charges. Still, thousands of outraged students and members of the local community jumped to their own quick conclusion and crushed this sixty-one-year-old man's reputation. Nobody was held accountable for the public denouncements that he was racist, sexist, and transphobic, including an article (littered with factual errors) published in the college's *Skidmore News*. In the absence of evidence to suggest he did anything wrong, students were able to tarnish a reputation built over thirty-one years of loyal employment. Isn't one purpose of college to acquire information and perspectives beyond what you previously possessed? Wouldn't it be valuable to inquire about someone's side of the story before demanding their termination? Instead of affirming norms of fairness and treating everyone with a sense of dignity, students in this case (and others) perpetrated a climate of fear that coarsened public discourse. We must be vigilant about becoming what we previously despised.

THE BIG IDEA

In addition to showing restraint and mustering empathy and charity for the Newly Powerless (even if they didn't show such generosity of spirit themselves), the Rebels Who Won should welcome good faith skepticism from all quarters, recognizing skepticism's power to reshape and refine orthodoxy to everyone's benefit. Relatedly, they should welcome humor.

Poking fun is a long-standing strategy for dealing with power shifts, so long as it comes from a place of understanding, good faith, and an honest desire to provoke thought. Elites and oppressed groups alike are quick to decry humor pointed at them, but a good deal of humor embodies exactly what principled insubordinates advocate:

mild transgressions of social norms. At their best, comedians are truth-tellers, saying what the rest of us notice but are afraid to touch. Humor allows us to pose questions about people or practices that that baffle and intrigue us. As I've suggested in relation to the false accusation against Professor Peterson, an attitude of "I can say whatever I want to whomever I want in any way that I want" is highly problematic, no matter who is saying it. But political correctness is equally problematic because it stifles debate. Society benefits when well-intentioned humorists notice something dysfunctional and nonsensical in any corner and poke fun.

When President George W. Bush vowed to avenge the September 11, 2001, attacks, we plunged headlong into an ill-fought war in Afghanistan that continued for another twenty *years.* Stephen Colbert skewered the president, the war on terror, all of it, in what is considered the most controversial comedy routine ever given at the White House Correspondents' Dinner (where journalists are supposed to roast the U.S. President in good fun). Colbert mocked Bush for his premature decision to start a war with Iraq and declare the Iraq War over:

> *I believe the government that governs best is the government that governs least. And by these standards, we have set up a fabulous government in Iraq.*

Brilliantly succinct. And then Colbert dug in:

> *I stand by this man because he stands for things. Not only for things, he stands on things. Things like aircraft carriers and rubble and recently flooded city squares. And that sends a strong message: that no matter what happens to America, she will always rebound—with the most powerfully staged photo ops in the world.*

But when Colbert first told these jokes, conservatives were outraged, and sent voluminous amounts of hate mail ("Mr. Colbert's employer, Comedy Central, said it had received nearly 2,000 e-mail messages" within forty-eight hours). As a member of an oppressed group gaining power today, you must hold the same standards of truth-telling—whether it goes for or against your tribe. If you lean liberal and enjoyed that ribbing of President Bush, you must show the same willingness to hear the truth about the foibles of your own tribe members.

It has become harder to joke about anyone without causing offense. Perhaps we *should* allow jokes about minorities for the sake of a thriving marketplace of ideas, so that society can continue to reap the benefits of insubordination. In their *Time* magazine essay titled "Make Fun of Everything," mixed-race comedians Keegan-Michael Key and Jordan Peele bemoan the assumption that being other than White, male, heterosexual, and able-bodied implies fragility. What's worse, they ask, "making fun of people or assuming that they're too weak to take it?" There is value in equality, and the true measure of progress might come when we can jest about societal overcorrections and hyperbolic statements and *not* cause offense. As comedian Bill Burr attempted to do in skewering disingenuous gestures:

> *Gotta @#$ing apologize to everybody. This is how screwed up my country is right now. You know Bryan Cranston, right? That dude did a movie. He played a quadriplegic and people gave him sh!t. . . . "Why is there an able-bodied person playing a quadriplegic?" It's like, "It's because it's called acting. . . ." See, if he was a quadriplegic playing a quadriplegic, that's not acting. That's just @#$ing laying there, saying sh!t that someone else wrote.*

Rooted in brutal albeit playful honesty, comedians offer society a gift. Regardless of which area of the political spectrum is being satirized, comedians provide warnings when society is adrift and slipping into nonsensical territory.

The desire to protect the Rebels Who Won from even the most modest of attacks is understandable given America's history of oppression. But members of these groups must ask themselves what the endgame is. Equality under the law and in the workplace is one thing. But as long as we view the disabled, particular races, sexes, and sexual orientation as too weak to be spoofed, we're putting them beneath members of the historical majority. In his most famous speech, President Teddy Roosevelt urged his audience to be the one who actually enters the arena, "whose face is marred by dust and sweat and blood; who strives valiantly; who errs, who comes short again and again, because there is no effort without error and shortcoming; but who does actually strive to do the deeds . . . and who at the worst, if he fails, at least fails while daring greatly." Allowing others to make fun of you and jesting in good faith—in short, breaking with a pernicious form of political correctness—is one portal that grants entry into the arena.

As the research in this chapter also suggests, protecting members of formerly underprivileged groups from attack can have serious and unintended consequences. Unless they're careful, members of these groups and their supporters risk fomenting new injustices upon taking power. The last thing our broken world needs is more trauma, aggression, and tit-for-tat competition, but that seems inevitable unless today's Rebels Who Won take it upon themselves to do better than previous generations of rebels have done and show compassion for those they've supplanted. Let's break from the zero-sum thinking that holds that we're right and our opponents are wrong. Let's break from the drive to consolidate power over the Newly Powerless at all costs. Let's protect not merely members of our own tribe, but the respect for insubordination that has always undergirded efforts at social change.

Rebels shoulder a great deal of responsibility once they've taken power. But the burden doesn't rest on them alone. The Newly Powerless must psychologically train themselves to remain open-minded in the face of unfamiliar or unwanted ideas. If you're in the majority, what's the healthiest way to react when someone identifies flaws in your existing assumptions? As we'll see in the next chapter, non-dissenters can help improve society by truly listening to others whose ideas differ from their own—with expressions of curiosity and intellectual humility. Only by exploring the messiness and discomfort of principled insubordination as it is, not as we hope or want it to be, can we access the best available ideas. Science has uncovered some principles and guidelines that just might help.

RECIPE STEPS

1. *Engage with the Newly Powerless.* Pushing against your tribal impulses, reach out to your former adversaries and shore up a shared identity to the extent you can. Provide assurances to everyone involved in the war of ideas—friends, foes, and neutral observers—that their opinions still count.
2. *Stay focused on the ways in which power compromises self-awareness.* Remind yourself frequently of your own established values. Setting aside your need to consolidate power, are your present actions truly consistent with your desired legacy? Do your utmost to keep the playing field leveled for the next generation of conformists and non-conformists alike.
3. *Nurture critical thinking.* Rebels Who Won should welcome good faith skepticism from all quarters, recognizing skepticism's power to reshape and refine orthodoxy to everyone's benefit.

PART III
HARNESSING DISOBEDIENCE

CHAPTER 8

Engage the Outrageous

How to overcome barriers that prevent us from heeding unconventional ideas

We've encountered many heroes thus far, intrepid non-conformists who took great risks for a greater good. I'm proud to say I've personally had a brush with one of them: a grant administrator at the University at Buffalo's Department of Biomedical Informatics. In 2007, Cheryl Kennedy, then a thirty-year-old graduate student and project coordinator at the university's Clinical and Research Institute on Addictions, became a whistleblower. She expressed grave concerns about her boss, Dr. William Fals-Stewart, our joint mentor and a prominent addictions researcher. For years, Fals-Stewart published numerous papers and secured tons of research grant money. Behind the scenes, some students (myself included) sensed something wasn't quite right. We wondered, for instance, where he recruited 120 couples for a study on the effectiveness of a substance abuse treatment program. He handled the consent forms. He handled the payments. Nobody other than Fals-Stewart ever met a research participant.

Cheryl decided to take action. She knew that accusing Fals-Stewart of academic fraud carried major career risks. Fals-Stewart paid her salary, and as a graduate student, she had little power. But Cheryl was convinced Fals-Stewart had committed academic fraud. "I'm a very strong person," she told me. "I'm not intimidated by people. I don't care what your job title is."

I wish I could say Cheryl emerged victorious and unscathed after her act of principled insubordination, but that's not what happened. The institute followed up on her information, summoning Fals-Stewart to appear before an ethics panel. They asked him for addresses of the therapy clinics where he collected data, and he provided them. Visiting the clinics, panel members found no evidence that he had ever performed research. Concerned, they asked Fals-Stewart for signed consent forms from study participants. Before he could produce them, a warehouse that apparently contained the sole copies of the research documents burned to the ground in a suspicious fire.

A formal misconduct inquiry launched by the university mandated a hearing for investigators to obtain testimony from Fals-Stewart's witnesses. Coincidentally, Fals-Stewart said each of these witnesses happened to be out of town. They could only testify by phone. If you can believe it, the inquiry panel accepted his story instead of delaying the investigation. Each witness testified that Fals-Stewart's research was legitimate. In a made-for-movie plot twist, the witnesses were actually paid actors who had no idea they were participating in a formal proceeding (I swear I'm not making this shit up). The script they read required them to impersonate Fals-Stewart's actual staff members and deliver false testimony in a real hearing. Each actor read a script that included the name of the person responsible for burning down the warehouse, destroying documents, and fabricating the data. That name was Cheryl Kennedy, the whistleblower. Somebody had leaked her identity to Fals-Stewart, and this was his revenge plan.

Based on "witness" testimony, the ethics panel acquitted Fals-

Stewart and, incredibly, fired Cheryl. But that wasn't enough for Fals-Stewart. Cheryl had engaged in fraud, Fals-Stewart insisted. He intended to sue the University at Buffalo for defamation of character. Here he overstepped—big-time. His lawsuit caught the attention of the New York State's attorney general. After looking into the case, the State of New York charged Fals-Stewart with fourteen felonies for defrauding the government by accepting grant dollars with fake data. A few weeks later, Fals-Stewart killed himself.

Although Cheryl ultimately succeeded in bringing Fals-Stewart to justice, the process devastated her. The institute's leadership accepted his accusations and fired her without due process. After the attorney general exonerated her, she received zero compensation in damages. Not a single person uttered, "I'm sorry." Nobody backed her up or offered protection, and as she relayed in our conversation, "it fucked with my life." To this day, she remains ostracized by fellow academics.

Listening to Cheryl tell her story, I felt both moved by her heroism and outraged by the shitty treatment she received. It was important, I thought, to prevent the next Cheryl from being disrespected and unfairly punished so that the rest of us could benefit from the important truths whistleblowers and other non-conformists tell. What might have helped members of the ethics panel and other institute leaders listen more carefully to Cheryl and take her more seriously? How might any of us better champion people living on the margins who, lacking the "right" credentials, nevertheless possess the best ideas and solutions?

Sifting through psychological research, I uncovered three powerful mental barriers that close our minds to alternative notions we encounter. Although listening to unfamiliar, provocative, or creative ideas is never easy, understanding and overcoming these barriers can help. Our psychology makes us vulnerable to the arguments and assumptions of authorities and the incurious among us who unthinkingly support the status quo and render certain beliefs and speakers off-limits. Fortunately, we can train ourselves to listen to non-conformists in a more even-handed manner, focusing less on the messenger and more on the value of the information itself. When we hear ideas that really do have merit, we can build on them, increasing the extent to which non-conformists persuade the majority.

THE BIG IDEA

Your own mind closes you off from accepting new ideas, without you even realizing it. Fortunately, you can take back control and learn to become more receptive.

BARRIER 1: PSYCHOLOGICAL DISTRESS

As members of a majority, we struggle to hear what people like Cheryl have to say because their ideas freak us out a little. Specifically, they prompt what people in my line of work call "anxious uncertainty." Humans are close-minded by nature. We hold tightly to our belief systems, especially if powerful authorities promote them, because they provide structure and meaning to our lives. When a rebel pipes up with a new and provocative idea, we feel unsettled. That uncertainty causes us distress. Yes, we *need* to feel unsettled and uncertain at times—that's how we grow. But it ain't fun. When adults feel anxious uncertainty about how to handle a situation, they recoil from creativity and cling to the familiar. Teachers say they want creative students, but they far prefer obedient rule-followers in their classes over those unruly creative kids. To make matters worse, new ideas don't just trigger negative emotions in us—they trigger emotions *about* those emotions. We feel uncertain about feeling uncertain, fearful of feeling afraid, embarrassed about being embarrassed.

How do we free ourselves from this emotional trap? One solution is to pull ourselves out of the situation entirely and look at it from afar. If we can get outside of our own egos, we might be able to understand an idea more clearly without our emotions coloring it. Scientists have developed and tested a mental strategy for doing this, what they call "self-distancing."

Rooted in gold-standard cognitive behavioral psychotherapies, self-distancing has us zoom out and notice in a more objective way the big picture of what is happening, including the players involved and their perspectives. The strategy shakes us out of a self-absorbed mindset and helps us take in relevant external information. By freeing our thinking from distortions due to past events, assumptions, or expectations, we gain wiser insights about the challenges we face and the best courses of action available to us.

When listening to the thoughts of a principled rebel, self-distancing has two key steps. First, *detail the challenge you face as a listener.* A non-conformist questions your viewpoint and offers an alternative. You form initial impressions about this non-conformist based on a number of factors: whether they belong to your in-group, their physical appearance (age, race, sex, gender, height, weight, physical attractiveness), their popularity (power and likability), and their personality (such as emotional volatility, enthusiasm, and politeness). Acknowledge how difficult it is to listen to this person's message with an open mind given the biases you harbor, as well as the plain old impulse you feel to stick with the status quo.

Second, *intentionally adopt a broader mindset.* You can do this in one of two ways. First, try talking to yourself in the third person. Instead of sitting in a meeting listening to what a non-conformist has to say, and thinking thoughts like, "I'm not getting this," or "This makes zero sense to me," try framing those thoughts in the third person. If an administrator named Brian used self-distancing while reviewing the evidence Cheryl brought against Dr. William Fals-Stewart, his internal narrative might have sounded like this:

> Brian read Dr. Fals-Stewart's statement. Brian wondered why nobody found it surprising that the only building to burn happened to be the one with the only files Dr. Fals-Stewart had. I mean, Dr. Fals-Stewart happened to be nearby when the fire happened. Brian almost raised his doubts to Clarence [another administrator]. Brian never voiced his thoughts because nobody else on the committee expressed skepticism. If he's the only skeptic, Brian figured he must be wrong.

Crafting an internal narrative like this for yourself might feel weird. Resist the natural urge to recount what happens in an egocentric way. You might try interrogating your feelings. But consider an alternative to asking, "Why do I feel this way?" If your name is Brian, get outside your own ego by asking, "Why does Brian feel this way?" Using the pronouns "I" and "my" doesn't allow you space to truly question what you believe and think, nor does it keep you open-minded to new perspectives.

To overcome personal biases, describe what is happening in an emotionally charged situation as if you are being observed by someone. An observer would use your name ("Todd, start acting like a professor instead of a fourteen-year-old boy"), second-person pronouns ("You are going to offend someone with this lust for foul language. Are you okay with offending a small portion of readers?"), or third-person pronouns ("To model rebellious behavior, he should gamble on a few carefully crafted linguistic risks"). Try to understand what you think and feel using the pronoun "you" and "[your own name]" as much as possible ("Todd is getting frustrated with a seventh round of paragraph edits. He might illustrate his point better with an extremely candid, self-conscious self-evaluation."). It's okay to talk about yourself, but you have to do it as if you are a "fly on the wall" observing; use self-talk just like highly narcissistic celebrities. Unlike narcissistic celebrities, however, you're engaging in an introspective strategy in the interest of coping with strong emotions and becoming more open-minded when confronted with unpopular, albeit potentially valuable ideas.

Typically, psychologists ask people using self-distancing to check in with their emotions in the third person, and then go deeper, probing into the underlying reasons for the thoughts or emotions. When we interrogate our reactions in the third person, we suspend the ordinary judgments we make about ourselves, freeing ourselves from prejudices. You've probably noticed that you solve problems much more effectively when a friend asks you for advice than when you face the same problems yourself. Now you have a tool to help unleash your best creative thinking when in the heat of a sticky situation. That's right, you can become your own problem-solving friend, just by modifying self-talk!

Scientists from Northwestern and Stanford University explored what happens when couples deploy self-distancing. The answer: good things. Couples in the study were asked to think about how they communicate and behave from the perspective of a third-party observing them (like a videographer sifting through surveillance footage). The couples were to imagine what this observer would think, what suggestions they would give, and then write down the imagined advice. This exercise, lasting only a few minutes, led couples to experience greater relationship satisfaction over the course of two years, irrespective of how much they fought. Soldiers in the military also adopt self-distancing when debriefing successful and unsuccessful missions—because it works.

A second way to self-distance is to broaden your time horizon.

Here are some guidelines for doing this during an emotionally charged situation:

> Close your eyes and try to imagine what your life will be like five years from today. Consider how you will feel about this event in five years. What emotions and thoughts, if any, might you experience as you reflect on your problem in the distant future? If you did not have to worry at all about social approval, what would you be saying or doing today that would make a positive impact in the distant future? How will you judge yourself in the distant future based on what you decided to avoid out of fear, and what you were courageous enough to do despite fear? By contemplating these questions and your answers, be willing to make decisions that might feel uncomfortable today but that in the distant future, you will appreciate. Minimize decisions that you will later regret.

When we encounter challenging ideas, we often react in ways that make us feel better in the short term without thinking of a longer time frame. We must overcome the impulse to reject the new, and the way to do that is to evoke a vivid image of an alternative future. Naysayers often get stuck pondering the minutiae required to put novel ideas into action, which pushes them toward inaction. We can avoid that trap by thinking ahead to an imagined future when those same novel ideas gain traction. Rather than getting bogged down by the burdensome reasons why we can't do something, we can produce a concrete vision of the potential benefits of novel ideas that might prompt us to choose action (over inaction).

Whichever technique you choose, self-distancing is a promising strategy for interacting with insubordinates. Linguistic shifts in self-talk cost little in terms of time and effort, and they offer a substantial return on investment. Research has found that the shift in perspective this strategy brings helps people deal better with emotionally intense events, leading to less distress, lower cardiovascular activity and blood pressure, more insight, and a greater ability to take positive action. People who self-distance become more comfortable feeling uncomfortable. They also become more intellectually humble and more receptive to the ideas of people who hold opposing ideological beliefs.

The simple act of self-distancing has a lasting effect. Studies have shown that days and weeks after adopting self-distancing, people cope better with psychological and physical pain, helping them derive a greater sense of meaning in life after making hard decisions. Studies have also suggested that self-distancing allows people to separate their judgment of ideas from the source articulating them. One recent study found that when asked "Who am I?" participants thought about their identity differently than when asked to think in the third-person: "Who is Todd?" Asked to describe themselves using "I am" statements, participants produced a long list of concrete group memberships (such as "liberal," "atheist," "Jewish," and so on). When asked to describe themselves from a distance using third-person statements (such as "Todd is . . ."), people responded with more abstract personality descriptions (such as "emotionally stable," "assertive," "purposeful," and "imaginative").

Something similar happened when participants evaluated their friends. When asked to judge their friend Juliana with the prompt "Who is Juliana?," people described her by the presence of personality and character traits as opposed to the mention of exclusive group memberships. Self-distancing thus seems to make us obsess less about the demographics of non-conformists, cueing us in more to their individuality and the merit of their messages. With distanced self-talk, we mentally represent ourselves and judge other people in more nuanced ways. We become more open-minded and more amenable to what dissenters say.

THE BIG IDEA

New ideas can cause unnecessary psychological distress. Use self-distancing to short-circuit this problem and render yourself more open to novelty.

BARRIER 2: OVERCONFIDENCE

We must do more than transcend our initial emotional reactions to engage well with principled insubordinates. A big reason we dismiss people like Cheryl too quickly is that we think we know more than we do. This problem becomes especially pronounced if we've either received specialized training on a topic or, conversely, are grossly ignorant about it. Adding alphabet soup after our name by getting a degree, license, or professional certification makes us feel overly competent, in turn obscuring our intellectual shortcomings, whether it's limited knowledge, blind spots, partisan bias, luck, or failure to account for the specifics of a situation. We also become entrenched in ideas because we identify with what we think we know, and feel close to members of groups with whom we affiliate. In studies, participants reminded of their political affiliations or other social identities showed stronger overconfidence in what they knew, making it harder for them to consider new arguments and ideas. Meanwhile, other research has found that the *less* someone knows about a topic, the more likely they are to hold strong opinions about it. We become close-minded when we possess either too much or too little knowledge, which often leaves us overly confident in existing knowledge.

THE BIG IDEA

We won't learn much from principled rebels if we think we know enough on our own to arrive at competent judgments and decisions. Fortunately, we can shrink our big heads by cultivating that most precious of virtues: curiosity.

Curiosity helps in all kinds of ways, leading us to superior intelligence and growth. The highly curious among us not only persevere longer during difficult tasks, but perform better and tire less. In one study, having a participant merely describe a past experience when they felt curious led to a 20 percent bump in mental and physical energy as compared with recalling moments of profound happiness. Intelligence, tenacity, and energy all matter when we're trying to overcome resistance and listen to principled insubordinates. Curiosity also helps us to listen *better* to others. Often, we fail to truly understand the rebels among us because we spend more time confidently explaining *our* positions than we do thinking about what they have to offer. Curiosity wrenches us from our self-absorption, leaving us more receptive to new, useful ideas.

It's not hard to cultivate more curiosity—just *ask more and better questions.* When you encounter an opposing or unfamiliar viewpoint, begin from a place of open skepticism about your own beliefs, asking: *What does this principled insubordinate know that I don't? What can I extract from their unique knowledge to improve my life and thinking?* And if you're participating in a conversation with someone else, rather than trying to show how smart or competent you are and detailing a rationale for why you're so unmistakably right and your interlocutor wrong, try asking that person to reflect on and explain how their preferred ideas work. Say the following: "I am interested in what you're saying. Can you tell me more about how you reached that conclusion?"

So often, we react to new ideas defensively in an effort to shore up our own arguments. But that's hardly the path to a productive encounter. As philosopher Alain de Botton observes, the exceptional conversationalist is not a good listener but rather a "skilled interrupter." They don't "interrupt to intrude their own ideas," as most people do, but rather "to help the other get back to their original, more sincere yet elusive concerns." Science bears this out. In one study, researchers had one group of participants focus on their own arguments when hearing someone present an opposing viewpoint, while other participants posed open-ended questions of the speaker designed to help them understand why they believe what they do. "The mere act of *formulating* elaboration questions was sufficient to change their reactions," said the study's lead researcher. Researchers found that when people let go of trying to persuade conversation partners and instead approached time together as an opportunity to learn something new, this led to greater enjoyment, more positive attitudes, and a greater desire to see each other again. Improve civil discourse by clarifying that the goal of conversation is learning, not persuading. Showcase your interest in what someone says with visible gestures such as head nods and tilts, directed gaze, squinted eyes in concentration, and mm'hmm noises. Being a learning- instead of a persuasion-oriented listener might be the difference in being able to profit from the liberating opening of the mind that dissenters stimulate.

In another study, posing a single curious question—an open-ended query posed with the goal of better understanding why someone feels or thinks as they do—altered debates between two people holding opposing views. With a single curious question, the questioner became more receptive to the other person's views, more eager to continue the conversation, and more likely to view the opposition as warm, open-minded, intelligent, reasonable, objective, and moral. The average person asks no more than six questions during a fifteen-minute initial one-on-one online chat with a stranger. In an online chat, all you can do is write, read, or think. Six questions in this venue offers an opportunity to get to know someone's personality, interests, and values. Yes, asking more questions helps. But what kind of questions you ask is far more important. Across two studies, researchers found that asking a high rate of follow-up questions led to greater friendliness and a greater desire to learn more about a conversation partner. The partners, meanwhile, found responsive questioners more likable and viewed them as more caring.

Following up on what someone is interested in shows that you are paying attention and seek to understand them. Increase your social attractiveness by asking a high rate of *follow-up questions* (they say, "I'm craving a freshwater eel sushi roll," and you respond, "Now, if you could only consume one food forever, what would it be?"). Contrast this powerful conversational tuning with strategies that are less likely to predict likability such as a high rate of *topic switch questions* (they say, "I regret buying a hedgehog" and you respond, "But do you read graphic comic books?"), *mirror questions* (they say, "What do you do when someone trolls you online?" and you respond, "I usually send a video of my dog sleeping on a hammock. What do you do?"), or *rhetorical questions* (they say, "When was the last time you felt really embarrassed?" and you respond, "I accidentally sliced off 22 percent of my tie with a guillotine paper trimmer. Isn't that a great name for an office product?"). Show you care. Show you are responsive. Let them know you want more information because you feel inspired or intrigued. Signal that what someone cares about is interesting to you. With frequent well-deployed follow-up questions, you give conversation partners an opportunity to flesh out their stories and thoughts with greater depth, and they will appreciate you for it.

Disrupt overconfidence with curiosity. Misconceptions about what makes for a great conversationalist prevent us from connecting with principled rebels, and indeed, everyone else. Most people experience conversations as fraught with decisions about what to say and how to act. Relying on instinct, we admire people who seem witty, tell intriguing stories, and are "smooth" in answering questions. We assume others will view us as great conversationalists if we're witty and smooth. No, no, no, says modern science.

Most people—ourselves included—crave conversation partners who show interest in what we feel or think—what bothers us, intrigues us, excites us. Be the highly skilled partner you crave by diving deeper into what other people are interested in. Ask questions such as, "What's on your mind?," "I want to know more about . . . ," "What initiated your interest in . . . ," "Why did that happen?," "How did you feel when . . . ," "And what else?" To excel in conversations, stop being so damn egocentric.

Redirect your attention to what others offer. Talk less and ask more. When talking to someone and you follow up their comments by asking "why," do so with curiosity, not judgment. The curious "why" tries to explore what another person is saying or doing in the present moment for the sole purpose of understanding it. The judgmental "why" criticizes the statement or behavior, pushing it away. If you ask why in the spirit of "Why are you even here?" or "What's wrong with you?" you'll not only come across as an asshole—you'll fail to draw out people around you, including those immensely valuable non-conformists. Curiosity is an antidote to defensiveness.

When it comes to dealing effectively with non-conformists or whistleblowers, asking questions and staking out a posture of curiosity makes all the difference. In Dr. William Fals-Stewart's case, Cheryl lodged a number of allegations. Although the good doctor had published an article referencing 120 couples participating in a therapy program, Cheryl perused the files and found only three. As Cheryl also noted, Dr. Fals-Stewart preferred not to use checks or credit cards but instead paid work-related expenses in cash, even though funding from government grants requires careful receipts and records. This alone, she felt, was highly suspect. Unfortunately, administrators failed to show a comparable level of curiosity in their evaluation of the facts. Not only didn't they probe these two issues; they didn't query the credibility of Dr. Fals-Stewart's witnesses, nor did they ask why Dr. Fals-Stewart was more credible than Cheryl. At key points, they felt overly confident in the information presented and therefore failed to ask follow-up questions.

Asking tough, even dangerous questions rarely feels good in the moment. A preference for cognitive simplicity leads us to fall back on assumptions. We generalize unduly, thinking that all African Americans are politically liberal, or that all Republicans unthinkingly support Trump. We assume that complex issues revert to binaries. You're either for open borders for immigrants or against them. You're either for freedom of speech or against it. And so, we decline to ask certain questions because we presume to know the answer.

To engage better with principled rebels, we must resist the urge to paint everything as either/or. There are few inherently good or bad people. Many of us are a blend of values and a wide range of ethical, unethical, and morally ambiguous decisions that make little sense when pulled out of context. Let's show some curiosity, people. Let's explore the novel, complex, ambiguous, and mysterious elements of our world. Let's embrace complexity and resist the temptation to categorize people or their views in an overly simplified way. Let's spend more time *asking*. You can't always be happy, but you can nearly always be curious.

BARRIER 3: INTOLERANCE

A burglary has taken place at a suburban home, and the police have apprehended three suspects. As the investigator in the case, you have a photograph of each suspect and you know their name, occupation, alibi, police record, what they had on them and how they behaved during their arrest. Reviewing all of this information below, whom do you most suspect of committing the crime?

NAME	PETER ALLEN	MARK MATHER	STEVEN JONES
ALIBI	Was playing bridge with church group	Was walking the dog	Was home alone watching TV
PREVIOUS RECORD	Speeding, 80 mph	None	Spent six months in jail for burglary in 2002
POSSESSIONS WHEN APPREHENDED	$35, deck of cards	Leash, cigarettes, golden retriever, $6 in loose change	$400 in cash, screwdriver, gum
ACTION WHEN APPREHENDED	Complied with officer	Verbally abused officer	Complied with officer
OCCUPATION	Accountant	Real estate agent	Unemployed

You might have noticed that one suspect, Steven Jones, lacked an alibi, had a previous criminal record, and had $400 in cash and a screwdriver on him when the police arrested him. He was also the only unemployed suspect. Everything points to him. He also happens to be the only Black suspect.

A fascinating study put participants in the position of investigators and asked them to consider these three potential perpetrators. Participants took a pen and drew a circle around Steven Jones's picture, then handed it in. But that wasn't the end of the experiment. Leaving the room, participants learned that another person in the study had previously completed the same task. Participants received a manila folder containing this other person's response. Opening the folder, participants found a handwritten note from this person stating, "I refuse to make a choice here—this task is obviously biased. I find it offensive to make a Black man the obvious suspect. I refuse to play this game." Pretty bold move, right? This other person had accused the researchers of being racist!

How do you suppose participants responded upon encountering this act of moral rebellion? You might have expected them to applaud the rebel who called out the racism, but they didn't. They loathed them, perceiving them as self-righteous, defensive, stubborn, judgmental, and easily offended. Watching the rebel take a stand they hadn't considered or had feared taking, the other "detectives" in the study declared they didn't want to be friends with the rebel, didn't want them as a roommate, and didn't want to work on a project with them.

We engage poorly with rebels not simply because their ideas unsettle us or we assume we know everything, but because we resent these individuals for making us painfully aware of our own limitations. If you worked at the Research Institute on Addictions when Dr. William Fals-Stewart engaged in fraud, you might have rejected Cheryl and her evidence because she exposed your failure to spot a criminal. As a highly educated person who spent every workday with Dr. Fals-Stewart, you might have felt embarrassed and ashamed that Cheryl could spot a problem that you failed to notice. So you might have denigrated Cheryl as a strategy to protect yourself from self-criticism.

Recognizing this dynamic leads us to another strategy we can use to become more receptive to non-conformist ideas, what we might call "deliberate humility" or *reminding ourselves of our own failings and limitations.* Deliberate humility might seem counterintuitive: if we fear self-criticism, why would we make a point of criticizing ourselves? The answer is that when we "own" the sense of intellectual and moral inferiority we feel when confronted by principled insubordinates, we can deem them as a hallmark of strength and feel better about ourselves. We become less inclined to cling to some notion of self-perfection only to have it dashed to pieces by a principled insubordinate. This leaves us more willing to fight for the underdog instead of resisting or cowering in silence. Deliberate humility also helps by making us wiser, since wisdom arises from understanding the limitations of our own knowledge, respecting others' viewpoints, remaining open and receptive to criticism, and communicating our ideas respectfully. Reminded of how much intellectual humility serves to boost our wisdom, we become more tolerant of people who differ in ideology, ideas, and manners.

Practicing deliberate humility can make us more open to divergent ideas. Choose a moment when you showed a lack of humility and modesty. This could be a time when you couldn't stop thinking about your good qualities or good deeds, or when someone shared an idea and you ignored them or shot them down. You could have spent more time as a skilled interrupter, asking questions, collecting information, and learning something—but you didn't. Now re-create this event in your mind as vividly as possible. Consider how you felt and reacted to the event in the days that followed. List the emotions you felt, bringing in the emotion-labeling skill from chapter 6. Scrutinize this event from the vantage point of another person watching video footage of it. How would they see it? What might you have done differently? Finally, consider how you might change your behavior going forward based on recollections of this event. This sort of contemplation and self-questioning really works. Multiple studies have found that people who underwent such a thought process emerged humbler, more forgiving, more patient, and less critical of themselves and others.

In studies conducted at six different universities, scientists discovered that during a disagreement, intellectually humble people showed more interest in the opposition's view, treated the opposition with more respect and dignity, and reflected more on the accuracy of their own position, all of which helped them acquire more knowledge. The next time you find yourself around someone challenging the status quo, tell yourself that they know something you don't, and make it your mission to find out what that is. Remember, you're *supposed* to update your belief system as you encounter new information. That's how you grow! How sad would it be if ten years from now you still harbored the same old beliefs. Unless you're seeking out new information in a spirit of humility, you're merely proselytizing, not showing real curiosity.

THE BIG IDEA

Society needs fewer street preachers and more intellectually humble thinkers who can bridge social and intellectual divides. Courageously resist simple falsehoods and instead make it your practice to explore complex truths fully and honestly.

EXPERIMENT BETTER

When it comes to improving society, non-conformists don't bear sole responsibility for convincing us of their truths. The rest of us must receive and assess their contributions with equanimity, so that we can accept ideas and solutions that improve on what already exists. But as we've seen in this chapter, engaging productively with rebels isn't simply a matter of *wanting* to hear them out. We need to overcome the emotional and mental baggage we carry around that causes us to recoil from new and unusual ideas before we've had a chance to evaluate them rationally.

Let's remember what's at stake. Whistleblowers, political activists, artists, scientists, and others who dare to "think differently" are agents of social improvement. We need the Cheryls of this world to identify immorality, injustice, inefficiency, irrationality, and malfeasance in our systems where it exists. We need them to shout, "This isn't right!" and "We can do better!" We also need them to show us what "better" could be by envisioning new solutions we haven't thought of yet.

Societies today are in flux, transforming more quickly than ever. Whether on account of pandemics, technological change, generational change, or other factors, many of us are abandoning decades-old habits and practices almost overnight. When even the most vaunted experts can't predict what will come next, we're left to experiment with how best to feed ourselves, work, educate our kids, take care of our elderly parents, and so on. These experiments work best when we have multiple alternative ideas at our disposal. We'll only get them if we open our minds by cultivating a mixture of perspective-taking, curiosity, and intellectual humility.

It's not just individuals who must learn to become more welcoming and responsive to non-conformists, but groups of people. A great deal of social improvement occurs in schools, businesses, communities, teams, and neighborhoods. Yet entrenched social conventions prevent us from considering unfamiliar and potentially threatening ideas. Let's consider how we might change the norms and cultures that arise in groups to render them more welcoming of the rebels in their midst, and more capable of benefitting from their unique insight.

RECIPE STEPS

1. *To interact more productively with insubordinates, practice self-distancing.* People who self-distance experience greater equanimity in emotionally intense situations. By using self-distancing, you become less defensive when exposed to the ideas of people who hold opposing ideological beliefs.
2. *Cultivate curiosity.* When you encounter an opposing or unfamiliar viewpoint, begin from a place of healthy skepticism about your own beliefs. Redirect your attention to what others offer. Talk less and ask more follow-up questions.
3. *To become more receptive of non-conformist ideas, practice "deliberate humility."* When we admit and "own" our fallibility, we feel greater appreciation for the value of principled insubordinates and offer them greater respect. When intellectually humble, we are more willing to fight for the underdog instead of resisting or cowering in silence.

CHAPTER 9

Extract Wisdom from "Weirdos"

How to cultivate rebel-friendly cultures in group settings

Everything seemed normal on October 25, 1994, as U.S. Navy combat pilot Lieutenant Kara Hultgreen attempted to land her F-14A Tomcat on the aircraft carrier U.S.S. *Abraham Lincoln.* The weather was clear, and as Hultgreen made her final turn a mere mile away from landing, her plane's engines were both working fine. But something happened during her final approach. Her left engine malfunctioned, and Hultgreen overshot the landing area's yellow centerline. Her plane turned over to the left, and to compensate Hultgreen caused it to roll over into the Pacific Ocean. Seated behind her, Lieutenant Matthew Klemish initiated the ejection sequence for Hultgreen and himself. Klemish escaped with his life. A fraction of a second later, Lieutenant Hultgreen's seat ejected downward, directly into the Pacific Ocean. She died on impact.

As horrible and tragic as it was, the accident also embroiled the navy in a major political controversy. The year before, over the objections of senior military leaders, Congress repealed decades-old legislation that excluded women from military combat positions. Pressured to comply, the navy's brass implemented a plan to activate the service's first female combat pilot by the end of 1994. That was

Hultgreen. Now that she had perished, everyone wanted to know why. Were women ill-suited for combat, as some male voices in the military argued? Had the navy rushed Hultgreen into a combat setting too quickly without the proper training? Or had she merely been the unlucky victim of equipment failure?

The navy's top legal authority, the Judge Advocate General, released an official accident report blaming equipment failure for Hultgreen's death. But in March 1995, someone leaked an internal investigation performed by the Navy Safety Council. Its conclusion: pilot error caused Hultgreen's death. A naval officer, Captain Patrick Burns, blew the case wide open, leaking Hultgreen's confidential training records to an independent organization, the Center for Military Readiness. The center in turn shared this information with the press. As those records showed, the navy had dealt more leniently with her during training than it had with other would-be fighter pilots. When a male pilot underwent training and received a down or disqualification for failing to land a plane successfully, they typically received two more chances before expulsion. Lieutenant Hultgreen's training transcript showed evidence of four downs.

A skeptic might feel tempted to write off Burns as an unreconstructed misogynist who never believed Hultgreen had what it took to fly combat missions. Without doubt, Lieutenant Hultgreen and other women met with considerable resistance in the navy, including hostility from male officers. Some officers didn't appreciate the media attention bestowed upon Lieutenant Hultgreen, with journalists often on base watching her. Some officers held strong beliefs about women's inferiority to men. Even when male officers weren't overtly misogynistic, many didn't know how to talk and act around women. "I think it's a mistake to open up bombers and fighters to women," testified General Merrill A. McPeak, the Air Force Chief of Staff at a 1993 meeting of the Defense Advisory Committee on Women in the Services. "I have a culturally based hang-up: I can't get over this image of old men ordering young women into combat."

Other conditions also made life harder for female pilots. For example, the navy's equipment was ill-suited for their bodies. Nearly everything in the cockpit was designed to fit the physical dimensions of men, who on average are 4.7 inches taller than women and have hands 0.8 inches longer. Women will have a harder time piloting safely when equipment is not designed for their bodies such as the seat height, shoulder and back support, distance to the pedals and stick, and distance between control panel buttons.

Lieutenant Hultgreen didn't want anyone to bend the navy's standards for her or other women. She just wanted a fair chance. "I don't think the navy owes women a career path. I think the point is that they should want the best person for the job," she said. "If people let me slide through on a lower standard, it's my life on the line. I could get killed." But this was precisely Burns's argument. As he saw it, the navy let Lieutenant Hultgreen slide in on a lower standard because of the pressure leaders felt to mint its first female combat pilot. Burns supported gender integration so long as clear evidence existed of women's combat readiness. He risked his twenty-eight-year military career to leak information because he saw no other way to push back against the political pressure the navy felt. "I owed it to the Navy," he testified to the Naval Inspector General. "It's a real disservice to the women who are out there who are doing a good job, that are fully capable of flying airplanes and fighting airplanes and dropping bombs on target. They're being measured by a different yardstick than their male contemporaries. And that's not fair to them. So this is not doing a service to anybody."

We'll never know for sure what caused Lieutenant Hultgreen's death. What does seem clear is that the navy didn't do enough to properly welcome the contributions of principled insubordinates—both pioneering female soldiers and a whistleblower like Burns. External political pressure won't magically eradicate the biases and prejudices that make a group unwelcoming to minority groups. Likewise, you can't expect people to serve as honest truth-tellers if an organization itself tries to hide important facts in an investigation. To make the most of principled insubordination, government agencies, companies, teams, and other groups must train people to think differently. They must intentionally design cultures in which stereotype-breaking mavericks such as Lieutenant Hultgreen receive a fair chance. They must also design cultures in which principled rebels like Captain Burns can openly express inconvenient facts without fearing punishment.

So many groups squelch the contributions of minority members, including principled insubordinates. Even groups that pride themselves on being "diverse" often fail to glean the expected benefits. Although demographic diversity receives a great deal of attention, researchers have found little relationship between such diversity in a group and its performance. Job-related diversity dimensions, such as a person's educational background, years of experience, and functional knowledge and skills minimally impact group performance. It isn't that diversity is useless. Rather, as researchers argue, "certain kinds of groups may be better able to capitalize on the advantages that diversity affords." To increase a group's ability to benefit from diversity of all kinds, including people who harbor ideas we might find "weird" or "strange," we must abandon the idea that merely recruiting diverse individuals and adding them into the mix will enhance performance.

From there, we must probe the conditions that allow the presence of diverse people and viewpoints to work for us and them, and we must make cultural changes based on those conditions. Researchers at the University of Amsterdam and University of Kiel uncovered two powerful pathways for groups seeking to do a better job of welcoming non-conformists, extracting their wisdom, and enhancing the group's performance. Let's examine each, investigating how the navy might have encouraged a more honest and open investigation of Hultgreen's death, or perhaps prevented it in the first place.

THE BIG IDEA

Diversity alone or the presence of non-conformists won't magically supercharge performance in team settings. We must make cultural changes based on an understanding of what allows the presence of diverse people and viewpoints to work for us.

PATHWAY 1: CREATE AN ENVIRONMENT THAT ENCOURAGES EVERYONE TO CONTRIBUTE

Groups often fail to make the most of diversity because they struggle to extract knowledge from people on the margins. As a leader, you want your group to be tightly knit and cohesive, since that allows it to operate efficiently. With a sense of harmony and positivity, like-minded people can coordinate their thoughts and actions quickly—think firefighters seamlessly collaborating to arrive promptly at an emergency scene. Yet cohesion can impede principled rebels, who by definition think differently than the majority, from sharing their messages. It can also prevent other group members from considering those messages fairly. You can only access rebels' valuable ideas—thereby enhancing the group's ability to seek, conquer, think, learn, and create—if you treat rebels as uniquely valuable contributors and if you draw them out, elaborating on and improving their ideas. Otherwise, you won't arrive at the best solutions, just the quickest. The group's collective intelligence will suffer.

THE BIG IDEA

To maximize a group's collective intelligence, build a culture that affirms certain values: autonomy, critical thinking, freedom of thought, and the desire to seek out useful information regardless of where it originates.

Psychologists call these values "epistemic motivation," defined as the "willingness to expend effort to achieve a thorough understanding of the world, including the group task or decision problem at hand." For a group to seek out creative solutions, group members must want to do something different and useful because old ways aren't working. A group with strong epistemic motivation understands that a deep, systematic search for new possibilities is worth the effort.

Groups rarely extract wisdom from principled rebels if members already feel they possess the information needed to make a decision. But groups where epistemic motivation runs strong tend to look more kindly on non-conformist ideas. One study found that when people remembered epistemic motivation norms and wrote about past behaviors consistent with them, they viewed dissenters twice as positively compared with people who had focused on unity and cohesion as defining elements of the group. Groups that commit to epistemic motivation values perform better in problem-solving, creativity, and innovation, perhaps because they tease out and develop intriguing ideas from the weirdos and rebels among them.

How do you embed values associated with epistemic motivation into your culture? You can't just proclaim them as norms—you must shape the thinking of individual members and influence how groups actually process information. Here are some specific practices to try:

- If you're leading a meeting, open by discussing how participants might best engage with others and their messages. Explicitly tell members what the group does and doesn't value. Offer stories and examples to make abstract values more concrete and easier to replicate. Remind everyone that you want people who disagree with the majority. To maintain momentum, you want people to voice disagreement in a constructive manner. Clarify that disagreements require a fair hearing in which people seek knowledge and wisdom rather than attempt to validate their existing viewpoints. Do this every time.
- Prominently display a list of behaviors for group members to keep in mind while speaking, listening, interacting, and during decision-making. You might, for instance, include a rule that each participant only receives three chances to speak per meeting unless someone specifically asks them to participate more so that they can share specialized knowledge. You want to prevent a few blabbermouths from dominating the conversation, making it easier for diverse voices to participate. Create a one-page handout for members to pick up, read, and sign before the group convenes.
- To increase commitment to autonomy, critical thinking, and the search for new and useful information, ask people to list what they have done in the past or seen others do that is consistent with these values.
- Ask group members to pair up and discuss behaviors they will adopt or avoid in meetings that will demonstrate commitment to each value. When you publicly commit to a specific course of action, you make adherence to values more likely.
- Build in time for contemplation and deliberation. Reduce the pressure people feel to make decisions quickly.

- Minimize the influence that status and power have on who speaks, how long they speak, and whose opinion matters most. Train high-status, popular group members to build off the comments of people who possess less status or power. Remind everyone that useful ideas can come from anyone. After a project or initiative has concluded, reinforce these norms by detailing exactly who shared ideas, had their ideas elaborated on, and as a result improved the final product.
- As group conversations conclude, ask people to reflect on several questions: What was the most useful idea you learned from others today? What did you not fully understand that you could only clarify by asking someone else? What can you take from the information-gathering process that unfolded during the meeting to improve how you engage intellectually the next time? These reflections help people remember that the group is a process and that we can constantly improve and ensure we do not fall back into bad habits.

To embed epistemic motivation into the group dynamic, encourage team members to rely on their strengths as they go about their work and turn to differently abled team members for help in areas where they lack expertise. Combining the unique strengths and areas of expertise that reside in the group leads to the posing of more questions and the generation of more ideas. With a larger reservoir of resources at the team's disposal, better, more creative solutions arise.

Of course, team members can only focus on their strengths and turn to others to round out their knowledge if an ethic of intellectual humility reigns. Your own humility and that of your team members spur on more inquiry into others' knowledge. Relatedly, a group friendly to principled rebels tends to focus on outcomes rather than the means of obtaining those outcomes. Focused on results, group members will welcome principled rebels, since anyone who asks questions, offers helpful criticisms and counterarguments, and identifies overlooked solutions will improve the team. To promote and sustain intellectual humility, create an incentive structure that rewards group effort and productivity, offering instructions on how to cooperate (sharing what you know and what you can do best).

Promoting epistemic motivation instills a healthy culture, one in which people regard disagreement as a springboard to progress, and differences among group members as portals to new information and solutions. As scientists have found, you can further optimize decision-making in groups, leveraging the unique information that principled rebels carry, by combining epistemic motivation along with a prosocial orientation—the desire to work for the good of the group rather than just the self. In three separate studies, groups that produced the greatest number of possible ideas to solve a problem, the most original ideas, and the most frequent constructive disagreements embraced the values of autonomy and critical thinking instead of conformity and loyalty. Groups valuing autonomy and critical thinking direct their energy toward what would best help the group succeed (a prosocial orientation that was lacking in groups embracing conformity and loyalty).

PATHWAY 2: LOSE THE CLIQUES

Let's say you're one of just a few female pilots seeking to integrate into a large, preexisting group of male pilots. The male pilots view the females as outsiders and act, frankly, like jackasses. The women cope with the strain by bonding with one another and looking to one another as sources of support. Such bonding feels good, but it allows a potentially debilitating fissure to arise. The men feel justified in giving unfavorable treatment to newcomers who on the surface appear unwilling to integrate into the larger group. The women feel justified in wanting to work together as a subgroup, since they feel psychologically safe there to express distinct impressions and ideas for modifying the workplace environment. The loser from such "intergroup bias," as psychologists call it, is the larger group, which has a harder time creating an environment in which non-conformists feel welcomed and empowered to contribute.

Does intergroup bias hobble your team? Ask yourself: Do some on your team physically distance themselves from others if left on their own? Do some exhibit closed body postures or whisper together when others in the group speak? Do some stop their friendly banter or change the subject when a person not in their subgroup appears? Do some tend to criticize or show cynicism toward others not in their subgroup? The presence of subgroup boundaries and social distancing diminishes a group's ability to extract wisdom from weirdos, and in general, to deliver kick-ass performance. To counteract such boundaries, mobilize "debiasing strategies," that, as one researcher put it, guide people "out of pattern recognition [or stereotyping] into a more analytic mode of thinking, providing a mental correction to optimize decision making."

One such strategy is to instruct people in advance how to see past the usual in-group, out-group barriers to better empathize with others. In a laboratory experiment, Dr. Inga Hoever and her colleagues at Erasmus University Rotterdam assembled 77 three-person teams and asked them to organize a creative community theater production. With one set of teams, researchers established functional diversity by assigning each team member a specialized role: the artistic director was responsible for the creative reputation and quality of the plays; the financial manager for the theater's financial success and profitability;

and the event manager for making the visit to the theater enjoyable for audiences. Each group member received different information (location plan, schedule of plays, production costs, etc.) and a distinct viewpoint about what would make for a successful production, mimicking the functional diversity in an organization dealing with competing objectives. In a second team, the three team members lacked functional diversity—they collaborated with the same information but no role assignments. All teams had twenty minutes to develop a final creative action plan for the theater company while independent observers watched the group process unfold.

Researchers trained half of the groups in a low-cost strategy called "perspective-taking" that helped them to bridge the divide between people with varying interests (that is, the experiment had four groups: two (diverse vs. homogenous) times two (received perspective training or not). "Training" is perhaps a little generous here: members of these teams just received a one-pager about perspective-taking that coached them on how to best interact with others who were different from them and "view matters as if you were in the other person's shoes." The one-pager encouraged team members to consider what others cared about, why they conduct themselves as they do, and where the seeds of any disagreements lay.

The results were striking. Diverse groups didn't perform better creatively than homogeneous groups. In fact, diverse groups receiving no instructions on how to relate to one another seemed to display the least amount of creative thinking, even lower than the groups that lacked functional diversity. But giving members of diverse groups a simple, one-page handout on perspective-taking enabled them to perform at the highest level creatively—twice as high as both the groups that lacked functional diversity and those that were diverse but hadn't received instructions for how to work with diverse team members.

These findings add to other research showing that if you proactively anticipate differences in opinions, you are more liable to understand and appreciate the reason for disagreements. In one field study, researchers gave Israelis and Palestinians five-hour workshops on perspective-taking skills, including the ability to take on another person's viewpoints and experience their emotions. They heard a story about a leader who failed to employ perspective-taking and how it hurt his relationships with employees, and they also learned about famous leaders like Martin Luther King, Jr., and Steve Jobs who benefited from perspective-taking. Participants practiced perspective-taking during a simulated negotiation and learned how perspective-taking helped in places like Northern Ireland. At no point did the workshop address the Israeli-Palestinian conflict. After the workshop, participants received weekly refreshers about perspective-taking that prompted them to think about how they were applying these skills. Researchers discovered that this single workshop led to a reduction of negative attitudes between Israelis and Palestinians, an increase in hopefulness that the Israeli–Palestinian conflict could be resolved, and increases in conciliatory behavior—changes that persisted for six months afterward or longer.

We can enhance our perspective-taking by training ourselves to look at the world—and in particular, the contentions of nonconformists—more objectively. When we categorize a person as an "other," we tend to seek out information that confirms that hypothesis, even though it actually helps us more to seek out evidence that clashes with our assumptions. If you believe a woman can't serve as a navy combat pilot, you'll selectively focus on data that seems to "prove" that they can't and avoid contradictory information. Scroll through online forums for military personnel, and you'll see confirmation bias at its ugliest. "We should dig up more examples of career-women crashing and burning (no pun intended) when propped up through affirmative action like this," one comment reads. Another observes that, "Theres [sic] a few biological studies . . . that show females are inherently worse at spatial awareness (flying in 3d) and logic (comprehending the flight computers on f14s . . . or anything)." And these are the relatively innocuous comments.

Think about the meaning of these two comments. The first states that instead of trying to determine objectively whether men and women differ in piloting skill, we should only unearth cases that fit the "women are worse" story line. The second explicitly verifies that studies exist showing differences between men and women, with no concern for the quality of the research or its relevance. We humans love to be right, which means we'll bust our butts to selectively find, ignore, and distort information that supports what we already think. We become even more entrenched in our intergroup biases and, as a team, less capable of extracting information from minorities and using it to improve.

THE BIG IDEA

To resolve conflicts with messengers that challenge our belief system and increase our ability to consider messages, we must wrench ourselves away from confirmation biases.

Make a habit of asking questions that challenge your preexisting beliefs, in particular by raising multiple possible explanations about the behavior of people who think, act, and look different from you. If you assume that someone on your team always contributes bad ideas, you might note that implementation of his last idea cost the team money. Ask questions like: "How many times did the group ignore his concerns about a project that ended up becoming a problem later on?" or "How many times did he suggest ideas that improved a project, whether or not he received credit?" If you assume that someone is a poor team player, you might think back to the times when others complained about them. Raise questions that potentially challenge this assumption, such as: "Why do other people in other settings enjoy working with them?" or "Why did they perform exceptionally in groups other than this one?"

Training ourselves to invalidate our preexisting hypotheses, rather than blithely confirming them, will help us reverse misperceptions that in turn allows us to generate more friendships and reduce social conflicts. In essence, we want to train ourselves to behave like scientists when evaluating principled insubordination rather than lawyers who seek to bury information that conflicts with preexisting conclusions.

Conditioning ourselves to get outside of our own heads and consider others' vantage points really works. In another study of whether brief psychological interventions work within intractable conflicts, Israeli participants instructed on how to get in touch with the thoughts and feelings of others responded less angrily toward Palestinians and in turn voiced greater support for reconciliation policies and less support for military aggression. Five months later, Israelis given these instructions continued to feel less anger toward Palestinians and still expressed more support for policies promoting peace instead of war.

BUILDING REBEL-FRIENDLY CULTURES

Congress's decision to allow women to assume roles as combat pilots was long overdue and an important step forward. But we can't just mandate inclusion of minority groups, including principled insubordinates, and expect to see instant progress. The mere presence of principled insubordinates doesn't mean that companies, teams, political parties, and other groups in society will succeed in harvesting their unique and valuable insights. Each of us as individuals must work to become more congenial to non-conformists and their views, and we must create groups adept at extracting wisdom from weirdos. We must carve out opportunities within groups for principled rebels to share what they know, and we must ensure that newcomers or marginal group members can wield influence to the same extent as established group members. Culture building takes time, and once we see progress, we must remain vigilant to prevent backsliding. With focus and determination, we can build groups in which disinterested inquiry and the ability to think in someone else's shoes become entrenched, maximizing group intelligence and creativity.

To round out this book, I'd like to challenge us to think even more ambitiously. Why should we wait until people enter teams and companies before increasing our hospitality toward those holding unpopular, minority opinions? To build a society fully capable of mobilizing the insights of non-conformists, we must also increase the total number of non-conformists among us. Over the long term, the most effective way of doing this is to educate children from a young age to break from the crowd and become principled rebels themselves. We must instill in youth the mindset and skills that produce and sustain non-conformity, and we must make dissent *cool.* Drawing on the latest science, the next chapter provides a science-based roadmap for creating a new generation of courageous and inspiring freethinkers.

RECIPE STEPS

1. *Treat rebels as uniquely valuable contributors.* To maximize a group's collective intelligence, build a culture that affirms certain values: autonomy, critical thinking, freedom of thought,

and the desire to seek out useful information regardless of where it originates.

2. *Fight back against confirmation bias.* Make a habit of asking questions that challenge your preexisting beliefs, in particular by raising multiple possible explanations about the behavior of people who think, act, and look differently than yourself.
3. *Repeatedly reinforce norms for permitting dissent and embracing it when present.* Notice stark shifts when particular non-conformist members speak in terms of a drop in attentiveness (turning to devices and side conversations), insufficient follow-up on what is said (squashing traction), and failing to offer charity (making no attempt to find the truth or rational basis behind someone's words). If you don't think this happens on your team, you are ignoring social activity. We now know that small behavioral shifts will help teams reap the benefits of people who are different and dissenting. We can build groups where intellectual humility, disinterested inquiry, and viewing matters from another person's perspective become commonplace.

CHAPTER 10

Raising Insubordinate Kids

Evidence-based strategies for training the next generation of heroes in waiting

In August 2020, high school sophomore Hannah Watters made national news by getting herself into what she called some "good and necessary trouble." Across the country, controversy swirled around whether schools should open for business in the midst of the raging COVID-19 pandemic or conduct classes virtually. President Donald J. Trump and others in government were pushing for schools nationwide to reopen. Many parents, teachers, students, and public health officials doubted schools could operate safely. The school Watters attended, North Paulding High School in suburban Atlanta, Georgia, decided to start in-person classes. Students who declined to attend risked expulsion. The school's reopening plan seemed so reckless that one teacher resigned rather than come back to work.

When Watters arrived for her first day of school, she was appalled at what she saw. The school had "ignorantly opened back up," she said. "Not only did they open, but they have not been safe." Although the Centers for Disease Control and other top public health authorities identified face masks as important for reducing the spread of COVID-19, the school made wearing them voluntary. Watters found that only a minority of students were wearing them. Meanwhile, hallways were packed during the course of the day, with students sometimes pressed shoulder to shoulder. Although the school had policies against using smartphones and posting pictures of students on social media sites without obtaining consent, Watters took and posted a video of crowded hallways on Twitter. "I was concerned for the safety of everyone in that building and everyone in the county because precautions and guidelines that the CDC has been telling us for months now, weren't being followed."

The images went viral and elicited a storm of media coverage. Did administrators applaud Watters for her act of principled rebellion? Not at all. They slapped her with a five-day suspension for breaking school policies. Meanwhile, the school's principal announced to students that they would be disciplined for posting pictures on social media. Happily, when Watters's mother called the school, she learned the suspension had been rescinded. Although the school district defended its performance, the superintendent acknowledged that "the photo does not look good" and suggested the school would have to make adjustments.

It couldn't have been easy for Watters to break the rules. She knew she'd piss people off. And yet she did it anyway because she felt it was the morally appropriate thing to do. She had an impact, raising awareness about a critically important issue that affects us all. Pretty amazing, if you ask me. What would our country look like if every school was teaming with students like Watters, and if getting yourself into "some good and necessary trouble" was not only common, but "cool"? Science reveals a number of principles that parents and teachers can use to train youth to disagree, defy, and deviate from problematic norms and standards. You might be using some of these principles right now without realizing it. The key is to make *all* of them prominent in your parenting approach or pedagogy so that your kids feel inclined and empowered to dissent. Let's all dedicate ourselves to raising a new generation of young people like Watters who care so damn much that they rise up and take a stand on behalf of progress.

THE BIG IDEA

We must dedicate ourselves to raising a new generation of youth who feel emboldened to disagree, defy, and deviate from problematic norms and standards for the sake of progress.

REBEL-MAKER PRINCIPLE 1: SHOW YOUR KIDS THAT YOU BELIEVE IN THEM

Do you remember the inspiring English teacher played by Robin Williams in the movie *Dead Poets Society*? I had a grade-school teacher like that—Dr. Frank Cacciutto. Once he stood on a desk just like Robin Williams did and read aloud a poem he'd written about grammar—in particular, the dejection felt by misunderstood semicolons and the pride felt by frequently used commas and exclamation points (the idea of describing punctuation with human attributes blew our minds). But Dr. Cacciutto didn't just read to us—he asked for constructive feedback on work in progress, and when we gave it, he listened. Imagine a teacher—with a Ph.D. no less—asking little old *me* for writing advice! While most educators treat students as oversized children, Dr. Cacciutto flattened the classroom's social hierarchy, showing us that he regarded us as fully formed, independent human beings with opinions worth hearing. No accident that my friends and I loved going to class and hung on his every word.

Setting high standards and regularly affirming students' potential boosts their performance, especially when youths belong to marginalized or stigmatized groups. But if you think about it, showing kids that you believe in them is also a great way of raising them to become principled insubordinates. To dissent from prevailing wisdom, kids must believe they have the ability to make a difference in the world. They must have a sense of their own power. When parents or teachers show confidence in their kids' competence, affirming that their kids can create workable strategies to surmount obstacles and persist in the long game of achieving goals, they help their kids to believe in themselves. As kids develop ideas that deviate from the norm, they become more inclined to pursue them.

The question then becomes: how can parents and teachers best help kids internalize a sense of competence? One way is to simply remind youth about their past successes. Ask your child about experiences *they* define as successes. Some kids might have persuaded a friend to change their mind on a topic, learned how to type without looking at their hands, auditioned for a role in a play (regardless of whether they made the cut), raised doubts about information presented in class, or finished a non-assigned book to ramp up their knowledge base. Have your kids list positive changes they've made, skills they've learned, accomplishments of which they are proud, times they took a bold stand. Probe for details, asking questions like: "When did you first start thinking about making a change or improving your skill set?"; "What was going on in your life at the time?"; "Did you improve all at once, or take small steps?"; "What were some of the steps?"; "How do you feel about what you did today?"; "How does it feel to remember this now?"

A second strategy is to help your child minimize what psychologists call "belonging uncertainty." When youths feel like outsiders, they tend to view social bonds as fragile. Constantly gauging whether you fit in is exhausting for anyone, much less youth who are still developing a firm sense of identity. We adults can reduce these feelings of uncertainty that undermine motivation and achievement. When youth are experiencing difficult transitions, let them hear from kids who were once in the exact same situation and are now on the other side.

Lowering standards in the hope of making youth feel good about themselves is not the answer (often adults do this so that *they can feel positive about themselves and virtuous for trying to even the playing field*). To become principled rebels, youth must believe they possess sufficient agency to make a difference. We adults must build our kids' confidence in their ability to surmount obstacles and persist in the long game of succeeding at their goals.

REBEL-MAKER PRINCIPLE 2: SHOW INTEREST IN YOUR KID'S INTERESTS

Former Delaware secretary of education Mark Murphy visited thousands of classrooms in over seven hundred schools. What he found disheartened him. Young people were eager to learn yet bored by traditional schooling. They had teachers who believed in them but lacked adults in their lives who took an interest in their efforts. "There are so many things I want to learn," they told him, "but nobody seems to care. I feel smothered by rules, regulations, and boundaries of what is right, what is acceptable, and what is valued. I am not in control, at all."

Determined to do something, Mark founded GripTape, an organization that allows teenagers to take ten-week learning journeys outside the classroom guided by their own interests. GripTape asks young people two questions: What is an idea, topic, or skill you've always wanted to learn? How is this related to your success, now or in the future? Based on satisfactory answers to both questions, they receive an invitation to start a learning journey. Young people who completed the program have learned about rap communities, computer coding, fashion design, blockchain technology, homelessness, drone photography, and the use of gene-editing techniques. GripTape is agnostic toward content, paying heed to research showing that kids learn best and are most motivated to persist through challenges and find alternative routes around roadblocks when engaged in personally meaningful pursuits. Critically, GripTape provides youth with an adult "champion" who provides emotional support, not advice. To minimize the risk that champions will veer back into advice-giving mode, the organization excludes adults who are subject experts in the topics kids are exploring. These adult figures are present simply to affirm, validate, and encourage kids as they learn, not to feed them specialized knowledge.

Champions ask reflective questions, trying to grasp what youth find most energizing or depleting as they proceed with their missions. Instead of giving in to the temptation to proffer advice, champions ask questions that guide youth in whatever it is that interests them, such as "How's it going?"; "What are you struggling with?"; "Did you talk to anyone about that?"; "Who would be a good person to contact who knows more than you?" Such questions allow youth to think about their actions and problem-solve the next move for themselves. Kids have enough adults in their lives telling them what to do. They want adults who will simply listen to them without feeling compelled to jump in with a story or piece of information.

Preliminary data show that GripTape's methodology is extremely effective, transforming kids' lives and turning them on to the power of learning. More broadly, science confirms how important it is for kids to have supportive, interested adults in their lives. Such adults not only enhance learning; they help kids grow into principled rebels. We become more curious and courageous when others let us feel safe to be ourselves and support our explorations. Also, when we share our interests with other people and they listen enthusiastically, what we share becomes more interesting and meaningful to us. We in turn become more curious and want to take more risks.

Provide this support system for your child. Be responsive when your child shares past explorations or future plans with you. If they feel uncomfortable, let them know that anxious thoughts and feelings are natural when trying new things and tackling challenges. When you accept their negative feelings, they will learn to do the same. Help your kid regulate their emotions. Start by setting an example yourself, expressing the right level of emotion for particular situations and breaking with entrenched cultural norms (for instance, affirm that boys can cry and girls can get angry). Not only will you enhance your kids' curiosity; you will strengthen your relationship with them by serving as a facilitator of their life's journey.

REBEL-MAKER PRINCIPLE 3: SUPPORT AUTONOMY

At GripTape, adult champions refrain from providing advice because they seek to advance another strategy critical for training in principled insubordination: providing kids with autonomy. Rebels by definition feel a strong sense of freedom to go their own way. That mentality has to come from somewhere. You instill it when you allow children to serve as a codirector of when, how, and what they learn. Doing so facilitates active engagement and an experience of joy and wonder. Letting youth direct their time and energy toward a meaningful goal in a way that is enriching to them offers the best opportunity for learning.

Research has shown that youth explore and discover best when they are in control and allowed to solve problems themselves. As parents and educators, we must set aside our fears and our impulse to intercede, allowing our kids to feel (and master!) moments of discomfort. Doing so helps them to become self-directed in their thinking and behavior. If you can't break with the idea that learning requires a student and teacher, then have kids teach other kids. There is no better way to consolidate learning and a deeper understanding of material than to verbalize and explain it to a peer with a deep interest in the subject at hand.

What Adults Can Say and Do to Support Autonomy

1. *Don't lecture your kids.* Instead, spend time listening to them. Show them that what they say matters. You should re-express what a child says with such clarity and vividness that they respond, "Damn, I wish you could be my speech writer."
2. Find moments for kids to enjoy independence, offering them space to work on problems and puzzles in their own way.
3. Provide your kids with frequent speaking opportunities. Even if their points are nearly inarticulate, find the useful nugget and validate it. Give them the floor to speak for themselves when around other adults.
4. Note indicators that your child is improving or mastering a skill and call it out. Try to connect what they do to their personal goals. For example, you might say, "And that is why you are going to be landing ollies on a skateboard soon!" or "Spoken like a future veterinarian."
5. *Don't bark out commands at your kids.* Instead, encourage them as they work, chiming in with "You got this" and "So close" along with reminders of what they've done in the past ("Keep plugging away and remember how well your efforts paid off last time").
6. When your kids get stuck on a problem, don't offer solutions but instead feed them helpful hints ("I wonder if you . . ." or "It might be easier if you started with . . ."). Remind them that making mistakes is part of the learning process.
7. Acknowledge your kids' perspective and experience. Show compassion for the difficulty of a task. Remind them of what it was like for you as a beginner. Explain why you aren't giving them the

answer ("You will remember this far better and longer by working through it on your own").

8. Avoid statements with words like "should" and "ought," as these suggest that there is a right and wrong way of arriving at solutions. Let kids experiment and come to their own conclusions.

REBEL-MAKER PRINCIPLE 4: HELP YOUR KIDS SPOT BULLSHIT

Principled insubordination hinges on a person's ability to sift through information at their disposal, filter out useful stuff from the bullshit, and convince others to accept the useful stuff as well. To raise young rebels, you must help them supercharge their critical thinking skills so that they are more alert to bullshit ideas when they appear. The point is not to render youth cynical, but rather to teach them to take a "trust but verify" approach to information. Youth must become comfortable asking questions and distinguishing between high- and low-quality data. They must make a habit of suspending judgment, slowing down their analytical process, and letting critical analysis run its course.

Parents and teachers can foster critical thinking skills by posing reflective questions when kids come to seemingly incorrect or ill-formed judgments. Let's say you're at a pool party, and your teenager and their friends are debating whether homosexuality is a choice. Don't bludgeon them with scientific evidence pro or con. Don't force them to change their belief systems. Ask them questions, and let them pose questions, too. Prompt them to engage in thought experiments such as the following: "Imagine a bomb is attached to your leg, and you are attached to a video monitor that shows you incredibly physically attractive men and women and a heart rate monitor to determine whether you are physically aroused. Could you change which sex you are physically attracted to? What if your life depended on it and the bomb would go off if you didn't stop your heart fluttering when you see a hot man and raise your heart rate when you see a hot woman?" As parents and educators, we must help kids learn *how* to think instead of *what* to think.

Middle and high school students should take classes in which they don't simply download information from lectures but learn, write, think, and argue about society's most controversial ideas. They should learn about the workings of the brain that prevent us from reacting in purely rational ways (see the list of cognitive distortions in chapter 3). And they should have fun. Kids can only improve their thinking skills when learning engages them emotionally, and when they have the freedom to mess up and become confused at times.

SIX QUESTIONS THAT ENCOURAGE KIDS TO EVALUATE INFORMATION QUALITY

1. "Are you putting too much trust in authority figures?" Fancy titles, age, and years of training do not tell us whether experts are giving us accurate information. Double-check their statements. Search for and read the exact information from which they draw conclusions. Check to see if they are exaggerating or misinterpreting the data.

2. "Do certain alleged experts have incentives to push particular claims?" Be skeptical of people who really, really (really!) want a claim to be true. Don't rely on people whose paycheck depends on a particular conclusion. Be on the lookout for psychological conflicts of interest, situations in which people invested substantial time, energy, and money to arrive at a particular outcome. Be wary when people start with the conclusion they want and then work backward to present supportive evidence and discard or dismiss contradictory evidence.

3. "Does a speaker encourage debate?" Be cautious when someone presents an idea and refuses critical questions, comments, and contradictions. Until you find out whether something is accurate, it remains a hypothesis. Stay cautious about ideas until genuine debate occurs, and seek out that debate. In doing so, think of yourself as a juror, editor, or scientist instead of a lawyer trying to "win" the case. The goal isn't to develop a hypothesis that turns out to be right. It's to separate fact from fiction, signal from noise.

4. "Does the information fit with the way the world works?" Although open-mindedness is a virtue, some possibilities are less plausible than others. Notice whether a piece of information or an explanation requires a number of mental leaps. When you notice weak links in the chain of an argument, treat this as a moment to be skeptical.

5. "Where does the preponderance of evidence point?" It's hard to resolve complicated, big issues with any single study or observation. If various lines of evidence point in the same direction, our confidence increases. If different people collect the evidence independently in different ways, our confidence increases even more. Resist seduction by a single, compelling person or story line in the moment and check for independent verification by others.

6. "Does verifiable evidence exist?" Be wary of people who rely on compelling, emotionally intense stories as evidence, and of arguments conveyed in ways that prevent you from testing their legitimacy.

REBEL-MAKER PRINCIPLE 5: TELL STORIES OF SUCCESSFUL AND UNSUCCESSFUL PRINCIPLED INSUBORDINATION

Youth benefit when they learn about the messy life stories of successful and unsuccessful insubordinates. Dr. Yannis Hadzigeorgiou from the University of the Aegean spent ten years testing the tantalizing hypothesis that teaching kids about the process of scientific discovery—the intellectual arguments between scientists, the emotions they experience during their work, the social relationships they form, and the politics of science—helps kids to appreciate STEM subjects (science, technology, engineering, and mathematics). Dr. Hadzigeorgiou had sixteen-year-olds learn about the life and times of Nikola Tesla, rival to Thomas Edison and known as "the forgotten genius of electricity." Edison and Tesla attempted to solve the same riddle: how can you best transmit wireless electrical currents in a safe, reliable manner? As Hadzigeorgiou found, the teenagers relished the drama of scientific discovery (in this case, they learned that the young Tesla worked for his hero Edison before a betrayal led him to quit). Tesla went on to produce over seven hundred registered patents but faced Edison's wrath throughout his career. Edison allegedly paid someone to burn down Tesla's laboratory and blocked funding opportunities.

Immersing themselves in Tesla's story, teenagers came away impressed by the workings of principled insubordination. "It was because Tesla's ideas sounded crazy that he was not fully accepted by the academic community," one student wrote in his science class journal. "Never pour scorn on scientific ideas however strange or even crazy they may seem and sound at first," wrote another student. Researchers found that students exposed to this story-based approach to teaching acquired and retained a larger number of scientific facts and experienced a greater sense of wonder. Both girls and boys showed a greater appreciation and willingness to contest widely accepted ideas compared with peers taught using a traditional, lecture-based approach.

Other work found that teaching middle school children about another underappreciated principled insubordinate, the civil rights figure Elizabeth Jennings (discussed in chapter 3), not only enhanced their understanding of history but promoted psychological strengths. Researchers asked kids to identify what they know about civil rights in the United States, what they want to learn, and what was surprising and interesting about the story of Elizabeth Jennings. Instead of regurgitating dysfunctional views held in the late nineteenth and early twentieth century, kids recognized the limitations of viewing the past through the morality of the present, articulating what they might have done differently had they lived during that period. Applying a historical lens, they showed signs of empathy, perspective-taking, and wisdom.

As this research suggests, educators and parents can train the next generation to fight unapologetically for unpopular yet socially beneficial causes by recounting stories of past insubordinates. Further, parents and teachers can encourage kids to develop nontraditional interpretations of principled insubordinates. Kids can closely study famous insubordinates, probing their missteps and moral failings as well as their nonlinear paths to success. Using biographical information, kids can reflect on the importance of getting out of one's comfort zone, taking risks, and acting on one's values.

Our kids also require exposure to the trade-offs of choosing the path of principled insubordination. By being honest about the negative consequences that come with questioning dominant thinking, kids can make better decisions about whether a mission is worth sacrifices they might have to make. Have kids relate the stories they encounter back to their own lives. Have them compare how they decided to stand out against the herd or not, why they believe their decision was good or bad, and what they learned and plan to apply to upcoming challenges.

REBEL-MAKER PRINCIPLE 6: TEACH BRAVERY

As we've seen throughout this book, principled insubordinates are nothing if not brave. If we want to raise kids capable of challenging the status quo, we must teach them what bravery is. Start by informing them that bravery comes in a number of flavors—it isn't just physical bravery. When someone proves themselves willing to defend a cause against powerful people and even an entire society, they exhibit *moral courage.* Think of Cheryl Kennedy and Marty Goddard traversing the rugged path between cowardice and recklessness. These rebels sacrificed health, well-being, and career prospects to stand up for moral causes. Or think of Nichelle Nichols, William Shatner, and Gene Roddenberry producing the first interracial kiss on television. When someone overcomes a personal limitation, they display *personal courage.* A courageous act for one person, such as speaking in front of a room full of people or confronting a father about favoritism toward siblings, may be trivial if performed by another. Other forms of courage include the calculated risk of *honesty* (speaking the truth) and *authenticity* (presenting yourself as you actually are) when the majority is not yet on your side. Think of Fugazi playing their own unique style of music and never selling out, or Rick Barry throwing underhanded "granny shots" as huge crowds of disgusted basketball fans looked on, or Dr. Ignaz Semmelweis attempting to convince his peers that washing hands saves patient lives.

Expose kids to various forms of courage and give them the language to describe ways they themselves are brave. Point out instances when your kids act bravely, when you behave courageously, and when others behave in cowardly ways. As regards the last of these, don't denigrate the actors. Instead, ask children and adolescents what they think and might feel and do in a similar situation. You don't want kids to feel pressured or strong-armed into behaving courageously. You don't want them to feel that affection is contingent on courageous behavior. Let kids know that you have behaved in brave ways, in cowardly ways, and in ambiguous ways as well.

Deepen your kids' understanding of courage by relating it to fear. The defining quality of courage is not fearless action, but the willingness to take a worthwhile risk *despite* feeling afraid. Thanks to the insights of philosophers and social scientists, we can convert courage into the following formula:

Courage = Willingness to Act ÷ Fear

As this formula suggests, there are two ways of being courageous. First, we can tackle our fears about whether we can overcome or subdue barriers. One of the biggest reasons 1,312 federal employees refused to be whistleblowers after obtaining "direct evidence of one or more illegal or wasteful activities" where they worked was a fear of retaliation. Fear of retribution is the number one reason why youth do not report bullying problems to adults. In chapter 6, we learned strategies for building mental fortitude: Understand what you are feeling. Create a space between what you feel and how you respond. Ask yourself about the function of these unwanted emotions. What is your fear trying to communicate?

Second, we can increase our capacity to make progress toward personally important goals despite our fears. In chapter 6, we learned to clarify what and who makes a cause important enough to risk physical, reputational, or financial damage. Courageousness is not some level you unlock after a sufficient number of training hours. Rather, it's a series of small choices that you make over time. Teach kids to anticipate and relish these decision points. They will have many opportunities to test their physical bravery, moral courage, persistence, honesty, and authenticity. Encourage them not only to accept the challenge but to seek it out. Each time they choose to behave courageously, they can take pride in it. Viewing courage as a series of choices in itself boosts their willingness to act.

Teach kids to think of themselves as heroes in waiting—the person who intervenes to protect a stranger from an aggressive bully or who takes the time to support a grieving friend. All too often, good-hearted people fail to step up and behave courageously because they fall prey to the "bystander effect." With others present, they feel less likely to intervene to assist or accomplish a task, assuming that those others will act. Psychologists identified five factors that increase the odds of taking action in dangerous and non-dangerous social situations: paying attention and noticing a problem; realizing that the situation is urgent; feeling a sense of personal responsibility; believing you have the skills to be helpful; and reaching a conscious decision to help. Teach your kids these five factors and their importance, celebrating those rare individuals who step up and do the right thing in the face of danger.

Unlike other forms of education, courage training requires that you carefully consider your child's unique qualities, including their temperament, personality, past history, and existing environment. Tailor the training to your child and how *they* view fear. Remember, their personal resources and limitations are much different from yours and those of any other adult. Don't alienate children by referring to their fears as unfounded. Don't impose your worldview. Instead, empathize with theirs. Offer choices and break down conquering fears into small, manageable steps, ratcheting down the pressure your kid might feel to perform. Approach a fearful child with patience. Build them up slowly, rewarding every bit of courage you can detect. Play the long game here, showing them that they can in fact learn to reframe fear and behave bravely over time.

WHAT ARE *YOU* GOING TO CHANGE TODAY?

Not long ago, I volunteered to assist the teacher in my youngest daughter's classroom. It was an ordinary scene that day. Bells ringing throughout the morning to tell kids where to go and when with near military precision. Lesson plans dutifully followed to cover the ABCs one minute and basic addition and subtraction the next. But then something unexpected happened. I went rogue. The teacher took a break and let me play guest teacher. After introducing myself, I proposed a little lesson of my own, writing a single formula on the board: 1 + 1 + 1 = 4. I paused for a moment to let it sink in, then asked the class, "How can this equation be true?"

The class sat in silence. Then one little girl raised her hand. Rather than calling on her, I simply handed her the chalk. She walked to the front of the room and began to draw lines on the board, counting as she went.

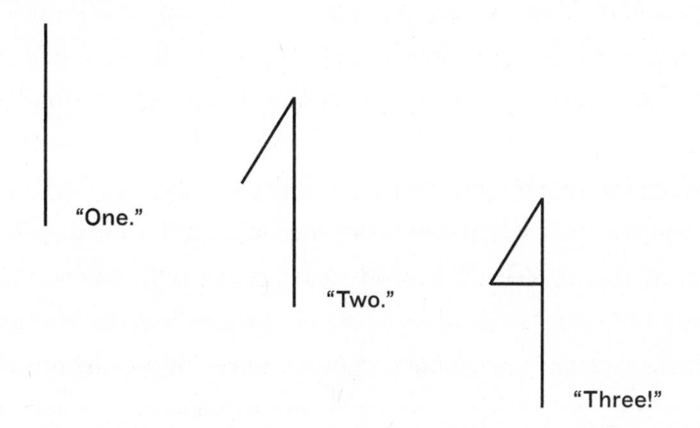

She handed back the chalk and walked to her seat as her fake teacher and the entire class soaked it in. She hadn't even made it to her chair before several kids nodded and said, "Oh yeah," and, "Of course." Then I saw it too. Obviously 1 + 1 + 1 add up to 3, but three distinct lines also make up the number four. Wow. Pretty damn cool. Not to mention bold. It took confidence for this little girl to respond to my provocation at all, but she did more, risking ridicule by proffering a rebellious answer. She might not have processed this risk in the handwringing way adults would, but she deviated from the crowd and the norm set by teachers and parents nonetheless. All of the children in the classroom knew how they were supposed to respond: "But Mr. Kashdan, 1 + 1 +1 doesn't equal 4!"

As this episode suggests, even a single insubordinate can liberate a group whose thoughts, ideas, and actions are otherwise frozen by social pressure to conform. A simple move, one both purposeful and open to whatever may follow, flips the balance of power. In the face of principled insubordination, the majority must once again prove the value of their ideas. They can no longer rely on an ethic of "This is the way we've always done it." When the status quo appears wanting, that same simple, open, and purposeful act reveals new possibilities. In this case, other kids suddenly felt inspired to present their own "deviant" ideas. A slew of hands went up, each child offering a new answer to this "impossibly true" equation. In an instant, the norm's oppressive power was broken. Play and possibility took over. New ideas formed. The desire to contribute skyrocketed. A tribe of future non-conformists was born.

I triggered this symphony of defiance because I wanted to do my part to educate kids that it was okay to take risks and speak out. If our species is to survive, all of us must steer the next generation to be more adept at non-conformity than we were. By incubating principled rebels, we'll put our future in the hands of courageous men and women who will have a voice and use it. Rather than punish or snuff out insubordinates, our kids will come to recognize rebelliousness as their generation's superpower—the key to its success—and unleash it. They'll courageously question, challenge, dismantle, and replace dysfunctional systems with something better.

THE BIG IDEA

Perhaps the most profound way to breed principled rebels is the simplest. You and I must lead by example, becoming more rebellious ourselves and more solicitous of others' insubordination.

Now that you've finished this book, you possess an arsenal of scientific research, tools, tactics, and strategies to win others to your cause and to render yourself and your social groups more welcoming of non-conformity. Put these assets to use. Dedicate yourself to cultivating principled insubordination. Even if you've tended to avoid "rocking the boat," even if you've resisted or denigrated those who have rebelled, it's not too late to change. There is too much needless pain in this world, too much injustice, inequality, inefficiency, and just plain wrongheadedness. It's up to you to do something about it. Before you put down this book, ask yourself one simple question: what am I going to change today? Our children are watching you. Do it for them.

RECIPE STEPS

1. *Foster a sense of agency in your kids.* To raise principled rebels, youth must believe they can make a difference. Be responsive when your children share past explorations or future plans. Let them know that anxious thoughts and feelings are natural when trying new things and taking on challenges. Help your kids regulate their emotions.

2. *Build your kids' critical thinking skills.* Principled insubordination hinges on a person's ability to sift through information at their disposal, filter out useful stuff from the bullshit, and convince others to accept the useful stuff as well. Youth must become comfortable asking questions and distinguishing between high- and low-quality data. They must make a habit of suspending judgment, slowing down their analytical process and letting critical analysis run its course.
3. *Expose kids to various forms of courage and give them the language to describe their own bravery.* Teach kids to see themselves as "heroes in waiting"—the person who intervenes when injustice presents itself.

Epilogue: Whipping Up Your Next Rebellion Masterpiece

How to get started with the non-conformist's cookbook

I've intended this book to be a most unusual kind of cookbook. You haven't learned how to roast a chicken or bake the perfect soufflé. There's nothing in here about preheating the oven to 350 degrees or where and how to buy fresh scrod. Those are important to know, but these days we have an existential need for a different kind of knowledge: how to unleash progress via principled insubordination. Follow the recipe steps in this book, and you'll become a stronger, wiser, principled insubordinate as well as a more open-minded, supportive ally. If millions of us follow these steps, we'll build a safer, more prosperous, more dynamic, and more harmonious society.

To get started, go back and reread Part I of the book. As we've seen, the act of advocating for ideas that might improve the longevity and vitality of groups is costly for the rebel and destabilizes groups in the short term. Creativity inspires a range of emotions, from appreciation to loathing. Guiding other people toward a better way is a journey fraught with anxious thoughts and feelings. Before you get started changing the world, take some time to really *feel* the dilemma that dissenters of the status quo confront every day.

Next, as you start applying the tools and guidance contained in

Parts II and III of this book, be patient. To influence as many people as possible with a new idea, you have to introduce it slowly and methodically. It also takes time to build new skills and aptitudes related to insubordination. As with an exercise or diet regimen, it's often hard and awkward at the beginning, and you need to pursue a routine diligently in the hope of seeing gains. Make it a habit to work with the uncomfortable thoughts, feelings, and bodily sensations that arise, bearing in mind that it often takes about six to eight weeks for self-improvement interventions to work.

As you work at being a better rebel, take good care of yourself. Questioning orthodoxy tests you mentally, physically, and emotionally. You cannot be an effective insubordinate without self-care. The basics are important: sleep, exercise, stress reduction. Also reflect on the toxic, energy-sapping characters in your social network and consider pruning them or at least finding a way to minimize contact. Also, use the concrete tools in the Psychological Flexibility Dashboard for handling emotionally intense situations.

At all times, stay principled. Remember, if you're fortunate enough to triumph as a longtime rebel, you'll be inclined to denigrate and reject those who failed to champion the cause early. Resist this vengeance impulse. Stay true to the same values that served you earlier in your rebellion. Continue to appreciate and welcome skepticism and criticism, regardless of its source. Extend an olive branch to former doubters and adversaries. Publicly affirm that differences of opinion, disagreement, and difference are worthy of celebration.

When you find yourself in the audience, questioning whether a principled rebel offers any value, rely on the twin virtues of humility and curiosity. Be realistic about how little you know. Upon discovering new information, be prepared to update your own thinking. The beauty of humility and curiosity is that it leaves you with a sense of ease. You no longer feel the pressure to defend your views, or show that you are right, smart, and likable. Be open to change and you will enjoy yourself more while also potentially improving your life with newer, better ideas.

In group settings, stay on the alert for signs of discord and discontents as well as the opposite: pressures on individuals to conform, cohere, cooperate, and put on a cheerful face. You won't get divergent thinking and unique perspectives unless you modify the culture to allow a wider range of voices to permeate. Support every measure that reduces the tendency of group members to follow the loudest, most popular, most talkative, or most distinguished. Let the best ideas arise from anyone, anywhere.

Non-conformity is a vital part of being human, a potential consequence of our inherent individuality. We all possess a unique genotype, life history, and personality profile. Our mix of interests, aspirations, and social relationships are different from anyone else's. As you use this book, remember that what will most benefit the world is not what you share in common with others but what sets you apart. Push hard into your uniqueness and help others do the same. Do it boldly and compassionately. Whether you succeed or not, it's the only way to reach your human potential.

Acknowledgments

This is a deeply personal book. My twin brother and I grew up as part of the racial minority in a predominantly Black neighborhood. Roxanne, the single mother who raised us, shouldered a large financial and social burden. I appreciated her then. Now that I'm a father, I appreciate her more.

Early on, I identified as a non-conformist, an outlier, someone who is different. In my youth, without a father figure, I possessed few role models for being a man. I learned by observing and deconstructing. In terms of how to play sports, how to ride a bike, how to be witty, how to attract friends and lovers, how to respond to verbal taunting and physical provocations, I learned through trial and error. Growing up, I had grade school teachers, neighbors, family, friends, and bosses who helped me rethink adversity. They helped me identify how being an outsider builds fortitude. I owe immense gratitude to each of these unnamed catalysts who kept me on a healthy path.

I wrote the book that would have benefitted me, a teenager whose mother died at the age of thirty-nine. A user-friendly handbook that would have helped me as a young adult trying to manage my own psychology. A touchstone to return to for advice throughout adulthood, especially while raising three daughters. It pains me that my mother will never see the culmination of her sacrifices. Never meeting three granddaughters who carry her legacy. Like all my writings, this book is devoted to my mother. Her legacy continues to expand outward.

I have a large set of family and friends who are responsible for transforming a fledgling idea into what is in your hands. For more than twenty years, I have been fortunate to lead a diverse set of intelligent, creative, insightful thinkers in my Well-Being Laboratory at George Mason University. I would be less productive, less creative, and derive far less pleasure, meaning, and moments of flow without them. Many have no idea how much I gained from their efforts and perspectives. Special thanks to the wide-ranging contributions of Anna Lewis (the female Sherlock Holmes), Angela Furst, Aslihan Imamogl, Bradley Brown, David Disabato, David Choi, David Hamlette, James Doorley, Kerry Kelso, Laura Wallace, Logan Craig, Sai Kanuri, and Shely Benitah. I also appreciate the hundreds of students enrolled in my "Science of Well-Being" course who allowed me to experiment with many of the ideas in this book.

Over twenty-three years I have collaborated with an amazing set of researchers. There are too many to name, but thankfully our work is immortalized in the annals of science. I feel intense gratitude when viewing the list of scientific articles we published together in journals and the hundreds of conference posters and talks we shared with the larger community. I will resist listing the large number of scientists who contributed to this book by sharing their unpublished research and answering a barrage of questions via email, phone call, and face-to-face conversation. You will find much of their work in the endnotes. Consider reading their original work referenced along with their additional contributions that can be found online.

Solitude is the most frequent state as a scientist and writer. To cope with these moments, I am grateful for the vitality, support, brilliance, wisdom, and playfulness of friends, relatives, colleagues, and acquaintances who unknowingly provided essential ideas, stories, and criticisms. As a hobby, I collect interesting characters who I want to meld worlds with. You know who you are. The fire pit gatherings, strolls, soccer sideline interactions, and long-lasting bouts of whiskey and cigars kept me sane and tranquil both before and during the pandemic. In times of war, I would sacrifice my body and livelihood to protect at least 71.8 percent of you.

I had a few members of my wise council who offered particularly significant contributions. Fallon Goodman, you are one of my favorite people on the planet. Your candor, integrity, and intellectual contributions cannot be easily quantified. Bouncing ideas off you is something I will always treasure. Our banter, laughter, discussions, and debates elevate the quality of my life and this book. Patrick McKnight, you are my lifelong collaborator. Brothers from a different mother on this journey through life and science. If there is one reason I relished sixteen years working at George Mason University, it is our time together. Robert Biswas-Diener, you are one of the most creative thinkers I've ever met. Writing the previous book with you, conducting workshops with you, and simply spending a dozen hours on the phone per week with you, supercharges me. The more lobes, the better; and the three of you continue to be my ultimate intellectual nourishment. I refuse to imagine an existence where I don't have access to your minds and hearts.

Seth Schulman, you are one of the most compelling writers I know. Working with you on this book has been a privilege. I will be touting your strengths until the end of my days.

Many writers dream of finding an agent, any agent. Christy Fletcher has been a blessing. She makes things happen with the ideal combination of skepticism and perseverance. As a compassionate sage, she often understands what I should be doing or could be doing better than I do. Since we started working together, I have known for every second that she is the ideal partner on this mission. Thank you for taking a chance on me.

There is something beautiful about working with the same editor on multiple books. You learn and grow together. Caroline Sutton, you know exactly how to motivate me, and how to tweak my thinking and writing. With exquisite agility, you know when to criticize and when to praise. Talking to you, working with you, is rewarding and effortless. I am infinitely richer for having you on my side. The same can be said for working with the league of extraordinary individuals at Avery: Casey Maloney, Farin Schlussel, Hannah Steigmeyer, Anne Kosmoski, and Roshe Anderson. When surrounded by people who know their craft so well, you relinquish the reins and observe in awe. I find myself doing this often with the Avery crew.

There are additional members of my wise council who keep my life in perspective. Barry and Marilyn Spitz are my second set of parents. I cherish watching them converse with seven grandchildren—never underestimating their capacities, always listening, always mesmerizing them with an unusual idea, tale, or question.

Barry is my role model for how to be a dad and grandfather. If a fulfilling life is about the capacity to love and be loved, and a collection of rich interesting experiences, then Barry is legendary. I took notes from his lessons. A lot of notes. I carry a little Barry on my shoulders, feeling the warmth and stability of his presence until the end of days. Barry died from COVID-19 during the early stages of writing this book. A preventable event if just a few f$#%ing principled insubordinates had stood up, spoken up, and challenged failed leadership in the United States. I waited for them to appear, and they never did. I write this book in hope of incubating an armada of principled insubordinates who will be ready and active in preventing the next tragedy. Do it for Barry and the hundreds of thousands of others who died needlessly.

My family is the most important part of my life, and Sarah is the fountainhead. We feel loved and cared for in her presence. She is intentional in creating a kinder, more benevolent world. Pushing everyone to offer a bit more generosity and concern for those in need. Anyone who knows her is in a better state of mind because of her.

This book is for my three daughters, Chloe, Raven, and Violet, who are my greatest sources of happiness, meaning, and psychological richness. I treasure your every act of principled rebellion and will always be your champion.

Notes

CHAPTER 1: THE CRITICAL IMPORTANCE OF CARTWHEELING IN THE LIBRARY

3 **Charles Darwin didn't invent:** We can boil down the theory of evolution into four words: variation, selection, retention, and competition. **Variation**: a variety of creatures exist with distinct qualities that may or may not help them survive and breed. **Selection:** creatures possessing qualities that improve their survival and reproductive success will outwit and outlast the rest. **Retention:** different survival rates for different qualities eventually produce creatures who function exquisitely well in their particular environments. **Competition:** there will always be pressures such as rivals and climatic conditions that test whether or not certain qualities remain best suited for maintaining a healthy lineage of descendants. Here are my eight favorite books on evolutionary theory: Richard Dawkins, *The Greatest Show on Earth: The Evidence for Evolution* (London: Bantam, 2009); Daniel Dennett, *Darwin's Dangerous Idea* (New York: Simon & Schuster, 1995); Jared Diamond, *Guns, Germs, and Steel: The Fates of Human Societies* (New York: Norton, 1997); Douglas T. Kenrick and Vladas Griskevicius, *The Rational Animal: How Evolution Made Us Smarter Than We Think* (New York: Basic Books, 2013); Geoffrey Miller, *Spent: Sex, Evolution and Consumer Behavior* (New York: Penguin/Putnam, 2009); Steven Pinker, *The Blank Slate* (New York: Viking, 2002); Christopher Ryan and Cacilda

Jethá, *Sex at Dawn: The Prehistoric Origins of Modern Sexuality* (New York: Harper, 2010); Robert Wright, *The Moral Animal: Evolutionary Psychology and Everyday Life* (New York: Vintage Books, 1994).

3 **preface to *On the Origin of Species*:** Charles Darwin, *On the Origin of Species by Means of Natural Selection* (London: Murray, 1859); Curtis Neal Johnson, "The Preface to Darwin's *Origin of Species*: The Curious History of the 'Historical Sketch,'" *Journal of the History of Biology* 40, no. 3 (2007): 529–56, https://doi.org/10.1007/s10739-006-9118-0.

3 **Al-Jahiz wondered why certain animals:** In his opus, he strove to grasp the mechanisms underlying animal competition to avoid being eaten and breed. Upon observing dozens of animal species, he pointed out, "Environmental factors influence organisms to develop new characteristics to ensure survival, thus transforming them into new species. Animals that survive to breed can pass on their successful characteristics to their offspring." His book, *Kitab al-Hayawan*, or *The Book of Animals*, mesmerized the Muslim world. A reminder of how luck and circumstance play a role in fame and fortune. See Abī 'Uthmān 'Amru Ibn Baḥr al-Jāḥiẓ, *Kitāb Al-ḥayawān* (Kairo: Maktabat Muṣṭafā al-Bābī al-Ḥalabī, n.d.).

3 **Al-Jahiz's patron:** Muḥammad ibn 'Abd al-Malik, nicknamed Ibn al-Zayyat. One might argue that trying to remember these names is one of the many reasons Darwin is given greater credit in the discovery of evolutionary theory. See Rebecca Stott, *Darwin's Ghosts: The Secret History of Evolution* (New York: Spiegel & Grau Trade Paperbacks, 2012), 57.

3–4 **executed him inside an iron maiden:** Stott, *Darwin's Ghosts*.

4 **Others on Darwin's list:** Johnson, "The Preface to Darwin's *Origin of Species*"; Stott, *Darwin's Ghosts*.

4 **doubting Biblical claims:** Here is a quick summary of the Biblical creation narrative. On Day 1, God created Light. On Day 2, He/She/It went on to create the atmosphere/firmament. On Day 3, dry ground and plants. On Day 4, the sun, moon, and stars. On Day 5, birds and sea animals. On Day 6, land animals and humans. And on the seventh day, God rested. A nasty debate exists whether God created animals and humans in two days or six days. See Genesis 1:1–31, 2:1–2.

4 **a countervailing idea:** A similar sentiment to what science writer Matt Ridley uncovered in that an evolutionary view offers a more accurate and elegant account than a creationist or intelligent designer view of cultural and technological transformations. See Matt Ridley,

The Evolution of Everything: How New Ideas Emerge (New York: HarperCollins, 2015).

5 **the speed of cultural evolution:** Jolanda Jetten and Matthew J. Hornsey, "Deviance and Dissent in Groups," *Annual Review of Psychology* 65, no. 1 (2014): 461–85, https://doi.org/10.1146/annurev-psych-010213-115151; Bibb Latané and Sharon Wolf, "The Social Impact of Majorities and Minorities," *Psychological Review* 88, no. 5 (1981): 438–53, https://doi.org/10.1037/0033-295x.88.5.438; Charlan Jeanne Nemeth and Brendan Nemeth-Brown, "Better than Individuals? The Potential Benefits of Dissent and Diversity for Group Creativity," in *Group Creativity: Innovation through Collaboration*, ed. Paul B. Paulus and Bernard Arjan Nijstad (New York: Oxford University Press, 2003), 63–84, http://doi.org/10.1093/acprof:oso/9780195147308.003.0004; Wendy Wood et al., "Minority Influence: A Meta-Analytic Review of Social Influence Processes," *Psychological Bulletin* 115, no. 3 (1994): 323–45, https://doi.org/10.1037/0033-2909.115.3.323.

5 **why was his insubordination:** Paul Johnson, *Darwin: Portrait of a Genius* (New York: Penguin Books, 2013); Randy Moore, "The Persuasive Mr. Darwin," *BioScience* 47, no. 2 (1997): 107–14, https://doi.org/10.2307/1313021; David Quammen, *The Reluctant Mr. Darwin: An Intimate Portrait of Charles Darwin and the Making of His Theory of Evolution* (New York: Atlas Books/Norton, 2007).

5 **how we might differ and disagree successfully:** Lisa Feldman Barrett and James A. Russell, *The Psychological Construction of Emotion* (New York: Guilford Press, 2014); Jolanda Jetten and Matthew J. Hornsey, *Rebels in Groups: Dissent, Deviance, Difference and Defiance* (Chichester, UK: Wiley-Blackwell, 2011); James C. Kaufman and Robert J. Sternberg, *The Cambridge Handbook of Creativity* (Cambridge, UK: Cambridge University Press, 2010); Robin Martin and Miles Hewstone, *Minority Influence and Innovation: Antecedents, Processes and Consequences* (Hove, UK: Psychology Press, 2010); Tom Postmes and Jolanda Jetten, *Individuality and the Group: Advances in Social Identity* (Thousand Oaks, CA: Sage, 2006); Kathleen D. Vohs and Eli J. Finkel, *Self and Relationships: Connecting Intrapersonal and Interpersonal Processes* (New York: Guilford Press, 2006).

6 **successful insubordination strategies:** Johnson, *Darwin: Portrait of a Genius*; Moore, "The Persuasive Mr. Darwin"; Quammen, *The Reluctant Mr. Darwin*.

6 **"the reception of analogous views":** Johnson, *Darwin: Portrait of a Genius.*

6 **overcome listeners' emotional resistance:** William D. Crano and Radmila Prislin, "Attitudes and Persuasion," *Annual Review of Psychology* 57, no. 1 (2006): 345–74, https://doi.org/10.1146/annurev.psych.57.102904.190034; Richard E. Petty and John T. Cacioppo, *Attitudes and Persuasion: Classic and Contemporary Approaches* (Boulder, CO: Westview Press, 1996).

6 **accessible, jargon-free style:** Darwin, *On the Origin of Species*; Johnson, *Darwin: Portrait of a Genius*; Moore, "The Persuasive Mr. Darwin."

6 **analogies as illustrations:** Scientific colleagues scoffed at this rhetorical device. Yet Darwin's communication style is what drew audiences in to read and enjoy the work. See Darwin, *On the Origin of Species.*

7 **allies play a critical role:** Ayelet Fishbach, Julia Steinmetz, and Yanping Tu, "Motivation in a Social Context: Coordinating Personal and Shared Goal Pursuits with Others," in *Advances in Motivation Science*, ed. Andrew Elliot (Cambridge, MA: Academic Press, 2016), 35–79; Gráinne M. Fitzsimons, Eli J. Finkel, and Michelle R. vanDellen, "Transactive Goal Dynamics," *Psychological Review* 122, no. 4 (2015): 648–73, https://doi.org/10.1037/a0039654; Edward Orehek, Amanda L. Forest, and Nicole Barbaro, "A People-as-Means Approach to Interpersonal Relationships," *Perspectives on Psychological Science* 13, no. 3 (2018): 373–89; Jordan E. Theriault, Liane Young, and Lisa Feldman Barrett, "The Sense of Should: A Biologically-Based Framework for Modeling Social Pressure," *Physics of Life Reviews* 36 (2021): 100–136.

8 **We humans are tribal creatures:** The differences between people who strongly identify with particular kinds of music and show disdain for other kinds is an underappreciated form of tribalism that affects much of what people consume and the social norms of behavior. See Gideon Nave et al., "Musical Preferences Predict Personality: Evidence from Active Listening and Facebook Likes," *Psychological Science* 29, no. 7 (2018): 1145–58; Peter J. Rentfrow and Samuel D. Gosling, "The Content and Validity of Music-Genre Stereotypes Among College Students," *Psychology of Music* 35, no. 2 (2007): 306–26; Peter J. Rentfrow and Samuel D. Gosling, "Message in a Ballad: The Role of Music Preferences in Interpersonal Perception," *Psychological Science* 17, no. 3 (2006): 236–42; Peter J. Rentfrow and Samuel D. Gosling, "The Do Re Mi's of Everyday Life: The Structure and

Personality Correlates of Music Preferences," *Journal of Personality and Social Psychology* 84, no. 6 (2003): 1236–56.

9 **odds of success as dissenters:** Insubordination is more than just dissent, defiance, or non-conformity. In a hierarchical social structure operating on the assumption that people on lower rungs will abide by the guidelines set by people on higher rungs, insubordination is a specific act of rebellion, the willful act of disobeying superiors or authorities. I favor this term because it carries the most negative connotations, despite depending on what authority figures, the mainstream, or the orthodoxy espouses. In 1851, a slave who attempted to escape their master was considered diseased. These slaves were afflicted with a condition termed "Drapetomania," "the disease that caused slaves to run away." Physicians and psychiatrists created this unfounded diagnosis, and the establishment accepted it—one of many reminders that the status quo is often completely wrong, and that we require insubordination to set things right. See Samuel A. Cartwright, "Report of the Diseases and Peculiarities of the Negro Race," *New Orleans Medical and Surgical Journal* (1851): 691–715.

10 **"the refusal to obey someone":** "Insubordination," Cambridge Dictionary Online, Google, accessed February 13, 2020, https://dictionary.cambridge.org/us/dictionary/english/insubordination.

CHAPTER 2: THE STRANGE THINGS WE DO TO BE LIKED

17 **he took 322 free throws:** Rick Barry and Bill Libby, *Confessions of a Basketball Gypsy: The Rick Barry Story* (New York: Dell Publishing Company, 1972).

17 **LeBron James, missed 132 overhand shots:** This is during the 2015–2016 season, which saw his highest free-throw percentage over the last five years of his career. I decided to be generous and not include the years 2016 to 2020, when he shot less accurately. See Barry and Libby, *Confessions.*

17 **according to multiple sports scientists:** Hiroki Okubo and Mont Hubbard, "Dynamics of the Basketball Shot with Application to the Free Throw," *Journal of Sports Sciences* 24, no. 12 (2006): 1303–14; Curtis Rist, "Physics Proves It: Everyone Should Shoot Granny-Style," *Discover*, July 19, 2008, https://www.discovermagazine.com/the-sciences/physics-proves-it-everyone-should-shoot-granny-style; Curtis Rist, "Underhanded Achievement," *Discover*, October 2000: 34–36; A. Tan and G. Miller, "Kinematics of the Free Throw in

Basketball," *American Journal of Physics* 49, no. 6 (1981): 542–44; Hannah Devlin, "'Granny Style' Is Best Way to Take a Basketball Free Throw, Study Shows," *Guardian*, April 25, 2017, https://www.theguardian.com/science/2017/apr/26/granny-style-is-best-way-to-take-a-basketball-free-throw-study-shows.

18 **Former NBA great Shaquille O'Neal:** He named his boat *Free Throw* . . . so he will "never sink it." See Rick Barry, "590: Choosing Wrong," interview by Malcolm Gladwell, *This American Life*, NPR, June 24, 2016, 10:00, https://www.thisamericanlife.org/590/transcript.

18 **"rather shoot zero percent":** Dan Feldman, "Shaq on Free Throws: 'I Told Rick Barry I'd Rather Shoot 0% Than Shoot Underhand,'" *NBC Sports*, December 11, 2017, https://nba.nbcsports.com/2017/12/11/shaq-on-free-throws-i-told-rick-barry-id-rather-shoot-0-than-shoot-underhand/.

18 **Andre Drummond, refused to adopt the granny shot:** Michelle Kaufman, "Rick Barry Was Known for 'Granny-Style' Free-Throws. His Son's Bringing Them Back," *Miami Herald*, March 23, 2017, https://www.miamiherald.com/sports/college/sec/university-of-florida/article140384263.html.

19 **He averaged a league record:** "Wilt Chamberlain," Career Regular Season Stats, NBA, https://stats.nba.com/player/76375/career/; Mayo Oshin, "The Wilt Chamberlain Effect: Why We Make Bad Decisions, Even When We Know Better," *The Ladders*, September 3, 2018, https://www.theladders. com/career-advice/the-wilt-chamberlain-effect-why-we-make-bad-decisions-even-when-we-know-better.

19 **he scored an astronomical one hundred points:** Still the record as of this writing in August 2020, even as the National Basketball Association transformed into a three-point shooting machine (fewer non-dunk two-point shots are taken). Michael Jordan, Hall of Famer, only scored sixty-nine points in a game. Kobe Bryant, Hall of Famer, only scored eighty-two points in a game. LeBron James, future Hall of Famer, only scored sixty-one points in a game. See "NBA Advanced Stats," NBA, last modified March 7, 2021, https://www.nba.com/stats/.

19 **hitting twenty-eight of thirty-two free-throw shots:** Oshin, "The Wilt Chamberlain Effect"; Colton Wesley, "Underhanded Free Throws Work, So Why Don't Players Shoot Them?," *Detroit Jock City*, May 31, 2017, https://detroitjockcity.com/2017/05/31/underhanded-free-throws-work-dont-players.

19 **he explained in his autobiography:** Wilt Chamberlain, *A View from Above* (New York: Signet, 1992).

19 **these averages haven't improved:** John Branch, "For Free Throws, 50 Years of Practice Is No Help," *New York Times*, March 3, 2009, https://www.nytimes.com/2009/03/04/sports/basketball /04freethrow .html.

20 **how powerful our tendency to conform:** Bert H. Hodges, "Conformity and Divergence in Interactions, Groups, and Culture," in *The Oxford Handbook of Social Influence*, ed. Stephen G. Harkins, Kipling D. Williams, and Jerry M. Burger (New York: Oxford University Press, 2017), 87–105; Tatsuya Kameda, Masanori Takezawa, and Reid Hastie, "The Logic of Social Sharing: An Evolutionary Game Analysis of Adaptive Norm Development," *Personality and Social Psychology Review* 7, no. 1 (2003): 2–19, https://doi.org/10.1207 /s15327957pspr0701_1; Theriault, Young, and Barrett, "The Sense of Should."

20 **muster the courage to buck convention:** Shahrzad Goudarzi et al., "Economic System Justification Predicts Muted Emotional Responses to Inequality," *Nature Communication* 11, no. 1 (2019): 1–9, https://doi .org/10.31219/osf.io/up8ay.

20 **the value of ideas or practices:** Scott Eidelman and Christian S. Crandall, "Bias in Favor of the Status Quo," *Social and Personality Psychology Compass* 6, no. 3 (2012): 270–81, https://doi.org/10.1111 /j.1751-9004.2012.00427.x; Scott Eidelman, Christian S. Crandall, and Jennifer Pattershall, "The Existence Bias," *Journal of Personality and Social Psychology* 97, no. 5 (2009): 765–75, https://doi.org/10.1037 /a0017058.

20 **acupuncture had been around for 250:** Scott Eidelman, Jennifer Pattershall, and Christian S. Crandall, "Longer Is Better," *Journal of Experimental Social Psychology* 46, no. 6 (2010): 993–98, https://doi.org /10.1016/j.jesp.2010.07.008.

21 **a painting was created a century ago:** Eidelman, Pattershall, and Crandall, "Longer Is Better."

21 **violent enhanced interrogation techniques:** Christian S. Crandall et al., "Status Quo Framing Increases Support for Torture," *Social Influence* 4, no. 1 (2009): 1–10.

21 **disliked and did not vote for the president:** Kristin Laurin, "Inaugurating Rationalization: Three Field Studies Find Increased Rationalization When Anticipated Realities Become Current,"

Psychological Science 29, no. 4 (2018): 483–95, https://doi.org/10.1177/0956797617738814.

21 **negative attitudes about the existence of all-Black colleges:** Herbert C. Kelman, "Reflections on Social and Psychological Processes of Legitimization and Delegitimization," in *Psychology of Legitimacy*, ed. John T. Jost and Brenda Major (Cambridge, UK: Cambridge University Press: 2001), 54–76.

22 **expressed disdain for Mexican immigrants:** Washington Post Staff, "Full Text: Donald Trump Announces a Presidential Bid," *Washington Post*, June 16, 2015, https://www.washington post.com/news/post-politics/wp/2015/06/16/full-text-donald-trump-announces-a-presidential-bid/.

22 **76 percent of Hispanics are Mexican:** Luis Noe-Bustamante, Antonio Flores, and Sono Shah, "Facts on Hispanics of Mexican Origin in the United States, 2017," Pew Research Center, September 16, 2019, https://www.pewresearch.org/hispanic/fact-sheet/u-s-hispanics-facts-on-mexican-origin-latinos/#:~:text=Mexicans%20are%20the%20largest%20population,36.6%20million%20over%20the%20period.

22 **treated no worse than Whites:** Juliana Menasce Horowitz, Anna Brown, and Kiana Cox, "2. Views of Racial Inequality," Pew Research Center, April 9, 2019, https://www.pewsocialtrends.org/2019/04/09/views-of-racial-inequality/.

23 **almost six times more likely to be imprisoned:** Jennifer Bronson and E. Ann Carson, "Prisoners in 2017," Bureau of Justice Statistics, April 25, 2019, https://www.bjs.gov/index.cfm?ty=pbdetail&iid=6546; "COVID-19 Spurs 25% Drop in Inmates Held in Local Jails," Bureau of Justice Statistics, June 2019–June 2020, https://www.bjs.gov/index.cfm?%20ty=pbdetail&iid=6546.

23 **41 percent of Black people polled in 2001:** Frank Newport, Jack Ludwig, and Sheila Kearney, "Black-White Relations in the United States, 2001 Update," Gallup Poll Social Audit, July 10, 2001, https://media.gallup.com/GPTB/specialReports/sr010711.PDF.

23 **have produced similar findings:** Gallup polls conducted from June 8 to July 24, 2020, show that one out of every three Black people say they are treated the same or better than Whites. See Megan Brenan, "New Highs Say Black People Treated Less Fairly in Daily Life," *Gallup*, August 19, 2020, https://news.gallup.com/poll/317564/new-highs-say-black-people-treated-less-fairly-daily-life.aspx.

23 **the psychological biases:** Some might take my argument as implying that Black people do not understand larger, long-standing problems in the criminal justice system, or that they are not reliable narrators of their own experience. I do not mean to single out Black people, or indeed, any minority group. I merely present these data to illustrate how humans across demographics remain unaware of existing status quo biases, and how they tend to prioritize stability over social change as a result.

23 **a theory of system justification:** John T. Jost and Mahzarin R. Banaji, "The Role of Stereotyping in System-Justification and the Production of False Consciousness," *British Journal of Social Psychology* 33, no. 1 (1994): 1–27, https://doi.org/10.1111/j.2044-8309.1994.tb01008.x; John T. Jost, Mahzarin R. Banaji, and Brian A. Nosek, "A Decade of System Justification Theory: Accumulated Evidence of Conscious and Unconscious Bolstering of the Status Quo," *Political Psychology* 25, no. 6 (2016): 881–919, https://doi.org/10.31234/osf.io/6ue35.

23 **"the revolutionary role of system rejection":** Chuma Kevin Owuamalam, Mark Rubin, and Russell Spears, "Addressing Evidential and Theoretical Inconsistencies in System-Justification Theory with a Social Identity Model of System Attitudes," *Current Directions in Psychological Science* 27, no. 2 (2018): 91–96, https://doi.org/10.1177/0963721417737136.

24 **our tendency to uphold and support oppressive systems:** Justin P. Friesen et al., "System Justification: Experimental Evidence, Its Contextual Nature, and Implications for Social Change," *British Journal of Social Psychology* 58, no. 2 (2018): 315–39, https://doi.org/10.1111/bjso.12278; John T. Jost, "A Quarter Century of System Justification Theory: Questions, Answers, Criticisms, and Societal Applications," *British Journal of Social Psychology* 58, no. 2 (2018): 263–314, https://doi.org/10.1111/bjso.12297; Chuma Kevin Owuamalam, Mark Rubin, and Russell Spears, "Revisiting 25 Years of System Motivation Explanation for System Justification from the Perspective of Social Identity Model of System Attitudes," *Journal of Social Psychology* 58, no. 2 (2018): 362–81, https://doi.org/10.31234/osf.io/y29xq.

25 **we tend to take comfort in the familiar:** Aaron C. Kay et al., "Panglossian Ideology in the Service of System Justification: How Complementary Stereotypes Help Us to Rationalize Inequality," *Advances in Experimental Social Psychology* 39 (2007): 305–58, https://doi.org/10.1016/S0065-2601(06)39006-5.

25 **participants to feel temporarily disempowered:** Bastiaan T. Rutjens, Frenk van Harreveld, and Joop van der Pligt, "Yes We Can: Belief in Progress as Compensatory Control," *Social Psychological and Personality Science* 1, no. 3 (2010): 246–52, https://doi.org/10.1177/1948550610361782; Bastiaan T. Rutjens et al., "Steps, Stages, and Structure: Finding Compensatory Order in Scientific Theories," *Journal of Experimental Psychology: General* 142, no. 2 (2013): 313–18, https://doi.org/10.1037/a0028716.

25 **uphold the system against critical detractors:** Steven Shepherd et al., "Evidence for the Specificity of Control Motivations in Worldview Defense: Distinguishing Compensatory Control from Uncertainty Management and Terror Management Processes," *Journal of Experimental Social Psychology* 47, no. 5 (2011): 949–58, https://doi.org/10.1016/j.jesp. 2011.03.026.

26 **Bush's job approval rose to 90 percent:** David W. Moore, "Bush Job Approval Highest In Gallup History," Gallup, September 24, 2001, https://news.gallup.com/poll/4924/bush-job-approval-highest-gallup-history.aspx.

26 **It remained high for a full two years:** "Presidential Approval Rating—George W. Bush," Gallup, last modified January 11, 2009, https://news.gallup.com/poll/116500/Presidential-Approval-Ratings-George-Bush.aspx. For research detailing the psychological mechanisms for the varying approval ratings of President Bush, see Mark J. Landau et al., "Deliver Us from Evil: The Effects of Mortality Salience and Reminders of 9/11 on Support for President George W. Bush," *Personality and Social Psychology Bulletin* 30, no. 9 (2004): 1136–50, https://doi.org/10.1177/0146167204267988; Thomas A. Pyszczynski, Sheldon Solomon, and Jeff Greenberg, *In the Wake of 9/11: The Psychology of Terror* (Washington, DC: APA Press, 2003).

26 **than a common nemesis:** Tom Douglas, *Scapegoats: Transferring Blame* (New York: Routledge Press, 1995); Mark J. Landau et al., "Deriving Solace from a Nemesis: Having Scapegoats and Enemies Buffers the Threat of Meaninglessness," in *Meaning, Mortality, and Choice: The Social Psychology of Existential Concerns*, ed. Phillip R. Shaver and Mario Mikulincer (Washington, DC: APA Press, 2012), 183–202; Daniel Sullivan, Mark J. Landau, and Zachary K. Rothschild, "An Existential Function of Enemyship: Evidence That People Attribute Influence to Personal and Political Enemies to Compensate for

Threats to Control," *Journal of Personality and Social Psychology* 98, no. 3 (2010): 434–49, https://doi.org/10.1037/a0017457.

26 **intentionally evoke symbolic links:** Steven Shepherd, Richard P. Eibach, and Aaron C. Kay, "'One Nation Under God': The System-Justifying Function of Symbolically Aligning God and Government," *Political Psychology* 38, no. 5 (2017): 703–20, https://doi.org/10.1111/pops.12353.

26–27 **why human beings favor the status quo:** Keisha M. Cutright et al., "When Your World Must Be Defended: Choosing Products to Justify the System," *Journal of Consumer Research* 38, no. 1 (2011): 62–77, https://doi.org/10.1086/658469.

27 **will feel hesitant to voice concerns:** David Skarbek, "Prison Gangs, Norms, and Organizations," *Journal of Economic Behavior & Organization* 82, no. 1 (2012): 96–109, https://doi.org/10.1016/j.jebo.2012.01.002.

28 **willing to sacrifice material payoffs:** Aaron C. Kay et al., "Inequality, Discrimination, and the Power of the Status Quo: Direct Evidence for a Motivation to See the Way Things Are as the Way They Should Be," *Journal of Personality and Social Psychology* 97, no. 3 (2009): 421–34, https://doi.org/10.1037 /a0015997; Jojanneke van der Toorn et al., "A Sense of Powerlessness Fosters System Justification: Implications for the Legitimation of Authority, Hierarchy, and Government," *Political Psychology* 36, no. 1 (2014): 93–110, https://doi.org/10.1111/pops.12183; Jojanneke van der Toorn, Tom R. Tyler, and John T. Jost, "More than Fair: Outcome Dependence, System Justification, and the Perceived Legitimacy of Authority Figures," *Journal of Experimental Social Psychology* 47, no. 1 (2011): 127–38, https://doi.org/10.1016/j.jesp.2010.09.003.

28 **conformity intensifies:** Chuma Kevin Owuamalam and Russell Spears, "Do Humans Possess an Autonomous System Justification Motivation? A Pupillometric Test of the Strong System Justification Thesis," *Journal of Experimental Social Psychology* 86 (2020), https://doi.org/10.31219/osf.io/jx7rs.

29 **tightening immigration policies:** Experiments 1 and 2. See Kristin Laurin, Steven Shepherd, and Aaron C. Kay, "Restricted Emigration, System Inescapability, and Defense of the Status Quo," *Psychological Science* 21, no. 8 (2010): 1075–82, https://doi.org/10.1177/0956797610375448.

30 **difficulty transferring to another institution:** Experiment 3. See Laurin, Shepherd, and Kay, "Restricted Emigration."

30 **policies that perpetuate existing inequalities:** Kay et al., "Inequality, Discrimination, and the Power of the Status Quo."

31 **When we feel hopeful:** Chuma Kevin Owuamalam, Mark Rubin, and Christian Issmer, "Reactions to Group Devaluation and Social Inequality: A Comparison of Social Identity and System Justification Predictions," *Cogent Psychology* 3, no. 1 (2016) 1188442, https://doi.org/10.1080/23311908.2016.1188442.

31 **As women make inroads in society:** Luca Caricati and Chuma Kevin Owuamalam, "System Justification Among the Disadvantaged: A Triadic Social Stratification Perspective," *Frontiers in Psychology* 11 (2020): 40, https://doi.org/10.3389/fpsyg.2020.00040.

31 **Experiments produced similar findings:** Chuma Kevin Owuamalam et al., "Why Do People from Low-Status Groups Support Class Systems That Disadvantage Them? A Test of Two Mainstream Explanations in Malaysia and Australia," *Journal of Social Issues* 73, no. 1 (2017): 80–98, https://doi.org/10.1111/josi.12205.

31 **hopeful defenders of oppressive systems:** Angela L. Duckworth et al., "Cognitive and Noncognitive Predictors of Success," *Proceedings of the National Academy of Sciences* 116, no. 47 (2019): 23499–504, https://doi.org/10.1073/pnas.1910510116; Angela Duckworth and James J. Gross, "Self-Control and Grit: Related but Separable Determinants of Success," *Current Directions in Psychological Science* 23, no. 5 (2014): 319–25, https://doi.org/10.1177/0963721414541462.

32 **congratulating yourself for grittiness:** These seven items come directly from the twelve-item John Henryism Scale for Active Coping. See Sherman A. James, "John Henryism and the Health of African-Americans," *Culture, Medicine and Psychiatry* 18, no. 2 (1994): 163–82, https://doi.org/10.1007/bf01379448.

32 **racial minorities to work too hard:** James, "John Henryism and the Health of African-Americans."

33 **Scientists followed 3,126 young adults:** Emiliano Albanese et al., "Hostile Attitudes and Effortful Coping in Young Adulthood Predict Cognition 25 Years Later," *Neurology* 86, no. 13 (2016): 1227–34, https://doi.org/10.1212/wnl.0000000000002517.

33 **It's difficult to embrace an aspirational vision:** Aaron C. Kay and Justin Friesen, "On Social Stability and Social Change: Understanding When System Justification Does and Does Not Occur," *Current*

Directions in Psychological Science 20, no. 6 (2011): 360–64, https://doi.org/10.1177/0963721411422059; Owuamalam, Rubin, and Spears, "Addressing Evidential and Theoretical Inconsistencies."

CHAPTER 3: RENEGADES ROCK

37 **Jennings could have nodded:** The current leading researcher on her life is Dr. Katherine Perrotta at Kennesaw State University. Here is a sampling of her work: Katherine Perrotta, "A Century Apart: An Evaluation of Historical Comparisons between Elizabeth Jennings and Rosa Parks in Narratives of the Black Freedom Movement," *American Educational History Journal* 44, no. 1 (2017): 33–48; Katherine Perrotta and Chara Haeussler Bohan, "Nineteenth Century Rosa Parks? Assessing Elizabeth Jennings' Legacy as a Teacher and Civil Rights Pioneer in Antebellum America," *Vitae Scholasticae: The Journal of Educational Biography* 30, no. 2 (2013): 5–23.

38 **"you are a good for nothing impudent fellow":** John H. Hewitt, "The Search for Elizabeth Jennings, Heroine of a Sunday Afternoon in New York City," *New York History* 71, no. 4 (1990): 386–415; Jerry Mikorenda, *America's First Freedom Rider: Elizabeth Jennings, Chester A. Arthur, and the Early Fight for Civil Rights* (Guilford, CT: Lyons Press, 2020).

38 **As a result of the struggle:** Chronicled in a March 1855 issue of New-Lisbon, Ohio's *Anti-Slavery Bugle*. See "Anti-Slavery Bugle," Library of Congress, "Chronicling America: Historic American Newspapers," March 10, 1855, https://chroniclingamerica.loc.gov/lccn/sn83035487/1855-03-10/ed-1/seq-3/.

38 **"bushiest and boldest mustache":** G. Clay Whittaker, "A History of West Wing Whiskers," *Men's Journal*, November 13, 2014, https://www.mensjournal.com/style/a-history-of-west-wing-whiskers-20141113/james-garfield/.

38 **policy giving Black people equal access:** Rhoda Golden Freeman, "The Free Negro in New York City in the Era before the Civil War" (PhD diss., Columbia University, 1966); Hewitt, "The Search for Elizabeth Jennings."

39 **New York retained racist laws:** Anne Farrow, Joel Lang, and Jenifer Frank, *Complicity: How the North Promoted, Prolonged, and Profited from Slavery* (New York: Ballantine Books, 2006); Leslie M. Harris, *In the Shadow of Slavery: African Americans in New York City, 1626–1863* (Chicago: University of Chicago Press, 2004); Mikorenda, *America's First Freedom Rider.*

39 **Over a hundred years before Rosa Parks:** Joyce A. Hanson, *Rosa Parks: A Biography* (Santa Barbara, CA: Greenwood Biographies, 2011).

39 **As Bill Clinton told an audience:** Bill Clinton, "Hillary Clinton and the Changing Political Landscape: The Daily Show," interview by Trevor Noah, *The Daily Show*, September 15, 2016, 9:34, https://www.youtube.com/watch?v=h-H1LddWxo8&feature=youtube.

40 **Egyptian dung ointments:** Evan Andrews, "7 Unusual Ancient Medical Techniques," History, last modified August 22, 2018, https://www.history.com/news/7-unusual-ancient-medical-techniques.

40 **44,000 patients die each year:** Juan Escrivá Gracia, Ricardo Brage Serrano, and Julio Fernández Garrido, "Medication Errors and Drug Knowledge Gaps among Critical-Care Nurses: A Mixed Multi-Method Study," *BMC Health Services Research* 19, no. 640 (2019), https://doi.org/10.1186/s12913-019-4481-7; Ghadah Asaad Assiri et al., "What Is the Epidemiology of Medication Errors, Error-Related Adverse Events and Risk Factors for Errors in Adults Managed in Community Care Contexts? A Systematic Review of the International Literature," *BMJ Open* 9, no. 5 (2018), https://doi.org/10.1136/bmjopen-2017-019101; Gili Kadmon et al., "Case Not Closed: Prescription Errors 12 Years after Computerized Physician Order Entry Implementation," *Journal of Pediatrics* 190 (2017): 236–40, https://doi.org/10.1016/j.jpeds.2017.08.013; Institute of Medicine (U.S.) Committee on Quality of Health Care in America, *To Err Is Human: Building a Safer Health System*, ed. Linda T. Kohn, Janet M. Corrigan, and Molla S. Donaldson (Washington, DC: National Academies Press, 2000).

40 **estimating the universe's age:** Adam G. Riess et al., "Large Magellanic Cloud Cepheid Standards Provide a 1% Foundation for the Determination of the Hubble Constant and Stronger Evidence for Physics beyond ΛCDM," *Astrophysical Journal* 876, no. 1 (2019): 85, https://doi.org/10.3847/1538-4357/ab1422; Corey S. Powell, "The Universe May Be a Billion Years Older than We Thought. Scientists Are Scrambling to Figure Out Why," NBC News, May 18, 2019, https://www.nbcnews.com/mach/science/universe-may-be-billion-years-younger-we-thought-scientists-are-ncna1005541.

40 **Our educational system is better:** Thomas D. Snyder, ed., *120 Years of American Education: A Statistical Portrait* (Washington, DC: U.S. Department of Education, January 1993).

41 **only 39 percent could name all three:** "Americans' Civics Knowledge Increases but Still Has a Long Way to Go," Annenberg

Public Policy Center, September 12, 2019, https://www.annenbergpublicpolicycenter.org/americans-civics-knowledge-increases-2019-survey/.

41 **sixteen minutes of physical movement:** John Cawley, Chad Meyerhoefer, and David Newhouse, "The Impact of State Physical Education Requirements on Youth Physical Activity and Overweight," *Health Economics* 16, no. 12 (2007): 1287–1301, https://doi.org/10.1002/hec.1218; John Cawley, Chad Meyerhoefer, and David Newhouse, "Not Your Father's PE: Obesity, Exercise, and the Role of Schools," *Education Next* 6, no. 4 (2006): 61–66; "Teens Only Active in Gym Class for 16 Minutes," NBC News, September 19, 2006, https://www.nbcnews.com/health/health-news/teens-only-active-gym-class-16-minutes-flna1C9438469.

42 **15,000 law enforcement professionals:** "PoliceOne's 2013 Gun Policy & Law Enforcement Survey Results: Executive Summary," *PoliceOne*, April 8, 2013, https://www.policeone.com/police-products/firearms/accessories/articles/policeones-2013-gun-policy-law-enforcement-survey-results-executive-summary-x02GJHRSJXGbGwH9/.

42 **shooters miss the target 82 percent of the time:** Bernard D. Rostker et al., *Evaluation of the New York City Police Department Firearm Training and Firearm-Discharge Review Process*, RAND Center on Quality Policing (Santa Monica, CA: RAND Corporation, 2008), http://www.nyc.gov/html/nypd/downloads/pdf/public_information/RAND_FirearmEvaluation.pdf.

43 **importance of psychological safety:** Bret Sanner and J. Stuart Bunderson, "When Feeling Safe Isn't Enough: Contextualizing Models of Safety and Learning in Teams," *Organizational Psychology Review* 5, no. 3 (2015): 224–43, https://doi.org/10.1177/2041386614565145.

43 **only when sufficient minority viewpoints exist:** Bernard A. Nijstad, Floor Berger-Selman, and Carsten K. W. de Dreu, "Innovation in Top Management Teams: Minority Dissent, Transformational Leadership, and Radical Innovations," *European Journal of Work and Organizational Psychology* 23, no. 2 (2012): 310–22, https://doi.org/10.1080/1359432x.2012.734038; Carsten K. W. de Dreu and Michael A. West, "Minority Dissent and Team Innovation: The Importance of Participation in Decision Making," *Journal of Applied Psychology* 86, no. 6 (2001): 1191–201, https://doi.org/10.1037/0021-9010.86.6.1191; Carsten K. W. de Dreu, "Team Innovation and Team Effectiveness: The Importance of Minority Dissent and Reflexivity," *European*

Journal of Work and Organizational Psychology 11, no. 3 (2002): 285–98, https://doi.org/10.1080/13594320244000175.

43 **"next best course of group action":** Katherine J. Klein and David A. Harrison, "On the Diversity of Diversity: Tidy Logic, Messier Realities," *Academy of Management Perspectives* 21, no. 4 (2007): 26–33, https://doi.org/10.5465/amp.2007.27895337.

44 **belong to an in-group:** Michael A. Hogg, "Social Identity Theory," in *Contemporary Social Psychological Theories*, ed. Peter James Burke (Palo Alto, CA: Stanford University Press, 2006), 111–36; Matthew J. Hornsey, "Social Identity Theory and Self-Categorization Theory: A Historical Review," *Social and Personality Psychology Compass* 2, no. 1 (2008): 204–22, https://doi.org/10.1111/j.1751-9004.2007.00066.x; Henri Tajfel and John C. Turner, "The Social Identity Theory of Intergroup Behavior," in *Political Psychology*, Key Readings in Social Psychology, ed. John T. Jost and Jim Sidanius (Hove, UK: Psychology Press, 2004), 276–93.

45 **"motivated certainty":** Cory J. Clark and Bo M. Winegard, "Tribalism in War and Peace: The Nature and Evolution of Ideological Epistemology and Its Significance for Modern Social Science," *Psychological Inquiry* 31, no. 1 (2020): 1–22, https://doi.org/10.1080/1047840x.2020.1721233.

47 **If you want to override the tendency:** A huge body of research suggests that the opinions of individuals become more radical when those individuals are" housed in groups with similarly minded individuals. For a classic review, see Helmut Lamm and David G. Myers, "Group-Induced Polarization of Attitudes and Behavior," in *Advances in Experimental Social Psychology*, vol. 11, ed. Leonard Berkowitz (San Diego, CA: Academic Press, 1978), 145–95.

48 **questioning attitude of groups with dissenters:** Stefan Schulz-Hardt, Marc Jochims, and Dieter Frey, "Productive Conflict in Group Decision Making: Genuine and Contrived Dissent as Strategies to Counteract Biased Information Seeking," *Organizational Behavior and Human Decision Processes* 88, no. 2 (2002): 563–86, https://doi.org/10.1016/s0749-5978(02)00001-8. A final discovery in this body of work deserves mention: genuine dissent produced far more benefits in terms of less bias and better decision-making than training someone to be the inauthentic devil's advocate in the group. In follow-up studies, these researchers once again found that groups seeded with genuine dissenters showed less confirmation bias, and this improvement in

information gathering and willingness to tolerate difficult conversations translated into better solutions and decision-making (far better than the homogeneous groups). See Stefan Schulz-Hardt et al., "Group Decision Making in Hidden Profile Situations: Dissent as a Facilitator for Decision Quality," *Journal of Personality and Social Psychology* 91, no. 6 (2006): 1080–93, https://doi.org/10.1037/0022-3514.91.6.1080.

48 **improved group problem-solving:** Robert S. Dooley and Gerald E. Fryxell, "Attaining Decision Quality and Commitment from Dissent: The Moderating Effects of Loyalty and Competence in Strategic Decision-Making Teams," *Academy of Management Journal* 42, no. 4 (1999): 389–402, https://doi.org/10.5465/257010; Charlan Nemeth, "Interactions Between Jurors as a Function of Majority vs. Unanimity Decision Rules," *Journal of Applied Social Psychology* 7, no. 1 (1977): 38–56, https://doi.org/10.1111/j.1559-1816.1977.tb02416.x; Elizabeth Levy Paluck, Hana Shepherd, and Peter M. Aronow, "Changing Climates of Conflict: A Social Network Experiment in 56 Schools," *Proceedings of the National Academy of Sciences* 113, no. 3 (2016): 566–71, doi:10.1073/pnas.1514483113; Floor Rink et al., "Team Receptivity to Newcomers: Five Decades of Evidence and Future Research Themes," *Academy of Management Annals* 7, no. 1 (2013): 247–93, https://doi.org/10.5465/19416520.2013.766405.

49 **creative trendsetters:** Mark A. Runco et al., "Torrance Tests of Creative Thinking as Predictors of Personal and Public Achievement: A Fifty-Year Follow-Up," *Creativity Research Journal* 22, no. 4 (2010): 361–68, https://doi.org/10.1080/10400419.2010.523393.

49 **amplified performance and creativity:** Linn Van Dyne and Richard Saavedra, "A Naturalistic Minority Influence Experiment: Effects on Divergent Thinking, Conflict and Originality in Work-Groups," *British Journal of Social Psychology* 35, no. 1 (1996): 151–67, https://doi.org/10.1111/j.2044-8309.1996.tb01089.x.

51 **altered people's way of seeing the world:** Charlan Nemeth and Cynthia Chiles, "Modelling Courage: The Role of Dissent in Fostering Independence," *European Journal of Social Psychology* 18, no. 3 (1988): 275–80, https://doi.org/10.1002/ejsp.2420180306. It is worth pointing out that this is a replication and extension of the seminal study that discovered that witnessing dissent mentally liberates us, especially for those who do not publicly agree with us initially. See Serge Moscovici, Elisabeth Lage, and Martine Naffréchoux, "Influence of a Consistent

Minority on the Responses of a Majority in a Color Perception Task," *Sociometry* 32, no. 4 (1969): 365–80, https://doi.org/10.2307/2786541.

52 **modifications in how others think and behave:** Anne Maass, S. G. West, and Robert B. Cialdini, "Minority Influence and Conversion," in *Group Processes: Review of Personality and Social Psychology*, vol. 8, ed. Clyde A. Hendrick (Newbury Park, CA: Sage, 2987), 55–79.

CHAPTER 4: TALK PERSUASIVELY

57 **according to Urban Dictionary:** The acronym spelled out is "Fucked Up Got Ambushed Zipped In" (to a body bag), which captures the daily threats faced by military veterans in the Vietnam War. As can be seen, the band name oozes political subversion. See "Fugaze/Fugazi," Urban Dictionary, June 7, 2018, https://www.urbandictionary.com/define.php?term=Fugaze%2FFugazi; Mark Baker, *Nam: The Vietnam War in the Words of the Men and Women Who Fought There* (New York: Berkley, 1981).

57 **According to one music journalist:** Vincent Caruso, "30 Years Ago: Fugazi Is Born," Diffuser, May 31, 2017, https://diffuser.fm/fugazi-formed/.

58 **They just didn't care about becoming rock stars:** For books about Fugazi, see Michael Azzerad, *Our Band Could Be Your Life: Scenes from the American Indie Underground, 1981–1991* (Boston: Back Bay: 2001); Daniel Sinker, *We Owe You Nothing, Punk Planet: The Collected Interviews* (New York: Akashic Books, 2007). For interviews with Fugazi members, see Ian MacKaye, "Ian MacKaye Doesn't Do Many Interviews, but This Is One of His Most Enlightening," interview by Daniel Dylan Wray, *Loud and Quiet*, May 26, 2015, https://www.loudandquiet.com/interview/ian-mackaye-dischord/; Ian MacKaye, "Special Guest: Ian MacKaye of Dischord Records, Fugazi, & Much More," interviewed by Brian Nelson-Palmer, DC Music Rocks, February 6, 2018, https://www.dcmusicrocks.com/episodes/2018-02-06-special-guest-ian-mackaye-of-dischord-records-fugazi-and-more. For articles about Fugazi, see Anthony Pappalardo, "Why Fugazi Are Still the Best Punk Band in the World—an Op-Ed," *Alternative Press*, November 20, 2014, https://www.altpress.com/features/fugazi_are_the_best_punk_band_in_the_world/; Andrea Kurland, "Getting Deep with Ian MacKaye, the Godfather of DIY Culture," *Huck*, May 27, 2020, https://www.huckmag.com/art-and-culture/ian-mackaye-survival-issue-interview/; Eric Brace, "Punk Lives! Washington's

Fugazi Claims It's Just a Band. So Why Do So Many Kids Think It's God?," *Washington Post*, August 1, 1993, https://www.washingtonpost.com/archive/lifestyle/style/1993/08/01/punk-lives-washingtons-fugazi-claims-its-just-a-band-so-why-do-so-many-kids-think-its-god/6c56fef5-780a-4a6e-8411-8c6b407e1eed/?noredirect=on&utm_term=.8b4b5f2e0312; Greg Kot, "Fugazi Making Punk Rock Relevant Again," *Chicago Tribune*, August 10, 1991, https://www.chicagotribune.com/news/ct-xpm-1991-08-10-9103270453-story.html; Karen Bliss, "Pearl Jam's Eddie Vedder Talks Surfing, Story behind 'Jeremy' in Rediscovered 1991 Interview," *Billboard*, April 6, 2017, https://www.billboard.com/articles/columns/rock/7751635/pearl-jam-eddie-vedder-1991-interview-vintage; Paul Brannigan, "Ian MacKaye on Minor Threat, Fugazi and the Power of Punk Rock," Louder, April 16, 2014, https://www. loudersound.com/features/ian-mackaye-on-minor-threat-fugazi-and-the-power-of-punk-rock; Ryan Reft, "Musical Fugazi: Politics, Post Punk, and Reevaluating D.C.'s Most Famous Rock Band 25 Years Later," Tropics of Meta, May 13, 2015, https://tropicsofmeta.com/2015/05/13/musical-fugazi-politics-post-punk-and-reevaluating-d-c-s-most-famous-rock-band-25-years-later/.

59 **the band has been on "hiatus" since 2003:** "Fugazi," Spotify, accessed February 19, 2020, https://open.spotify.com/artist/62sC6lUEWRjbFqXpMmOk4G; "Fugazi," last.fm, accessed February 19, 2020, https://www.last.fm/music/Fugazi; "Fugazi—Topic," YouTube channel, accessed February 19, 2020, https://www.youtube.com/channel/UC2cjwtJB5rzpMetjDlnjGHg; "Fugazi," Pandora, accessed February 19, 2020, https://www.pandora.com/artist/full-bio/fugazi/ARP5Kb9dKXPZvxm; "Fugazi," deezer, accessed February 19, 2020, https://www.deezer.com/us/artist/2873.

59 **Kurt Cobain and Eddie Vedder invoked the names of Fugazi:** For behavioral evidence of their influence, see Brendan Kelly, "Forget Nirvana, Pearl Jam Was the Most Influential Band of the 90s," Vice, October 29, 2015, https://www.vice.com/en_us/article/6vgpn9/pearl-jam-vs-nirvana-as-the-most-influential-90s-band. Examples of interviews with the intentional mention of Fugazi and even tendencies to write the band's name on their bodies and clothing, see Bliss, "Pearl Jam's Eddie Vedder"; Lauren Spencer, "Nirvana: The 1992 'Nevermind' Cover Story, 'Heaven Can't Wait,'" *Spin*, January 1, 1992, https://www.spin.com/1992/01/nirvana-cover-1992-kurt-cobain-heaven-cant-wait/; Raul Rossell II, "Why Did Kurt Cobain Write Fuhgawz on His

Shoe???," feelnumb, October 13, 2009, http://www.feelnumb.com/2009/10/13/why-did-kurt-cobain-wrote-fuhgawz-on-his-shoe/.

60 **Conversion Theory:** Serge Moscovici, "Toward a Theory of Conversion Behavior," in *Advances in Experimental Social Psychology*, vol. 13, ed. Leonard Berkowitz (San Diego, CA: Academic Press, 1980), 209–39.

60 **Conflict Elaboration Theory:** Juan Antonio Pérez and Gabriel Mugny, "The Conflict Elaboration Theory of Social Influence," in *Understanding Group Behavior: Small Group Processes and Interpersonal Relations*, vol. 2, ed. Erich H. Witte and James H. Davis (Mahwah, NJ: Erlbaum, 1996), 191–210.

60 **Context/Comparison Model:** William D. Crano, "Social Influence, Social Identity, and Ingroup Leniency," in *Group Consensus and Minority Influence: Implications for Innovation*, ed. Carsten K. W. de Dreu and Nanne K. de Vries (Oxford, UK: Blackwell, 2001), 122–43.

60 **Source-Context-Elaboration Model:** Robin Martin and Miles Hewstone, "Majority versus Minority Influence, Message Processing, and Attitude Change: The Source-Context-Elaboration Model," in *Advances in Experimental Social Psychology*, vol. 40, ed. Mark P. Zanna (San Diego, CA: Elsevier, 2008), 237–326.

60 **Elaboration Likelihood Model:** Richard E. Petty and Duane T. Wegener, "The Elaboration Likelihood Model: Current Status and Controversies," in *Dual Process Theories in Social Psychology*, ed. Shelley Chaiken and Yaacov Trope (New York: Guilford Press, 1999), 41–72.

62 **they can better catalyze change:** An exception to this: when outsiders possess specialized, exceptional skill sets, group members are more likely to listen to their messages. See Ben Goldacre, *Bad Science: Quacks, Hacks, and Big Pharma Flacks* (London, UK: McClelland & Stewart, 2010); Michael Shermer, *Why People Believe Weird Things: Pseudoscience, Superstition, and Other Confusions of Our Time* (New York: Henry Holt, 2002).

63 **the "four humours":** Noga Arikha, *Passions and Tempers: A History of the Humours* (New York: Harper Perennial, 2007).

63 **organic matter from corpses:** Nicholas Kadar, Roberto Romero, and Zoltán Papp, "Ignaz Semmelweis: The 'Savior of Mothers': On the 200th Anniversary of His Birth," *American Journal of Obstetrics & Gynecology* 219, no. 6 (2018): 519–22; Ignaz P. S. Semmelweis, *The Etiology, Concept, and Prophylaxis of Childbed Fever*, trans. K. Codell Carter (1859; Madison, WI: University of Wisconsin Press, 1983).

63 **the death rate plummeted to nearly zero:** Theodore G. Obenchain, *Genius Belabored: Childbed Fever and the Tragic Life of Ignaz Semmelweis*

(Tuscaloosa, AL: University of Alabama Press, 2016); Cailin O'Connor and James Owen Weatherall, *The Misinformation Age: How False Beliefs Spread* (New Haven, CT: Yale University Press, 2019).

63 **handwashing as standard protocol:** World Health Organization, *WHO Guidelines on Hand Hygiene in Health Care* (Geneva, Switzerland: World Health Organization, 2009).

64 **publications to attack a single obstetrician:** Ignaz P. S. Semmelweis, "Open Letters to Sundry Professors of Obstetrics," 1861; Irvine Loudon, "Semmelweis and His Thesis," *Journal of the Royal Society of Medicine* 98, no.12 (2005): 555.

64 **a sense of wonder and curiosity:** Robin Martin and Miles Hewstone, "Majority versus Minority Influence: When, Not Whether, Source Status Instigates Heuristic or Systematic Processing," *European Journal of Social Psychology* 33, no. 3 (2003): 313–30.

64 **statements that appear objective and verifiable:** Wood et al., "Minority Influence," 323–45.

65 **college admission officers:** Daniel W. Gorenflo and William D. Crano, "Judgmental Subjectivity/Objectivity and Locus of Choice in Social Comparison," *Journal of Personality and Social Psychology* 57, no. 4 (1989): 605; Gerd Bohner et al., "Framing of Majority and Minority Source Information in Persuasion: When and How Consensus Implies Correctness," *Social Psychology* 39, no. 2 (2008): 108–16; William D. Crano and Katherine A. Hannula-Bral, "Context/Categorization Model of Social Influence: Minority and Majority Influence in the Formation of a Novel Response Norm," *Journal of Experimental Social Psychology* 30, no. 3 (1994): 247–76.

65 **a "prevention" or "defensive" mindset:** Andrew J. Elliot and Todd M. Thrash, "Approach-Avoidance Motivation in Personality: Approach and Avoidance Temperaments and Goals," *Journal of Personality and Social Psychology* 82, no. 5 (2002): 804; Judith M. Harackiewicz et al., "Revision of Achievement Goal Theory: Necessary and Illuminating," *Journal of Educational Psychology* 94 (2002): 638–45.

67 **jury members regard dissenters:** Robert S. Baron and S. Beth Bellman, "No Guts, No Glory: Courage, Harassment and Minority Influence," *European Journal of Social Psychology* 37, no. 1 (2007): 101–24.

67 **are then more receptive:** Richard E. Petty et al., "Individual versus Group Interest Violation: Surprise as a Determinant of Argument Scrutiny and Persuasion," *Social Cognition* 19, no. 4 (2001): 418–42.

68 **understand how scary it is:** Leaf Van Boven, George Loewenstein, and David Dunning, "The Illusion of Courage in Social Predictions: Underestimating the Impact of Fear of Embarrassment on Other People," *Organizational Behavior and Human Decision Processes* 96, no. 2 (2005): 130–41.

68 **In 1994, Duke University's Dr. Wendy Wood:** Wood et al., "Minority Influence," 323–45.

69 **your consistent advocacy:** When the last few minutes of an encounter are colored by mutual respect, this endpoint impacts people's overall evaluation of whether it's a smart idea to change. See Daniel Kahneman, "Evaluation by Moments: Past and Future," in *Choices, Values, and Frames*, ed. Daniel Kahneman and Amos Tversky (New York: Cambridge University Press, 2000), 693–708; Daniel Kahneman, "A Perspective on Judgment and Choice: Mapping Bounded Rationality," *American Psychologist* 58, no. 9 (2003): 697–720.

70 **The first reaction to a new idea:** Angelica Mucchi-Faina and Stefano Pagliaro, "Minority Influence: The Role of Ambivalence toward the Source," *European Journal of Social Psychology* 38, no. 4 (2008): 612–23.

70 **will naturally feel uncertain:** The pain of not taking action is far more intense and long-lasting than the regret of taking a risk and realizing it was a mistake. See Thomas Gilovich, Victoria Husted Medvec, and Daniel Kahneman, "Varieties of Regret: A Debate and Partial Resolution," *Psychological Review* 105, no. 3 (1998): 602. The particular pain associated with regretting inaction is not limited to the United States: Thomas Gilovich et al., "Regrets of Action and Inaction across Cultures," *Journal of Cross-Cultural Psychology* 34, no. 1 (2003): 61–71.

70 **the "sleeper effect":** G. Tarcan Kumkale and Dolores Albarracín, "The Sleeper Effect in Persuasion: A Meta-Analytic Review," *Psychological Bulletin* 130, no. 1 (2004): 143.

70 **Ambivalent people update:** For a package of eight studies on the topic, see Laura E. Wallace et al., "Perceived Knowledge Moderates the Relation between Subjective Ambivalence and the 'Impact' of Attitudes: An Attitude Strength Perspective," *Personality and Social Psychology Bulletin* 46, no. 5 (2020): 709–22.

70 **Thanks to the advocacy of minorities:** Wallace et al., "Perceived Knowledge."

71 **when the message is fully internalized:** Barbara David and John C. Turner, "Studies in Self-Categorization and Minority Conversion:

The In-Group Minority in Intragroup and Intergroup Contexts," *British Journal of Social Psychology* 38, no. 2 (1999): 115–34.

CHAPTER 5: ATTRACT PEOPLE WHO'VE GOT YOUR BACK

74 **at 30 degrees:** Dennis R. Proffitt et al., "Perceiving Geographical Slant," *Psychonomic Bulletin and Review* 2, no. 4 (1995): 409–28.

74 **The hill seemed even steeper:** Dennis R. Proffitt et al., "The Role of Effort in Perceiving Distance," *Psychological Science* 14, no. 2 (2003): 106–12.

74 **10-degree ascent as steeper:** Mukul Bhalla and Dennis R. Proffitt, "Visual–Motor Recalibration in Geographical Slant Perception," *Journal of Experimental Psychology: Human Perception and Performance* 25, no. 4 (1999): 1076–96.

74 **The physical challenge seemed easier:** Simone Schnall et al., "Social Support and the Perception of Geographical Slant," *Journal of Experimental Social Psychology* 44, no. 5 (2008): 1246–55.

74 **less worrisome than men standing alone:** Daniel M. T. Fessler and Colin Holbrook, "Friends Shrink Foes: The Presence of Comrades Decreases the Envisioned Physical Formidability of an Opponent," *Psychological Science* 24, no. 5 (2013): 797–802.

75 **Our brains interpret the presence of an ally:** Lane Beckes and James A. Coan, "Social Baseline Theory: The Role of Social Proximity in Emotion and Economy of Action," *Social and Personality Psychology Compass* 5, no. 12 (2011): 976–88; James A. Coan, Casey L. Brown, and Lane Beckes, "Our Social Baseline: The Role of Social Proximity in Economy of Action," in *Nature and Formation of Social Connections: From Brain to Group*, ed. Mario Mikulincer and Phillip R. Shaver (Washington, DC: APA Press, 2014), 89–104; James A. Coan and David A. Sbarra, "Social Baseline Theory: The Social Regulation of Risk and Effort," *Current Opinion in Psychology* 1 (2015): 87–91.

75 **resources of close, trustworthy allies:** Julia L. Briskin et al., "For Better or for Worse? Outsourcing Self-Regulation and Goal Pursuit," *Social Psychological and Personality Science* 10, no. 2 (2019): 181–92; Gráinne M. Fitzsimons and Eli J. Finkel, "Outsourcing Self-Regulation," *Psychological Science* 22, no. 3 (2011): 369–75; Hans IJzerman et al., "The Human Penguin Project: Climate, Social Integration, and Core Body Temperature," *Collabra: Psychology* 4, no. 1 (2018): 37.

75 **Just like climbing a hill:** Theriault, Young, and Barrett, "The Sense of Should."

75 **We need not be the master of all trades:** Erica J. Boothby et al., "The World Looks Better Together: How Close Others Enhance Our Visual Experiences," *Personal Relationships* 24, no. 3 (2017): 694–714; David S. Lee et al., "I-Through-We: How Supportive Social Relationships Facilitate Personal Growth," *Personality and Social Psychology Bulletin* 44, no. 1 (2018): 37–48; Shigehiro Oishi, Jamie Schiller, and E. Blair Gross, "Felt Understanding and Misunderstanding Affect the Perception of Pain, Slant, and Distance," *Social Psychological and Personality Science* 4, no. 3 (2013): 259–66; Dean Keith Simonton, "The Social Context of Career Success and Course for 2,026 Scientists and Inventors," *Personality and Social Psychology Bulletin* 18, no. 4 (1992): 452–63.

76 **seeking out allies:** Anita Williams Woolley, "Evidence for a Collective Intelligence Factor in the Performance of Human Groups," *Science* 330, no. 6004 (2010): 686–88; Wendy M. Williams and Robert J. Sternberg, "Group Intelligence: Why Some Groups Are Better Than Others," *Intelligence* 12, no. 4 (1988): 351–77.

76 **a great candidate to recruit as an ally:** Gordon Hodson et al., "Intergroup Contact as an Agent of Cognitive Liberalization," *Perspectives on Psychological Science* 13, no. 5 (2018): 523–48; Elizabeth Mannix and Margaret A. Neale, "What Differences Make a Difference? The Promise and Reality of Diverse Teams in Organizations," *Psychological Science in the Public Interest* 6, no. 2 (2005): 31–55.

76 **great for self-expansion:** If you want a good read, here are my top suggested titles from the past decade: Todd B. Kashdan, "10 Books to Ramp Up Your Intellect," *Psychology Today*, December 9, 2019, https://www.psychologytoday.com/us/blog/curious/201912/10-books-ramp-your-intellect.

76 ***The Imposter:*** Chelsea Duff, "Breaking Down 'The Imposter,' the True Crime Documentary That's Creepy AF," *In Touch Weekly*, June 13, 2018, https://www.intouchweekly.com/posts/the-imposter-documentary-155882/.

76 ***Spellbound:*** Amy Crawford, "Thirteen Years Later, Did *Spellbound* Show Us the Power or the Myth of the American Dream?," *Smithsonian Magazine*, May 28, 2015, https://www.smithsonianmag.com/arts-culture/thirteen-years-later-did-spellbound-show-us-power-or-myth-american-dream-180955434/.

76 ***Searching for Sugar Man:*** Terrence McCoy, "The Incredible Story Behind 'Searching for Sugar Man,'" *Washington Post*, May 14, 2014, https://www.washingtonpost.com/news/morning-mix/wp/2014/05/14/the-incredible-story-behind-searching-for-sugar-man/.

76 **strengthen the self is through relationships:** Arthur Aron, Elaine N. Aron, and Christina Norman, "Self-Expansion Model of Motivation and Cognition in Close Relationships and Beyond," in *Blackwell Handbook of Social Psychology Interpersonal Processes*, ed. Garth J. O. Fletcher and Margaret S. Clark (Malden, MA: Blackwell Publishers, 2001), 478–501.

77 **the concept of "emotionships":** Elaine O. Cheung, Wendi L. Gardner, and Jason F. Anderson, "Emotionships: Examining People's Emotion-Regulation Relationships and Their Consequences for Well-Being," *Social Psychological and Personality Science* 6, no. 4 (2015): 407–14.

77 **calls "net positive energizers":** Kim S. Cameron, *Positive Leadership: Strategies for Extraordinary Performance* (San Francisco, CA: Berrett-Koehler, 2008); Bradley P. Owens et al., "Relational Energy at Work: Implications for Job Engagement and Job Performance," *Journal of Applied Psychology* 101, no. 1 (2016): 35–49.

79 **select dissimilar over similar partners:** Arthur Aron et al., "When Similars Do Not Attract: Tests of a Prediction from the Self-Expansion Model," *Personal Relationships* 13, no. 4 (2006): 387–96.

80 **taking it personally:** Todd B. Kashdan, Justin W. Weeks, and Antonina A. Savostyanova, "Whether, How, and When Social Anxiety Shapes Positive Experiences and Events: A Self-Regulatory Framework and Treatment Implications," *Clinical Psychology Review* 31, no. 5 (2011): 786–99; David A. Moscovitch, "What Is the Core Fear in Social Phobia? A New Model to Facilitate Individualized Case Conceptualization and Treatment," *Cognitive and Behavioral Practice* 16, no. 2 (2009): 123–34.

80 **a motivational push:** Researchers found that after contemplating a self-expansion message (compared with seeking stability), White adults actively sought out interactions with people of a different race as opposed to their own. The practical implications are clear. Being around people who do not share our values, skills, and perspective can be fraught with tension and difficulty, and yet, by leaving the safety and security of our in-group, we grow more rapidly, with broader horizons. Shifting away from the pull of safe, familiar circles can be

boosted by five minutes of reflection on why self-expansion is beneficial. See Odilia Dys-Steenbergen, Stephen C. Wright, and Arthur Aron, "Self-Expansion Motivation Improves Cross-Group Interactions and Enhances Self-Growth," *Group Processes and Intergroup Relations* 19, no. 1 (2016): 60–71; Stefania Paolini et al., "Self-Expansion and Intergroup Contact: Expectancies and Motives to Self-Expand Lead to Greater Interest in Outgroup Contact and More Positive Intergroup Relations," *Journal of Social Issues* 72, no. 3 (2016): 450–71.

80 **People will find you far more likable:** Mitch Prinstein, *Popular: The Power of Likability in a Status-Obsessed World* (New York: Viking, 2017).

81 **six fundamental features of friendship:** Michael Argyle and Monika Henderson, "The Rules of Friendship," *Journal of Social and Personal Relationships* 1, no. 2 (1984): 211–37. Although this article has received minimal attention, the rules it lays out are supported by other research. See Brooke C. Feeney and Nancy L. Collins, "A New Look at Social Support: A Theoretical Perspective on Thriving through Relationships," *Personality and Social Psychology Review* 19, no. 2 (2015): 113–47; Jeffrey A. Hall, "Sex Differences in Friendship Expectations: A Meta-Analysis," *Journal of Social and Personal Relationships* 28, no. 6 (2011): 723–47; Lukasz D. Kaczmarek et al., "Give and Take: The Role of Reciprocity in Capitalization," *Journal of Positive Psychology* (2021), https://doi.org/10.1080/17439760.2021.1885054; Brett J. Peters, Harry T. Reis, and Shelly L. Gable, "Making the Good Even Better: A Review and Theoretical Model of Interpersonal Capitalization," *Social and Personality Psychology Compass* 12, no. 7 (2018): e12407.

81 **hardwired to connect through pain:** Lane Beckes, James A. Coan, and Karen Hasselmo, "Familiarity Promotes the Blurring of Self and Other in the Neural Representation of Threat," *Social Cognitive and Affective Neuroscience* 8, no. 6 (2013): 670–77. For similar findings, see Sören Krach et al., "Your Flaws Are My Pain: Linking Empathy to Vicarious Embarrassment," *PloS One* 6, no. 4 (2011): e18675.

81 **found that trust emerges as we *share* adversity:** Simone McKnight, Patrick E. McKnight, Todd B. Kashdan, L. Alexander, E. J. de Visser, and James A. Coan, "The Psychology of Trust: A Review and Reconceptualization," manuscript in preparation.

82 **cooperate more with one another:** Brock Bastian, Jolanda Jetten, and Laura J. Ferris, "Pain as Social Glue: Shared Pain Increases Cooperation," *Psychological Science* 25, no. 11 (2014): 2079–85.

82 **endure pain together:** Brock Bastian et al., "Shared Adversity Increases Team Creativity through Fostering Supportive Interaction," *Frontiers in Psychology* 9 (2018), https://doi.org/10.3389/fpsyg.2018.02309.

82 **facilitate long-term friendships:** Martin P. Paulus et al., "A Neuroscience Approach to Optimizing Brain Resources for Human Performance in Extreme Environments," *Neuroscience and Biobehavioral Reviews* 33, no. 7 (2009): 1080–88.

82 **"transforms strangers into friends":** Alain de Botton, *The School of Life: An Emotional Education* (London: School of Life Press, 2019).

83 **satisfy two conflicting psychological needs:** Optimal distinctiveness theory addresses the competing motivations that individuals must resolve to function well in society. See Marilynn B. Brewer, "The Social Self: On Being the Same and Different at the Same Time," *Personality and Social Psychology Bulletin* 17, no. 5 (1991): 475–82; Marilynn B. Brewer, "The Role of Distinctiveness in Social Identity and Group Behaviour," in *Group Motivation: Social Psychological Perspectives*, ed. Michael Hoff and Dominic Abrams (Hemel Hempstead, UK: Harvester Wheatsheaf, 1993), 1–16; Marilynn B. Brewer and Cynthia L. Pickett, "Distinctiveness Motives as a Source of the Social Self," in *The Psychology of the Social Self*, ed. Tom R. Tyler, Roderick M. Kramer, and Oliver P. John (Hillsdale, NJ: Lawrence Erlbaum, 1999), 71–87.

83 **dissatisfied with their social lives:** Brewer and Pickett, "Distinctiveness Motives as a Source of the Social Self."

83 **zero close friends:** 2019 YouGov survey of 1,254 adults. See "Friendship," YouGov RealTime, data gathered July 3–5, 2019, https://d25d2506sfb94s.cloudfront.net/cumulus_uploads/document/m97e4vdjnu/Results%20for%20YouGov%20RealTime%20(Friendship)%20164%205.7.2019.xlsx%20%20[Group].pdf.

83 **In a survey of 20,096 adults:** For this 2018 Cigna survey of 20,096 adults aged eighteen and over, see "New Cigna Study Reveals Loneliness at Epidemic Levels in America," Cigna's U.S. Loneliness Index, May 1, 2018, https://www.multivu.com/players/English/8294451-cigna-us-loneliness-survey/.

83 **how often they felt lonely:** Davy Vancampfort et al., "Leisure-Time Sedentary Behavior and Loneliness among 148,045 Adolescents Aged 12–15 Years from 52 Low- and Middle-Income Countries," *Journal of Affective Disorders* 251 (2019): 149–55.

84 **questions about the future:** When I left my job working on the New York Stock Exchange floor and switched careers from finance to psychology, I started as an unpaid research assistant for Dr. Arthur Aron at the State University of New York at Stony Brook. Art began iterating on a new method for creating intimacy among strangers within forty-five minutes or less. That work led to this highly cited research article: Arthur Aron et al., "The Experimental Generation of Interpersonal Closeness: A Procedure and Some Preliminary Findings," *Personality and Social Psychology Bulletin* 23, no. 4 (1997): 363–77. I used this method in my own research (including my master's thesis): Todd B. Kashdan and John E. Roberts, "Social Anxiety's Impact on Affect, Curiosity, and Social Self-Efficacy during a High Self-Focus Social Threat Situation," *Cognitive Therapy and Research* 28, no. 1 (2004): 119–41. Some of the questions presented in the text are variants from this research. Read these scientific articles for the full list of original questions.

84 **interrupting with curious comments:** For a fantastic compendium of powerful questions, see Michael Bungay Stanier, *The Coaching Habit: Say Less, Ask More and Change the Way You Lead Forever* (Toronto, Can.: Box of Crayons Press, 2016).

86 **break out and do their own thing:** However, there is other research evidence for a paradoxical approach where thinking about how similar they are to other people introduces a mindset to strive to end this and become more original. See Kimberly Rios and Zhuoren Chen, "Experimental Evidence for Minorities' Hesitancy in Reporting Their Opinions: The Roles of Optimal Distinctiveness Needs and Normative Influence," *Personality and Social Psychology Bulletin* 40, no. 7 (2014): 872–83.

86 **noticeable gestures of deviance:** Michael Lynn and Charles Snyder, "Uniqueness Seeking," in *Handbook of Positive Psychology*, ed. Charles. R. Snyder and Shane J. Lopez (London: Oxford University Press, 2002), 395–410.

86 **red Converse sneakers:** Silvia Bellezza, Francesca Gino, and Anat Keinan, "The Red Sneakers Effect: Inferring Status and Competence from Signals of Nonconformity," *Journal of Consumer Research* 41, no. 1 (2014): 35–54.

88 **"you are their hero":** Nichelle Nichols, "A Conversation with Nichelle Nichols," interview by Neil deGrasse Tyson, *StarTalk* podcast, July 11,

2011, https://www.startalkradio.net/show/a-conversation-with-nichelle-nichols/.

CHAPTER 6: BUILD MENTAL FORTITUDE

90 **a standardized rape kit:** Along with six women, Kilpatrick in 1974 established the first rape crisis center in the state of South Carolina. Dean Kilpatrick, personal communication with author, May 2020.

90 **The advantage of a rape kit:** World Health Organization, "3. Service Provision for Victims of Sexual Violence," in *Guidelines for Medio-Legal Care for Victims of Sexual Violence* (2003), https://www.who.int/violence_injury_prevention/resources/publications/en/guidelines_chap3.pdf.

90 **"conviction of rapists in Illinois":** Betty Greudenheim, "Chicago Hospitals Are Using New Kit to Help Rape Victims Collect Evidence," *New York Times*, December 2, 1978, https://www.nytimes.com/1978/12/02/archives/chicago-hospitals-are-using-new-kit-to-help-rape-victims-collect.html.

90 **"But *Playboy*?":** Marty Goddard, "Marty Goddard Interview Transcript," interview by Anne Seymour, *An Oral History of the Crime Victim Assistance Field*, University of Akron, February 26, 2003.

91 **preserving DNA that officers:** Jay D. Aronson, *Genetic Witness: Science, Law and Controversy in the Making of DNA Profiling* (Piscataway, NJ: Rutgers University Press, 2007); Patricia Yancey Martin et al., "Controversies Surrounding the Rape Kit Exam in the 1980s: Issues and Alternatives," *Crime and Delinquency* 31, no. 2 (1985): 223–46.

91 **identify suspects and support a criminal prosecution:** Dean Kilpatrick, personal communication.

91 **fewer than a quarter of survivors:** Lisa Anderson, "Why Are We So Bad at Prosecuting Sexual Assault?," *Dallas Morning News*, September 15, 2019, https://www.dallasnews.com/opinion/commentary/2019/09/15/why-are-we-so-bad-at-prosecuting-sexual-assault/.

91 **even judges defended rape:** Shirley Feldman-Summers and Gayle C. Palmer, "Rape as Viewed by Judges, Prosecutors, and Police Officers," *Criminal Justice and Behavior* 7, no. 1 (1980): 19–40.

92 **trying to reduce distress can cause *more* suffering:** Steven C. Hayes et al., "Acceptance and Commitment Therapy: Model, Processes and Outcomes," *Behaviour Research and Therapy* 44, no. 1 (2006): 1–25; Steven C. Hayes, Kirk D. Strosahl, and Kelly G. Wilson,

Acceptance and Commitment Therapy: The Process and Practice of Mindful Change, 2nd ed. (New York: Guilford Press, 2011); Steven C. Hayes et al., "Experiential Avoidance and Behavioral Disorders: A Functional Dimensional Approach to Diagnosis and Treatment," *Journal of Consulting and Clinical Psychology* 64, no. 6 (1996): 1152–68.

92 **what scientists call "psychological flexibility":** Todd B. Kashdan and Jonathan Rottenberg, "Psychological Flexibility as a Fundamental Aspect of Health," *Clinical Psychology Review* 30, no. 7 (2010): 865–78.

93 **A powerful tool . . . the Psychological Flexibility Dashboard:** This is a variant of what my colleagues built. A few of my colleagues created the Acceptance and Commitment Therapy (ACT) Matrix: Kevin L. Polk et al., *The Essential Guide to the ACT Matrix: A Step-by-Step Approach to Using the ACT Matrix Model in Clinical Practice* (Oakland, CA: New Harbinger Publications, 2016); Kevin L. Polk and Benjamin Schoendorff, *The ACT Matrix: A New Approach to Building Psychological Flexibility across Settings and Populations* (Oakland, CA: New Harbinger Publications, 2014). Other colleagues built the Choice Point Framework: Joseph Ciarrochi et al., "Measures That Make a Difference: A Functional Contextualistic Approach to Optimizing Psychological Measurement in Clinical Research and Practice," in *The Wiley Handbook of Contextual Behavioral Science*, ed. Robert D. Zettle et al. (Chichester, UK: Wiley, 2016), 320–46; Russ Harris, *ACT Made Simple: An Easy-to-Read Primer on Acceptance and Commitment Therapy* (Oakland, CA: New Harbinger Publications, 2019). My colleagues created these models for therapists and health professionals. My goal is to describe this model for the everyday person to use on their own.

94 **Clarity about your mission:** Yoona Kang et al., "Purpose in Life and Conflict-Related Neural Responses during Health Decision-Making," *Health Psychology* 38, no. 6 (2019): 545–52; Patrick E. McKnight and Todd B. Kashdan, "Purpose in Life as a System That Creates and Sustains Health and Well-Being: An Integrative, Testable Theory," *Review of General Psychology* 13, no. 3 (2009): 242–51.

94 **reacted less to the number of "likes":** Anthony L. Burrow and Nicolette Rainone, "How Many Likes Did I Get?: Purpose Moderates Links between Positive Social Media Feedback and Self-Esteem," *Journal of Experimental Social Psychology* 69 (2017): 232–36.

94 **panic attack symptoms:** Brian J. Cox,, Norman S. Endler, and Richard P. Swinson, "Anxiety Sensitivity and Panic Attack Symptomatology," *Behaviour Research and Therapy* 33, no. 7 (1995): 833–36.

95 **"no conviction of the culprit":** From the Chandler Museum Public History Program on Women Leaders and Activists, Chandler, Arizona.

95 **The following exercises:** Jennifer Crocker, Yu Niiya, and Dominik Mischkowski, "Why Does Writing about Important Values Reduce Defensiveness? Self-Affirmation and the Role of Positive Other-Directed Feelings," *Psychological Science* 19, no. 7 (2008): 740–47; Amber S. Emanuel et al., "Spontaneous Self-Affirmation Is Associated with Psychological Well-Being: Evidence from a US National Adult Survey Sample," *Journal of Health Psychology* 23, no. 1 (2018): 95–102; Rebecca A. Ferrer and Geoffrey L. Cohen, "Reconceptualizing Self-Affirmation with the Trigger and Channel Framework: Lessons from the Health Domain," *Personality and Social Psychology Review* 23, no. 3 (2019): 285–304; Philine S. Harris, Peter R. Harris, and Eleanor Miles, "Self-Affirmation Improves Performance on Tasks Related to Executive Functioning," *Journal of Experimental Social Psychology* 70 (2017): 281–85; Kristin Layous et al., "Feeling Left Out, but Affirmed: Protecting against the Negative Effects of Low Belonging in College," *Journal of Experimental Social Psychology* 69 (2017): 227–31.

96 **Value Trade-Offs to Know Yourself:** Items 1 and 2, and variants of items 3 and 9, are drawn from an activity in this study: Virginia R. Hash, "An Evaluation of a Values Clarification Seminar in the Preservice Education of Teachers," Ph.D. diss., Iowa State University, 1975.

98 **acknowledge the distress:** Here are a few reviews of empirical research detailing the importance of identifying felt experiences as a first step in being able to engage in healthy self-regulation (the self's capacity for altering what happens next): Pablo Briñol and Kenneth G. DeMarree, "Social Metacognition: Thinking about Thinking in Social Psychology," in *Frontiers of Social Psychology: Social Metacognition*, ed. Pablo Briñol and Kenneth G. DeMarree (New York: Psychology Press, 2012); Brett Q. Ford and James J. Gross, "Emotion Regulation: Why Beliefs Matter," *Canadian Psychology/Psychologie Canadienne* 59, no. 1 (2018): 1–14; Richard G. Tedeschi and Lawrence G. Calhoun, "Posttraumatic Growth: Conceptual Foundations and Empirical Evidence," *Psychological Inquiry* 15, no. 1 (2004): 1–18.

99 **skillfulness at "emotional labeling":** Todd B. Kashdan, Lisa Feldman Barrett, and Patrick E. McKnight, "Unpacking Emotion Differentiation: Transforming Unpleasant Experience by Perceiving Distinctions in Negativity," *Current Directions in Psychological Science* 24, no. 1 (2015): 10–16.

99 **consumed 40 percent less alcohol:** Todd B. Kashdan et al., "Emotion Differentiation as Resilience against Excessive Alcohol Use: An Ecological Momentary Assessment in Underage Social Drinkers," *Psychological Science* 21, no. 9 (2010): 1341–47.

99 **less likely to retaliate:** Richard S. Pond et al., "Emotion Differentiation Buffers Aggressive Behavior in Angered People: A Daily Diary Analysis," *Emotion* 12, no. 2 (2011): 326–37.

99 **better able to handle:** Todd B. Kashdan et al., "Who Is Most Vulnerable to Social Rejection? The Toxic Combination of Low Self-Esteem and Lack of Negative Emotion Differentiation on Neural Responses to Rejection," *PLoS One* 9, no. 3 (2014): e90651.

99 **When you label your emotions effectively:** Brad A. Brown et al., "Does Negative Emotion Differentiation Influence Daily Self-Regulation after Stressful Events? A 4-Year Daily Diary Study," *Emotion* (in press).

99 **physically handling spiders:** Katharina Kircanski, Matthew D. Lieberman, and Michelle G. Craske, "Feelings into Words: Contributions of Language to Exposure Therapy," *Psychological Science* 23, no. 10 (2012): 1086–91.

100 **less progress on their most important goals:** Todd B. Kashdan, William E. Breen, and Terri Julian, "Everyday Strivings in War Veterans with Posttraumatic Stress Disorder: Suffering from a Hyper-Focus on Avoidance and Emotion Regulation," *Behavior Therapy* 41, no. 3 (2010): 350–63. For an extension of this work with adults suffering from social anxiety disorder, see Fallon R. Goodman et al., "Personal Strivings to Understand Anxiety Disorders: Social Anxiety as an Exemplar," *Clinical Psychological Science* 7, no. 2 (2019): 283–301.

100 **gradients of particular emotions:** From a variety of sources: Robert Plutchik, *Emotions and Life: Perspectives from Psychology, Biology, and Evolution* (Washington, DC: APA Press, 2003); Phillip Shaver et al., "Emotion Knowledge: Further Exploration of a Prototype Approach," *Journal of Personality and Social Psychology* 52, no. 6 (1987): 1061–86.

103 **Cognitive defusion is a psychological exercise:** Steven C. Hayes, Kirk D. Strosahl, and Kenneth G. Wilson, *Review of Acceptance and Commitment Therapy: An Experiential Approach to Behavior Change* (New York: Guilford Press, 2002).

103 **write them down on a piece of paper:** Pablo Briñol et al., "Treating Thoughts as Material Objects Can Increase or Decrease Their Impact on Evaluation," *Psychological Science* 24, no. 1 (2013): 41–47.

103 **say them aloud:** Akihiko Masuda et al., "The Effects of Cognitive Defusion and Thought Distraction on Emotional Discomfort and Believability of Negative Self-Referential Thoughts," *Journal of Behavior Therapy and Experimental Psychiatry* 41, no. 1 (2010): 11–17. For replications and extensions, see Chloe Brandrick et al., "A Comparison of Ultra-Brief Cognitive Defusion and Positive Affirmation Interventions on the Reduction of Public Speaking Anxiety," *Psychological Record* (2020): 1–9; Brett J. Deacon, "Cognitive Defusion versus Cognitive Restructuring in the Treatment of Negative Self-Referential Thoughts: An Investigation of Process and Outcome," *Journal of Cognitive Psychotherapy* 25, no. 3 (2011): 218–32; Maria Karekla et al., "Cognitive Restructuring vs. Defusion: Impact on Craving, Healthy and Unhealthy Food Intake," *Eating Behaviors* 37 (2020), https://doi.org/10.1016/j.eatbeh.2020.101385.

104 **neutralize thoughts and feelings:** Many of these are modifications of exercises created by psychological flexibility practitioners. See George H. Eifert and John P. Forsyth, *Acceptance and Commitment Therapy for Anxiety Disorders: A Practitioner's Treatment Guide to Using Mindfulness, Acceptance, and Values-Based Behavior Change Strategies* (Oakland, CA: New Harbinger, 2005); Hayes, Strosahl, and Wilson, *Review of Acceptance and Commitment Therapy*; Russ Harris, *The Happiness Trap: How to Stop Struggling and Start Living* (Boston: Trumpeter, 2008).

105 **An extension of the immortal words:** Rollo May, *Freedom and Responsibility Re-Examined* (New York: Bureau of Publications, Columbia University, 1963): 101-2. This statement probably inspired the widely used quote attributed to Holocaust survivor Viktor Frankl, "Between stimulus and response there is a space. In that space is our power to choose our response. In our response lies our growth and our freedom." Interestingly, many people cite this supposed Viktor Frankl quote without reference or source. It is unclear who invented these words. Rollo May's words are equally, if not more, profound.

106 **"I would say the most important strategy":** Goddard, "Marty Goddard Interview Transcript."

106 **keeping a journal of lessons learned:** For the past seven years, I have kept a daily journal on the three most exceptional moments each day. Three is a manageable number. Exceptional moments can be healthy, unhealthy, or just interesting. If someone says something memorable, I enter verbatim quotes. You fail to retain many of the best moments in your life because they are fleeting. By jotting them down, I have a

running tabulation of what inspires me, what influences me, what makes me laugh and cry, poignant moments, and how I have changed or stayed the same. In truth, your life is nothing more than a tapestry of moments. Fail to capture them and you fail to live. This is captured nicely in a 2014 TEDx talk by my longtime collaborator, Robert Biswas-Diener, titled "Your Happiest Days Are Behind You." All of this is relevant to principled insubordinates who can easily forget to savor the milestones along the journey as they mistakenly hold out for the so-called finality of their mission (which rarely ever happens, as detailed in chapter 7). See Robert Biswas-Diener, "Your Happiest Days Are Behind You," TEDxUNLV, Las Vegas, April 11, 2014, 13:18, https://www.youtube.com/watch?v=-QTVv9tAlIE.

107 **separate out the real "you":** This notion that each of us regularly puts on a performance in front of others face-to-face, online, or even when we're alone contemplating what others might think of us is part of a theatrical production metaphor for human living. See Erving Goffman, *The Presentation of Self in Everyday Life* (Garden City, NY: Doubleday Anchor Books, 1959).

107 **how you might frame goals:** Brian R. Little, "The Integrative Challenge in Personality Science: Personal Projects as Units of Analysis," *Journal of Research in Personality* 56 (2015): 93–101; Dan P. McAdams, "Personality, Modernity, and the Storied Self: A Contemporary Framework for Studying Persons," *Psychological Inquiry* 7, no. 4 (1996): 295–321.

107 **strivings are a pretty cool way of describing yourself:** For two modern comprehensive accounts of personality traits, see Colin G. DeYoung, "Cybernetic Big Five Theory," *Journal of Research in Personality* 56 (2015): 33–58; William Fleeson and Eranda Jayawickreme, "Whole Trait Theory," *Journal of Research in Personality* 56 (2015): 82–92.

108 **try to compose six strivings:** Robert A. Emmons, "Personal Strivings: An Approach to Personality and Subjective Well-Being," *Journal of Personality and Social Psychology* 51, no. 5 (1986): 1058–68; Brian R. Little, Katariina Salmela-Aro, and Susan D. Phillips, eds., *Personal Project Pursuit: Goals, Action, and Human Flourishing* (Mahwah, NJ: Erlbaum, 2007).

108 **negative emotional experiences fell:** Todd B. Kashdan and Patrick E. McKnight, "Commitment to a Purpose in Life: An Antidote to the

Suffering by Individuals with Social Anxiety Disorder," *Emotion* 13, no. 6 (2013): 1150–59.

108 **sixteen-week "Internet-mediated walking program":** Caroline R. Richardson et al., "An Online Community Improves Adherence in an Internet-Mediated Walking Program. Part 1: Results of a Randomized Controlled Trial," *Journal of Medical Internet Research* 12, no. 4 (2010): e71. Here are additional examples for the benefits of sharing goals with other people as a strategy to increase behavioral commitment and effort expenditure: Lorraine R. Buis et al., "Evaluating Active U: An Internet-Mediated Physical Activity Program," *BMC Public Health* 9, no. 331 (2009), https://doi.org/10.1186/1471-2458-9-331; Paul J. Resnick et al., "Adding an Online Community to an Internet-Mediated Walking Program. Part 2: Strategies for Encouraging Community Participation," *Journal of Medical Internet Research* 12, no. 4 (2010): e72.

108–9 **Sharing your mission plans:** See the methodological details of all four studies in: Howard J. Klein et al., "When Goals Are Known: The Effects of Audience Relative Status on Goal Commitment and Performance," *Journal of Applied Psychology* 105, no. 4 (2020): 372–89.

109 **the hard work of Hunting Meaning:** Klein et al., "When Goals Are Known."

109 **Ahmet Altan:** Ahmet Altan, *I Will Never See the World Again: The Memoir of an Imprisoned Writer* (New York: Other Press, 2019).

109 **Marcus Aurelius:** Marcus Aurelius, *Meditations* (Chicago: Henry Regnery Company, 1949).

110 **envision the multiple paths available:** C. Richard Snyder, "Hope Theory: Rainbows in the Mind," *Psychological Inquiry* 13, no. 4 (2002): 249–75.

110 **hope for the best, but brace for the worst:** Julie K. Norem, "Defensive Pessimism, Anxiety, and the Complexity of Evaluating Self-Regulation," *Social and Personality Psychology Compass* 2, no. 1 (2008): 121–34; Julie K. Norem, "Defensive Pessimism as a Positive Self-Critical Tool," in *Self-Criticism and Self-Enhancement: Theory, Research, and Clinical Implications*, ed. Edward C. Chang (Washington, DC: APA Press, 2008), 89–104.

110 **Positivity alone won't help you:** James D. Doorley et al., "Psychological Flexibility: What We Know, What We Do Not Know, and What We Think We Know," *Social and Personality Psychology Compass* 14, no. 12 (2020): 1–11.

110 **dissent despite pain:** Todd B. Kashdan et al., "Understanding Psychological Flexibility: A Multimethod Exploration of Pursuing Valued Goals despite the Presence of Distress," *Psychological Assessment* 32, no. 9 (2020): 829–50; Kashdan and Rottenberg, "Psychological Flexibility as a Fundamental Aspect of Health."

CHAPTER 7: WIN RESPONSIBLY

113 **legalize production of the coca plant:** Coca is the main ingredient in cocaine, hence the controversy over whether to ban the plant and criminalize cultivation. See Martín Sivak, *Evo Morales: The Extraordinary Rise of the First Indigenous President of Bolivia* (New York: Macmillan, 2010). For the medicinal properties of coca, see Douglas H. Boucher, "Cocaine and the Coca Plant," *BioScience* 41, no. 2 (1991): 72–76.

113–14 **Officials also arrested farmers:** Drugs and Democracy, "Human Rights Violations Stemming from the 'War on Drugs' in Bolivia," Transnational Institute, December 23, 2005, https://www.tni.org/es/node/12035.

114 **three to four times greater gross national income:** Isabella Gomez Sarmiento, "How Evo Morales Made Bolivia a Better Place . . . Before He Fled the Country," NPR, November 26, 2019, https://www.npr.org/sections/goatsandsoda/2019/11/26/781199250/how-evo-morales-made-bolivia-a-better-place-before-he-was-forced-to-flee; "Bolivia," Social Security Programs Throughout the World: The Americas, 2011, Social Security Administration, https://www.ssa.gov/policy/docs/progdesc/ssptw/2010-2011/americas/bolivia.html.

114 **Latin America's fastest growing economy:** Stansfield Smith, "Eleven Years of the 'Process of Change' in Evo Morales' Bolivia," Council on Hemispheric Affairs, January 3, 2018, http://www.coha.org/eleven-years-of-the-process-of-change-in-evo-morales-bolivia/.

115 **disband civil society organizations:** José Miguel Vivanco, "Bolivia: Letter to President Evo Morales on Human Rights Legislation," Human Rights Watch, December 15, 2014, https://www.hrw.org/news/2014/12/15/bolivia-letter-president-evo-morales-human-rights-legislation#_ftn3.

115 **blacklisted dissenters:** Mariano Castillo, "Bolivian Journalist's Family Wants to Know Who Was behind Attack," CNN, November 1, 2012, https://www.cnn.com/2012/11/01/world/americas/bolivia-journalist-attacked/index.html; John Otis, "Forced Out of Jobs and Sidelined, Bolivia's Independent Journalists See Their

Audience Slipping Away," Committee to Protect Journalists, October 10, 2019, https://cpj.org/blog/2019/10/forced-out-of-jobs-and-sidelined-bolivias-independ.php.

115 **highway across a protected reserve:** Jon Lee Anderson, "The Fall of Evo Morales," *New Yorker*, March 23, 2020, https://www.newyorker.com/magazine/2020/03/23/the-fall-of-evo-morales.

115 **police brutally attacked protesters:** Emily Achtenberg, "Police Attack on Tipnis Marches Roils Bolivia," North American Congress on Latin America, September 28, 2011, https://nacla.org/blog/2011/9/28/police-attack-tipnis-marchers-roils-bolivia.

115 **"police bound their faces with duct tape":** Jim Shultz, "The Rise and Fall of Evo Morales," *New York Review of Books*, November 21, 2019, https://www.nybooks.com/daily/2019/11/21/the-rise-and-fall-of-evo-morales/.

115 **We share in our fellow group members' pride and joy:** Marilynn B. Brewer, "The Psychology of Prejudice: Ingroup Love and Outgroup Hate?," *Journal of Social Issues* 55, no. 3 (1999): 429–44. For a recent study limited to sports, see Charles E. Hoogland et al., "The Joy of Pain and the Pain of Joy: In-Group Identification Predicts Schadenfreude and Gluckschmerz Following Rival Groups' Fortunes," *Motivation and Emotion* 39, no. 2 (2015): 260–81.

115 **We ignore when members of our group behave aggressively:** Rachael Goodwin, Jesse Graham, and Kristina A. Diekmann, "Good Intentions Aren't Good Enough: Moral Courage in Opposing Sexual Harassment," *Journal of Experimental Social Psychology* 86 (2020): 103894; Aaron C. Weidman et al., "Punish or Protect? How Close Relationships Shape Responses to Moral Violations," *Personality and Social Psychology Bulletin* 46, no. 5 (2020): 693–708.

116 **we assign outsiders as our nemesis:** Groups often define themselves in relation to an antagonist. Think of Democrats rousing themselves in opposition to Republicans, or vegans identifying as the healthy, moral alternative to heartless carnivores. Identifying a nemesis is a psychologically sound strategy for bonding together as a tribe, because the presence of a nemesis motivates the tribe to build, create, and sustain a clear sense of what the tribe is and isn't, what the tribe stands for and will fight against. Contrary to common wisdom, an arch-nemesis offers something beyond addictive story lines in superhero comic books. Research shows that in certain situations, such as the experience of extended unemployment or the loss of a romantic

partner, people stave off the worst of their pain by blaming someone or something other than themselves. Viable scapegoats help people regain control and confidence. Unfortunately, by taking advantage of such psychological benefits, you initiate unnecessary conflict, leading to casualties. Without realizing it, you've provided justification for your nemesis to target you in the future. See Douglas, *Scapegoats*; Landau et al., "Deriving Solace from a Nemesis"; Sullivan, Landau, and Rothschild, "An Existential Function of Enemyship."

116 **blame someone or something other than ourselves:** Nigel P. Field and George A. Bonanno, "The Role of Blame in Adaptation in the First 5 Years Following the Death of a Spouse," *American Behavioral Scientist* 44, no. 5 (2001): 764–81; Michael V. Miller and Sue Keir Hoppe, "Attributions for Job Termination and Psychological Distress," *Human Relations* 47, no. 3 (1994): 307–27.

116 **As Martin Luther King, Jr., said:** Martin Luther King, Jr., *The Trumpet of Conscience* (New York: Harper & Row, 1967).

117 **cutting-edge experiments conducted by Dr. Radmila Prislin:** I find it mind-blowing that each of her primary empirical articles on the changing of majority and minority positions within a group has been cited less than seventy-five times in the past twenty years (as revealed by Google Scholar on March 30, 2021), even though Prislin published her work in the most prestigious social psychology outlet, the *Journal of Personality and Social Psychology*. I hope my discussion of her findings and their implications brings more attention to this underappreciated and eminent scholar. See "Radmila Prislin, Ph.D.," San Diego State University, https://psychology.sdsu.edu/people/radmila-prislin/.

117 **This is the gist of Prislin's research:** Studies differ on other elements of the design. For instance, Dr. Prislin often manipulates another feature of the group. Sometimes the reactions of the other members of the group are made publicly and immediately so the participant knows exactly who said what. Sometimes participants are given reasons for why people supported or opposed their position. The reasons can be superficial, having nothing to do with the arguments made ("I just wanted to get over with it"), versus genuine support (they "made me rethink my position"). Sometimes there is another task after the debate or campaign and there is an option to continue working with the same people in the group or leave to work with strangers. Sometimes the new majority gets to devise rules for a second task and has an opportunity to show favoritism toward supporters and create

rules that disadvantage opponents. Sometimes there is peer pressure applied by actors to be friendly or hostile to factions in the group, or be egalitarian. Sometimes the group interactions occur more than once, over the course of days or weeks. Like I said, she is a creative scientist trying to mimic what causes people to behave in various ways.

117 **After a structural change in the group:** Radmila Prislin and P. Niels Christensen, "The Effects of Social Change within a Group on Membership Preferences: To Leave or Not to Leave?," *Personality and Social Psychology Bulletin* 31, no. 5 (2005): 595–609.

117 **As Prislin provocatively noted:** Prislin and Christensen, "The Effects of Social Change." A summary of her discoveries is provided here: Radmila Prislin and P. Niels Christensen, "Social Change in the Aftermath of Successful Minority Influence," *European Review of Social Psychology* 16, no. 1 (2005): 43–73.

118 **the world's most dangerous amusement rides:** Andy Mulvihill, with Jake Rossen, *Action Park: Fast Times, Wild Rides, and the Untold Story of America's Most Dangerous Amusement Park* (New York: Penguin, 2020).

119 **"we must develop a world perspective":** King, Jr., *The Trumpet of Conscience.*

119 **Yale University admitted 588 women to join its class of 1973:** For an archive of documents about the fiftieth anniversary of women entry into Yale, see "History of Women at Yale," Yale University, https://celebratewomen.yale.edu/history-women-yale.

119 **forfeit any game in which a female athlete played:** For interviews with the first Yale class of women, to capture their firsthand accounts, see "First-Person Stories: Yale Men," *Yale Alumni Magazine*, Sept./Oct. 2019, https://yalealumnimagazine.com/articles/4967-first-person-stories-yale-men. Check them out. You will find a wide-ranging mix of negative, positive, ambiguous, and neutral memories of their time as Yale students. See Anne Gardiner Perkins, *Yale Needs Women: How the First Group of Girls Rewrote the Rules of an Ivy League Giant* (Naperville, IL: Sourcebooks, 2019).

119 **expecting hostility and a lack of helpfulness:** Radmila Prislin, Wendy M. Limbert, and Evamarie Bauer, "From Majority to Minority and Vice Versa: The Asymmetrical Effects of Losing and Gaining Majority Position within a Group," *Journal of Personality and Social Psychology* 79, no. 3 (2000): 385–97.

120 **"women were not going to be considered":** Anne Gardiner Perkins, "Unescorted Guests: Yale's First Women Undergraduates and the

Quest for Equity, 1969–1973," Ph.D. diss., University of Massachusetts Boston, 2018, https://scholarworks.umb.edu/doctoral_dissertations/389/.

120 **"I picked that up from the institution":** Perkins, "Unescorted Guests."

122 **old antagonisms faded:** Prislin and Christensen, "The Effects of Social Change."

122 **thousands more died in prison:** There is no exact number but this appears to be the minimum number confirmed by a wide range of advisers and experts among the editors at *Encyclopaedia Britannica* (1998): The Editors of Encyclopaedia Britannica, "Reign of Terror," *Encyclopaedia Britannica*, accessed May 8, 2020, https://www.britannica.com/event/Reign-of-Terror.

122 **"wanting to wind them up too strongly":** Maximilien Robespierre, "On the Death Penalty," June 22, 1791, trans. Mitch Abidor, https://www.marxists.org/history/france/revolution/robespierre/1791/death-penalty.htm.

122 ***suspected* someone of dissenting:** Rebecca Abrams, "The Monstrous Puzzle of the Revolution," *Guardian*, May 19, 2006, https://www.theguardian.com/books/2006/may/20/featuresreviews.guardianreview4.

122 **"[W]e must exterminate all our enemies":** John Kekes, "Why Robespierre Chose Terror: The Lessons of the First Totalitarian Revolution," *City Journal*, Spring 2006, https://www.city-journal.org/html/why-robespierre-chose-terror-12935.html.

123 **"the punishment of the people's enemies is death":** Kekes, "Why Robespierre Chose Terror."

123 **"atrocities only strengthen the utter certainty":** Kekes, "Why Robespierre Chose Terror."

123 **immediately after a power shift:** Radmila Prislin, Vanessa Sawicki, and Kipling Williams, "New Majorities' Abuse of Power: Effects of Perceived Control and Social Support," *Group Processes and Intergroup Relations* 14, no. 4 (2011): 489–504.

123 **If they don't aggressively reinforce their power:** Prislin, Sawicki, and Williams, "New Majorities' Abuse of Power." For a replication and extension, see Radmila Prislin, John M. Levine, and P. Niels Christensen, "When Reasons Matter: Quality of Support Affects Reactions to Increasing and Consistent Agreement," *Journal of Experimental Social Psychology* 42, no. 5 (2006): 593–601.

124 **the playwright George Bernard Shaw:** George Bernard Shaw, *Man and Superman* (Cambridge, MA: The University Press, 1903).

125 **racial minorities are poised to become:** Maureen A. Craig, Julian M. Rucker, and Jennifer A. Richeson, "Racial and Political Dynamics of an Approaching 'Majority-Minority' United States," *ANNALS of the American Academy of Political and Social Science* 677, no. 1 (2018): 204–14.

126 **quietly attend a rally with his wife:** Chris Churchill, "Churchill: At Skidmore, Curiosity Might Get You Canceled," *Times Union*, September 10, 2020, https://www.timesunion.com/news/article/Churchill-At-Skidmore-curiosity-might-get-you-15553968.php.

127 **published in the college's *Skidmore News*:** Samantha Sasenarine, "The Petersons & 'Blue Lives Matter': Students Reveal a Pattern of Racism among Skidmore Faculty and Staff," *Skidmore News*, August 31, 2020, http://skidmorenews.com/new-blog/2020/8/31/opinion-the-petersons-amp-blue-lives-matter-students-reveal-a-pattern-of-racism-among-skidmore-faculty-and-staff.

128 **the White House Correspondents' Dinner:** Chris Cillizza, "This Is the Most Controversial Speech at the Correspondents' Dinner Ever. But Nobody Knew It at the Time," *Washington Post*, April 24, 2015, https://www.washingtonpost.com/news/the-fix/wp/2015/04/24/this-is-the-most-controversial-speech-ever-at-the-correspondents-dinner-and-i-was-there/.

129 **conservatives were outraged:** Jacques Steinberg, "After Press Dinner, the Blogosphere Is Alive with the Sound of Colbert Chatter," *New York Times*, May 3, 2006, https://www.nytimes.com/2006/05/03/arts/03colb.html.

129 ***Time* magazine essay titled "Make Fun of Everything":** Front cover of the March 13, 2014, issue of *Time magazine*, Keegan-Michael Key and Jordan Peele, "Make Fun of Everything," *Time*, March 13, 2014, https://time.com/22993/key-and-peele-make-fun-of-everything/.

129 **As comedian Bill Burr attempted to do:** *Bill Burr: Paper Tiger*, directed by Mike Binder, written by Bill Burr, featuring Bill Burr, aired September 10, 2019, on Netflix, https://www.netflix.com/title/81060174.

130 **President Teddy Roosevelt urged:** These lines are from a famous speech President Theodore Roosevelt gave on April 23, 1910, that has been given the unofficial title "The Man in the Arena." I think Teddy would be honored that Brené Brown was inspired enough by this speech

to reference it in the title of her book *Daring Greatly: How the Courage to Be Vulnerable Transforms the Way We Live, Love, Parent, and Lead* (New York: Avery, 2012). Questions remain about how Teddy would feel about an incomplete excerpt from his speech appearing as a tattoo on the arm of actress Miley Cyrus only to be completed by a continuation on the arm of actor and ex-husband Liam Hemsworth. Instead of removing the ink, they can each find new partners who can complete the sentences on their arms. Reference to his oratorical masterpiece in a television commercial for Cadillac cars might have been even more disturbing to Teddy. See *US Weekly* Staff, "Liam Hemsworth Gets Tattoo to Match Miley Cyrus' Theodore Roosevelt Quote!," *US Weekly*, October 12, 2012, https://www.usmagazine.com/celebrity-news/news/liam-hemsworth-gets-tattoo-to-match-miley-cyrus-theodore-roosevelt-quote-20121210/; David Gianatasio, "Ad of the Day: Cadillac's 'Dare Greatly' Launch Spot Has Teddy Roosevelt but No Car," *Adweek*, February 18, 2015, https://www.adweek.com/brand-marketing/ad-day-cadillacs-dare-greatly-launch-spot-has-teddy-roosevelt-no-car-163017/. Admiration for Teddy led my coauthor Robert Biswas-Diener and I to write an ode to his unusual personality strengths in our previous book, *The Upside of Your Dark Side: Why Being Your Whole Self—Not Just Your "Good" Self—Drives Success and Fulfillment* (New York: Avery, 2014): see chapter 6, "The Teddy Effect."

CHAPTER 8: ENGAGE THE OUTRAGEOUS

135 **In 2007, Cheryl Kennedy:** I worked with Fals-Stewart on several projects, two of them leading to scientific publications. See William Fals-Stewart et al., "Behavioral Couples Therapy for Drug-Abusing Patients: Effects on Partner Violence," *Journal of Substance Abuse Treatment* 22, no. 2 (2002): 87–96. My other research article with him is: William Fals-Stewart et al., "An Examination of Indirect Risk of Exposure to HIV among Wives of Substance-Abusing Men," *Drug and Alcohol Dependence* 70, no. 1 (2003): 65–76. One of our studies asked which intervention—couples or individual therapy—most effectively prevented drug-addicted men from physically abusing their romantic partners. Our tentative answer: couples therapy. I say tentative because the story I then share raises questions about the integrity of our research.

136 **Cheryl was convinced Fals-Stewart:** Cheryl Kennedy, phone interview with author, July 22, 2019; Cheryl Kennedy, e-mail with author, July 22–23, 2020.

136 **witnesses were actually paid actors:** Dan Herbeck, "Researcher Accused of Using Actors at Hearing Testimony at UB Led to Misconduct Acquittal," *Buffalo News*, February 17, 2010, https://buffalonews.com/2010/02/16/researcher-accused-of-using-actors-at-hearing-testimony-at-ub-led-to-misconduct-acquittal/; "AG Charges Ex-UB Researcher in Fraud," *Business Journals*, February 16, 2010, https://www.bizjournals.com/buffalo/stories/2010/02/15/daily10.html.

137 **three powerful mental barriers:** Jan-Willem van Prooijen and André P. M. Krouwel, "Psychological Features of Extreme Political Ideologies," *Current Directions in Psychological Science* 28, no. 2 (2019): 159–63.

138 **unsettled and uncertain at times:** A message aligned with the work of my brilliant colleague Dr. Susan David: Susan David, *Emotional Agility: Get Unstuck, Embrace Change, and Thrive in Work and Life* (London: Penguin, 2016).

138 **recoil from creativity and cling to the familiar:** Young Soo Lee, Jae Yoon Chang, and Jin Nam Choi, "Why Reject Creative Ideas? Fear as a Driver of Implicit Bias against Creativity," *Creativity Research Journal* 29, no. 3 (2017): 225–35; Jennifer S. Mueller, Shimul Melwani, and Jack A. Goncalo, "The Bias against Creativity: Why People Desire but Reject Creative Ideas," *Psychological Science* 23, no. 1 (2012): 13–17.

138 **they far prefer obedient rule-followers:** Ellis Paul Torrance, "The Creative Personality and the Ideal Pupil," *Teachers College Record* 65, (1963): 220–26; Erik L. Westby and V. L. Dawson, "Creativity: Asset or Burden in the Classroom?," *Creativity Research Journal* 8, no. 1 (1995): 1–10.

139 **what they call "self-distancing":** Ethan Kross and Özlem Ayduk, "Self-Distancing: Theory, Research, and Current Directions," in *Advances in Experimental Social Psychology*, vol. 55, ed. James M. Olson (Cambridge, MA: Academic Press, 2017), 81–136.

139 **cognitive behavioral psychotherapies:** Steven C. Hayes and Stefan G. Hofmann, *Process-Based CBT: The Science and Core Clinical Competencies of Cognitive Behavioral Therapy* (Oakland, CA: New Harbinger, 2018); Steven C. Hayes and Stefan G. Hofmann, "The Future of Intervention Science: Process-Based Therapy," *Clinical*

Psychological Science 7, no. 1 (2019): 37–50; Michael E. Levin et al., "The Impact of Treatment Components Suggested by the Psychological Flexibility Model: A Meta-Analysis of Laboratory-Based Component Studies," *Behavior Therapy* 43, no. 4 (2012): 741–56.

139 **talking to yourself in the third person:** Igor Grossmann, "Wisdom in Context," *Perspectives on Psychological Science* 12, no. 2 (2017): 233–57; Ethan Kross and Özlem Ayduk, "Making Meaning Out of Negative Experiences by Self-Distancing," *Current Directions in Psychological Science* 20, no. 3 (2011): 187–91.

141 **a "fly on the wall" observing:** Kanye West, hip-hop billionaire, does it best in interviews with reporters. Here are some excerpts: "I'm sure even a Steve Jobs has compromised. Even a Rick Owens has compromised. You know, even a *Kanye West* has compromised . . . The idea of *Kanye* and vanity are like, synonymous . . . I think what *Kanye West* is going to mean is something similar to what Steve Jobs means" (emphasis added). See Jon Caramanica, "Behind Kanye's Mask," *New York Times*, June 11, 2013, https://www.nytimes.com/2013/06/16/arts/music/kanye-west-talks-about-his-career-and-album-yeezus.html.

141 **self-distancing to check in with their emotions:** Modification and extension of the commonly used instructions in Ethan Kross et al., "Self-Talk as a Regulatory Mechanism: How You Do It Matters," *Journal of Personality and Social Psychology* 106, no. 2 (2014): 304–24.

141 **modifying self-talk:** Igor Grossmann and Ethan Kross, "Exploring Solomon's Paradox: Self-Distancing Eliminates the Self-Other Asymmetry in Wise Reasoning about Close Relationships in Younger and Older Adults," *Psychological Science* 25, no. 8 (2014): 1571–80. Notably, different scientists were able to replicate these findings. See Alex C. Huynh et al., "The Wisdom in Virtue: Pursuit of Virtue Predicts Wise Reasoning about Personal Conflicts," *Psychological Science* 28, no. 12 (2017): 1848–56.

141 **greater relationship satisfaction:** Eli J. Finkel et al., "A Brief Intervention to Promote Conflict Reappraisal Preserves Marital Quality over Time," *Psychological Science* 24, no. 8 (2013): 1595–1601.

141 **Soldiers in the military also adopt self-distancing:** A lieutenant general who wishes to remain anonymous, personal communications with the author, July 2019–May 2020. Teams often laugh when doing

"after action reviews" (AAR). With practice, they become an ingrained habit. The awkwardness and the effectiveness are a combination that bonds officers and enlisted soldiers together.

142 **Minimize decisions that you will later regret:** For modification and extension of instructions that are widely used in the psychological distance literature, see Emma Bruehlman-Senecal, Özlem Ayduk, and Oliver P. John, "Taking the Long View: Implications of Individual Differences in Temporal Distancing for Affect, Stress Reactivity, and Well-Being," *Journal of Personality and Social Psychology* 111, no. 4 (2016): 610–35.

143 **Linguistic shifts in self-talk:** Ariana Orvell et al., "Linguistic Shifts: A Relatively Effortless Route to Emotion Regulation?," *Current Directions in Psychological Science* 28, no. 6 (2019): 567–73.

143 **deal better with emotionally intense events:** Here is a sampling of studies supporting these statements: Özlem Ayduk and Ethan Kross, "From a Distance: Implications of Spontaneous Self-Distancing for Adaptive Self-Reflection," *Journal of Personality and Social Psychology* 98, no. 5 (2010): 809–29; Özlem Ayduk and Ethan Kross, "Enhancing the Pace of Recovery: Self-Distanced Analysis of Negative Experiences Reduces Blood Pressure Reactivity," *Psychological Science* 19, no. 3 (2008): 229–31; Anna Dorfman et al., "Self-Distancing Promotes Positive Emotional Change after Adversity: Evidence from a Micro-Longitudinal Field Experiment," *Journal of Personality* 89, no. 1 (2021): 132–44; Ethan Kross, Özlem Ayduk, and Walter Mischel, "When Asking 'Why' Does Not Hurt Distinguishing Rumination from Reflective Processing of Negative Emotions," *Psychological Science* 16, no. 9 (2005): 709–15; Jason S. Moser et al., "Third-Person Self-Talk Facilitates Emotion Regulation without Engaging Cognitive Control: Converging Evidence from ERP and fMRI," *Scientific Reports* 7, no. 1 (2017): 1–9.

143 **more intellectually humble and more receptive:** Ethan Kross and Igor Grossmann, "Boosting Wisdom: Distance from the Self Enhances Wise Reasoning, Attitudes, and Behavior," *Journal of Experimental Psychology: General* 141, no. 1 (2012): 43–48.

143 **more abstract personality descriptions:** Izzy Gainsburg and Ethan Kross, "Distanced Self-Talk Changes How People Conceptualize the Self," *Journal of Experimental Social Psychology* 88 (2020) 103969, https://doi.org/10.1016/j.jesp.2020.103969.

144 **we think we know more than we do:** Ethan Zell and Zlatan Krizan, "Do People Have Insight into Their Abilities? A Metasynthesis," *Perspectives on Psychological Science* 9, no. 2 (2014): 111–25.

144 **makes us feel overly competent:** Dan M. Kahan et al., "Motivated Numeracy and Enlightened Self-Government," *Behavioural Public Policy* 1, no. 1 (2017): 54–86.

144 **participants reminded of their political affiliations:** Ian G. Anson, "Partisanship, Political Knowledge, and the Dunning-Kruger Effect," *Political Psychology* 39, no. 5 (2018): 1173–92.

144 **the *less* someone knows about a topic:** David Dunning, "The Dunning–Kruger Effect: On Being Ignorant of One's Own Ignorance," in *Advances in Experimental Social Psychology*, vol. 44, ed. Mark Zanna and James Olson (San Diego, CA: Elsevier, 2011), 247–96; Joyce Ehrlinger et al., "Why the Unskilled Are Unaware: Further Explorations of (Absent) Self-Insight among the Incompetent," *Organizational Behavior and Human Decision Processes* 105, no. 1 (2008): 98–121.

145 **Curiosity helps in all kinds of ways:** Rachit Dubey and Thomas L. Griffiths, "Reconciling Novelty and Complexity through a Rational Analysis of Curiosity," *Psychological Review* 127, no. 3 (2020): 455–76; Todd B. Kashdan et al., "The Five-Dimensional Curiosity Scale Revised (5DCR): Briefer Subscales While Separating Overt and Covert Social Curiosity," *Personality and Individual Differences* 157 (2020) 109836, https://doi.org/10.31219/osf.io/pu8f3; Todd B. Kashdan and Paul J. Silvia, "Curiosity and Interest: The Benefits of Thriving on Novelty and Challenge," in *Handbook of Positive Psychology*, vol. 2, ed. Charles R. Synder and Shane J. Lopez (New York: Oxford University Press, 2009), 367–74; Todd B. Kashdan et al., "The Five-Dimensional Curiosity Scale: Capturing the Bandwidth of Curiosity and Identifying Four Unique Subgroups of Curious People," *Journal of Research in Personality* 73 (2018): 130–49; Celeste Kidd and Benjamin Y. Hayden, "The Psychology and Neuroscience of Curiosity," *Neuron* 88, no. 3 (2015): 449–60.

145 **describe a past experience when they felt curious:** There is a paradox in this discovery—being curious is effortful and requires intense concentration yet we feel more energized after exerting this effort. Strong bouts of positivity are not nearly as helpful in replenishing our energy supply as moments of curiosity. The bottom line: if you want grit, get curious. See Dustin B. Thoman, Jessi L. Smith, and Paul J.

Silvia, "The Resource Replenishment Function of Interest," *Social Psychological and Personality Science* 2, no. 6 (2011): 592–99.

145 **It's not hard to cultivate more curiosity:** Julia A. Minson, Varda Liberman, and Lee Ross, "Two to Tango: Effects of Collaboration and Disagreement on Dyadic Judgment," *Personality and Social Psychology Bulletin* 37, no. 10 (2011): 1325–38.

146 **explain how their preferred ideas work:** Philip M. Fernbach et al., "Explanation Fiends and Foes: How Mechanistic Detail Determines Understanding and Preference," *Journal of Consumer Research* 39, no. 5 (2013): 1115–31.

146 **As philosopher Alain de Botton observes:** De Botton, *The School of Life*.

146 **"*formulating* elaboration questions":** Frances S. Chen, Julia A. Minson, and Zakary L. Tormala, "Tell Me More: The Effects of Expressed Interest on Receptiveness during Dialog," *Journal of Experimental Social Psychology* 46, no. 5 (2010): 850–53.

146 **let go of trying to persuade:** Hanne Collins et al., "Why Won't You Learn about Me? Self-Other Differences in Conversational Goals," presentation, Society for Personality and Social Psychology Virtual Convention, online, February 9, 2021.

147 **the questioner became more receptive:** Collins et al., "Why Won't You Learn about Me?"

147 **more likable and viewed them as more caring:** Karen Huang et al., "It Doesn't Hurt to Ask: Question-Asking Increases Liking," *Journal of Personality and Social Psychology* 113, no. 3 (2017): 430–52.

148 **diving deeper into what other people are interested in:** For a truly profound book on the art of asking questions, turn to one of my favorite teachers: Stanier, *The Coaching Habit*.

149 **they didn't query the credibility:** New York State Office of the Attorney General, press release, "The New York State Attorney General Andrew M. Cuomo Announces Charges against Former UB Researcher for Hiring Actors to Testify during Misconduct Hearing and Attempting to Siphon $4 Million in Taxpayer Funds," February 16, 2010, https://ag.ny.gov/press-release/2010/new-york-state-attorney-general-andrew-m-cuomo-announces-charges-against-former.

149 **all African Americans are politically liberal:** A concept that a large number of African Americans cannot even accept. See Renée Graham, "Memo to Black Men: Stop Voting Republican," *Boston Globe*, November 8, 2018, https://www.bostonglobe.com/opinion/2018/11/08

/memo-black-men-stop-voting-republican/v9kJPzVMQcdr0szp78gumJ/story.html; Vanessa Williams, "What's Up with All Those Black Men Who Voted for the Republican in the Georgia Governor's Race?," *Washington Post*, November 23, 2018, https://www.washingtonpost.com/politics/2018/11/23/whats-up-with-all-those-black-men-who-voted-republican-georgia-governors-race/; Kenya Evelyn, "How Black Republicans Are Debunking the Myth of a Voter Monolith," *Guardian*, March 12, 2020, https://www.theguardian.com/us-news/2020/mar/12/black-republicans-african-american-voters.

149 **Republicans unthinkingly support Trump:** Maggie Astor, "Trump Pushes Young Republicans Away. Abortion Pulls Them Back," *New York Times*, May 6, 2020, https://www.nytimes.com/2020/05/06/us/politics/young-republicans-trump.html.

149 **Let's explore:** Kashdan et al., "The Five-Dimensional Curiosity Scale"; Todd B. Kashdan, "The Five Dimensions of Curiosity," *Harvard Business Review* (Sept.–Oct. 2018): 47–61; Todd B. Kashdan et al., "Curiosity Has Comprehensive Benefits in the Workplace: Developing and Validating a Multidimensional Workplace Curiosity Scale in United States and German Employees," *Personality and Individual Differences* 155 (2020) 109717, https://doi.org/10.1016/j.paid.2019.109717.

149–50 **resist the temptation to categorize people:** Todd B. Kashdan et al., "How Are Curious People Viewed and How Do They Behave in Social Situations? From the Perspectives of Self, Friends, Parents, and Unacquainted Observers," *Journal of Personality* 81, no. 2 (2013): 142–54.

151 **consider these three potential suspects:** Benoît Monin, Pamela J. Sawyer, and Matthew J. Marquez, "The Rejection of Moral Rebels: Resenting Those Who Do the Right Thing," *Journal of Personality and Social Psychology* 95, no. 1 (2008): 76–93. For a replication of this study, see Kieran O'Connor and Benoît Monin, "When Principled Deviance Becomes Moral Threat: Testing Alternative Mechanisms for the Rejection of Moral Rebels," *Group Processes and Intergroup Relations* 19, no. 5 (2016): 676–93.

152 **we might call "deliberate humility":** Monin, Sawyer, and Marquez, "The Rejection of Moral Rebels."

152 **Deliberate humility also helps:** For definitions of intellectual humility, see Elizabeth J. Krumrei-Mancuso and Steven V. Rouse, "The Development and Validation of the Comprehensive Intellectual Humility Scale," *Journal of Personality Assessment* 98, no. 2 (2016):

209–21; Mark R. Leary et al., "Cognitive and Interpersonal Features of Intellectual Humility," *Personality and Social Psychology Bulletin* 43, no. 6 (2017): 793–813; Benjamin R. Meagher et al., "Contrasting Self-Report and Consensus Ratings of Intellectual Humility and Arrogance," *Journal of Research in Personality* 58 (2015): 35–45; Stacey E. McElroy-Heltzel et al., "Embarrassment of Riches in the Measurement of Humility: A Critical Review of 22 Measures," *Journal of Positive Psychology* 14, no. 3 (2019): 393–404.

152 **intellectual humility serves to boost our wisdom:** Grossmann, "Wisdom in Context"; Henri C. Santos, Alex C. Huynh, and Igor Grossmann, "Wisdom in a Complex World: A Situated Account of Wise Reasoning and Its Development," *Social and Personality Psychology Compass* 11, no. 10 (2017): e12341, https://doi.org/10.1111/spc3.12341.

152 **humbler and more open to divergent ideas:** From the PROVE workbook, which has been shown to be an effective intervention. PROVE is an acronym for the steps: First, *Pick* a time when you showed a lack of humility. Second, *Remember* to situate your knowledge, skills, and achievements within the larger picture—you are not as important or significant as believed. Third, *Open* yourself to the wisdom of being around people who think differently and be adaptable (replacing tried-and-true ways with other ways when relevant). Fourth, *Value* what is happening that is not directly involving or linked to you. Fifth, *Examine* your limitations and commit to a humble approach to communicating with others. See Caroline R. Lavelock et al., "The Quiet Virtue Speaks: An Intervention to Promote Humility," *Journal of Psychology and Theology* 42, no. 1 (2014): 99–110.

153 **contemplation and self-questioning really works:** The findings by Lavelock et al., "The Quiet Virtue Speaks," were extended and replicated. See Caroline R. Lavelock et al., "Still Waters Run Deep: Humility as a Master Virtue," *Journal of Psychology and Theology* 45, no. 4 (2017): 286–303. Similar findings exist in trying to increase intellectual humility when there is a conflict between two groups differing in cultural beliefs. See Benjamin R. Meagher et al., "An Intellectually Humbling Experience: Changes in Interpersonal Perception and Cultural Reasoning across a Five-Week Course," *Journal of Psychology and Theology* 47, no. 3 (2019): 217–29.

153 **In studies conducted at six different universities:** Elizabeth J. Krumrei-Mancuso et al., "Links between Intellectual Humility and

Acquiring Knowledge," *Journal of Positive Psychology* 15, no. 2 (2020): 155–70.

CHAPTER 9: EXTRACT WISDOM FROM "WEIRDOS"

157 **Congress repealed decades-old legislation:** Kristy N. Kamarck, *Women in Combat: Issues for Congress* (Washington, DC: Congressional Research Service Report Prepared for Members and Committees of Congress, December 13, 2016), https://fas.org/sgp/crs/natsec/R42075.pdf; Eric Schmitt, "Senate Votes to Remove Ban on Women as Combat Pilots," *New York Times*, August 1, 1991.

158 **the Judge Advocate General:** Victoria L. Sadler, "Military Reports and the Problem with Technological Agency," *Discourse and Writing/Rédactologie* 22, no. 1 (2008): 72–85.

158 **leaked an internal investigation**: From a 2002 U.S. District Court case in the District of Columbia between Carey Dunai LOHRENZ Plaintiff v. Elaine DONNELLY, et al. Defendants. See Royce C. Lamberth, "Lohrenz *v.* Donnelly, 223 F. Supp. 2d 25 (D.D.C. 2002)," *Court Listener*, August 16, 2002, https://www.courtlistener.com/opinion/2345633/lohrenz-v-donnelly/.

158 **pilot error caused Hultgreen's death:** H. G. Reza, "Navy Pilot's Errors Contributed to Fatal Crash, Report Says," *Los Angeles Times*, March 22, 1995, https://www.latimes.com/archives/la-xpm-1995-03-22-mn-45801-story.html; Philip Kaplan, *Naval Air: Celebrating a Century of Naval Flying* (South Yorkshire, UK: Pen and Sword, 2013).

158 **Lieutenant Hultgreen's training transcript:** Center for Military Readiness, "Double Standards in Naval Aviation," *CMR Report*, June 1995, https://www.cmrlink.org/data/Sites/85/CMRDocuments/CMRRPT09-0695.pdf; William H. McMichael, "A Question of Standards," *Daily Press*, December 14, 1997, https://www.dailypress.com/ news/dp-xpm-19971214-1997-12-14-9712140060-story.html.

159 **"old men ordering young women into combat":** Alice W. W. Parham, "The Quiet Revolution: Repeal of the Exclusionary Statutes in Combat Aviation—What We Have Learned from a Decade of Integration," *William & Mary Journal of Women and the Law* 12 (2006): 377–40.

159 **designed to fit the physical dimensions of men:** NCD Risk Factor Collaboration, "A Century of Trends in Adult Human Height," *eLife* 5 (2016), https://doi.org/10.7554/eLife.13410; Caroline Criado-Perez, *Invisible Women: Exposing Data Bias in a World Designed for Men*

(London: Chatto & Windus, 2019); Todd Rose, *The End of Average: How We Succeed in a World That Values Sameness* (New York: HarperCollins, 2015).

159 **"they should want the best person for the job":** Michael Kirk, dir., "The Navy Blues," *Frontline*, show #1502, PBS, aired Oct. 15, 1996, transcript, https://www.pbs.org/wgbh/pages/frontline/shows/navy/script.html.

159 **"slide through on a lower standard":** New York Times News Service, "Female Combat Pilot's Death Sparks Debate," *Chicago Tribune*, October 30, 1994, https://www.chicagotribune.com/news/ct-xpm-1994-10-30-9410300206-story.html.

159 **He risked his twenty-eight-year military career:** R. Greiner, "Navy Whistle-blower Leaked Records of Female-pilot Errors," 1997, https://www.questia.com/read/1G1-20000517/navy-whistle-blower-leaked-records-of-female-pilot.

159 **"this is not doing a service to anybody":** Greiner, "Navy Whistle-blower Leaked."

160 **little relationship between such diversity in a group:** Suzanne T. Bell et al., "Getting Specific about Demographic Diversity Variable and Team Performance Relationships: A Meta-Analysis," *Journal of Management* 37, no. 3 (2011): 709–43; Clint A. Bowers, James A. Pharmer, and Eduardo Salas, "When Member Homogeneity Is Needed in Work Teams: A Meta-Analysis," *Small Group Research* 31, no. 3 (2000): 305–27; Sujin K. Horwitz and Irwin B. Horwitz, "The Effects of Team Diversity on Team Outcomes: A Meta-Analytic Review of Team Demography," *Journal of Management* 33, no. 6 (2007): 987–1015; Sheila Simsarian Webber and Lisa M. Donahue, "Impact of Highly and Less Job-Related Diversity on Work Group Cohesion and Performance: A Meta-Analysis," *Journal of Management* 27, no. 2 (2001): 141–62.

160 **minimally impact group performance:** Hans Van Dijk, Marloes L. Van Engen, and Daan Van Knippenberg, "Defying Conventional Wisdom: A Meta-Analytical Examination of the Differences between Demographic and Job-Related Diversity Relationships with Performance," *Organizational Behavior and Human Decision Processes* 119, no. 1 (2012): 38–53.

160 **"capitalize on the advantages":** Dominic J. Packer, Christopher T. H. Miners, and Nick D. Ungson, "Benefiting from Diversity: How Groups' Coordinating Mechanisms Affect Leadership Opportunities for Marginalized Individuals," *Journal of Social Issues* 74, no. 1 (2018): 56–74.

160 **diverse people and viewpoints to work for us and them:** Elizabeth Mannix and Margaret A. Neale, "What Differences Make a Difference," 31–55.

161 **two powerful pathways:** For the Leading Diversity or LeaD model, see Astrid C. Homan et al., "Leading Diversity: Towards a Theory of Functional Leadership in Diverse Teams," *Journal of Applied Psychology* 105, no. 10 (2020): 1101–28.

161 **the group's ability to seek, conquer:** These ideas come from the Theoretical Intellectual Framework of Dr. Patrick Mussel, who offers insights into the process and operation of creativity. *Process* is the motivational part of creative performance that hinges on two components: seek and conquer. *Seek* refers to the emotions that arise in intellectually challenging situations, and the general openness to approach rather than avoidance of these situations. *Conquer* refers to the effort and perseverance required to work through the uncertainty, complexity, and incongruities to master an intellectual challenge. *Operation* is the ability part of creative performance where there is *thinking* (reasoning, synthesizing, and drawing conclusions), *learning* (obtaining information, asking questions, testing hypotheses, filling knowledge gaps), and *creating* (which is putting all of these processes and abilities toward the development of new ideas, strategies, and products). With this framework, it is easy to argue for the benefits of a team composed of people with complementary motivational and ability profiles working together toward a common creative goal (as opposed to a team with generally identical profiles). See Patrick Mussel, "Intellect: A Theoretical Framework for Personality Traits Related to Intellectual Achievements," *Journal of Personality and Social Psychology* 104, no. 5 (2013): 885–906.

162 **"epistemic motivation," defined:** Carsten K. W. de Dreu et al., "Group Creativity and Innovation: A Motivated Information Processing Perspective," *Psychology of Aesthetics, Creativity, and the Arts* 5, no. 1 (2011): 81–89.

162 **they viewed dissenters twice as positively:** See Study 1 and Study 2 for a replication of the findings, in Matthew J. Hornsey et al., "The Impact of Individualist and Collectivist Group Norms on Evaluations of Dissenting Group Members," *Journal of Experimental Social Psychology* 42, no. 1 (2006): 57–68.

162 **Groups that commit to epistemic motivation values:** For findings on the value of internalizing explicit group norms to be an

independent, critical thinker, see Myriam N. Bechtoldt et al., "Motivated Information Processing, Social Tuning, and Group Creativity," *Journal of Personality and Social Psychology* 99, no. 4 (2010): 622–37; Jolanda Jetten, Tom Postmes, and Brendan J. McAuliffe, "'We're All Individuals': Group Norms of Individualism and Collectivism, Levels of Identification and Identity Threat," *European Journal of Social Psychology* 32, no. 2 (2002): 189–207; Brendan J. McAuliffe et al., "Individualist and Collectivist Norms: When It's OK to Go Your Own Way," *European Journal of Social Psychology* 33, no. 1 (2003): 57–70; Charlan J. Nemeth et al., "The Liberating Role of Conflict in Group Creativity: A Study in Two Countries," *European Journal of Social Psychology* 34, no. 4 (2004): 365–74; Tom Postmes, Russell Spears, and Sezgin Cihangir, "Quality of Decision Making and Group Norms," *Journal of Personality and Social Psychology* 80, no. 6 (2001): 918–30; Lotte Scholten et al., "Motivated Information Processing and Group Decision-Making: Effects of Process Accountability on Information Processing and Decision Quality," *Journal of Experimental Social Psychology* 43, no. 4 (2007): 539–52; Mark D. Seery et al., "Alone against the Group: A Unanimously Disagreeing Group Leads to Conformity, but Cardiovascular Threat Depends on One's Goals," *Psychophysiology* 53, no. 8 (2016): 1263–71.

162 **some specific practices to try:** Based on Table 1 in Carsten K. W. de Dreu, Bernard A. Nijstad, and Daan Van Knippenberg, "Motivated Information Processing in Group Judgment and Decision Making," *Personality and Social Psychology Review* 12, no. 1 (2008): 22–49.

163 **Create a one-page handout:** Susan Cain raises similar points about challenges faced by introverts in environments dominated by louder, aggressive, attention-seeking people: Susan Cain, *Quiet: The Power of Introverts in a World That Can't Stop Talking* (New York: Crown, 2013). See also research on differences between introverts and extraverts: Michael C. Ashton, Kibeom Lee, and Sampo V. Paunonen, "What Is the Central Feature of Extraversion? Social Attention versus Reward Sensitivity," *Journal of Personality and Social Psychology* 83, no. 1 (2002): 245–52.

163 **make adherence to values more likely:** Robert B. Cialdini and Noah J. Goldstein, "Social Influence: Compliance and Conformity," *Annual Review of Psychology* 55 (2004): 591–621.

164 **With a larger reservoir of resources:** Lauren E. Coursey et al., "Linking the Divergent and Convergent Processes of Collaborative

Creativity: The Impact of Expertise Levels and Elaboration Processes," *Frontiers in Psychology* 10 (2019): 699.

164 **a group friendly to principled rebels:** A principled-rebel–friendly group or organization is ends or outcome focused instead of means focused. With clarity of mission, it does not matter who produces the best ideas. Anyone who asks questions, offers helpful criticisms and counterarguments, and points out solutions missed improves the team. If you are means focused, then being a good solider who follows orders and the hierarchy of command and conforms becomes valued; each of these behaviors is the wrong metric unless it facilitates instead of frustrates the endgame. The problem with most diversity initiatives is that they are means focused instead of ends focused. Know the particulars of why diversity matters to convince the nonbelievers. See Packer, Miners, and Ungson, "Benefiting from Diversity."

165 **Groups valuing autonomy and critical thinking:** Bechtoldt et al., "Motivated Information Processing."

166 **mobilize "debiasing strategies":** Michelle Daniel et al., "Cognitive Debiasing Strategies: A Faculty Development Workshop for Clinical Teachers in Emergency Medicine," *MedEdPORTAL* 13 (2017).

166 **In a laboratory experiment, Dr. Inga Hoever:** Inga J. Hoever et al., "Fostering Team Creativity: Perspective Taking as Key to Unlocking Diversity's Potential," *Journal of Applied Psychology* 97, no. 5 (2012): 982–96.

168 **five-hour workshops on perspective-taking skills:** Amit Goldenberg et al., "Testing the Impact and Durability of a Group Malleability Intervention in the Context of the Israeli–Palestinian Conflict," *Proceedings of the National Academy of Sciences* 115, no. 4 (2018): 696–701.

168 **When we categorize a person as an "other":** Mark Snyder and William B. Swann, "Hypothesis-Testing Processes in Social Interaction," *Journal of Personality and Social Psychology* 36, no. 11 (1978): 1202–12.

168 **seek out evidence that clashes:** Anne-Laure Sellier, Irene Scopelliti, and Carey K. Morewedge, "Debiasing Training Improves Decision Making in the Field," *Psychological Science* 30, no. 9 (2019): 1371–79.

169 **"more examples of career-women crashing":** A. V. Yader, "The Deadly Consequences of Feminist Propaganda in the US Navy," essay, Return of Kings, July 11, 2014, https://www.returnofkings.com/39218/the-deadly-consequences-of-feminist-propaganda-in-the-us-navy.

169 **"Theres [sic] a few biological studies":** "Talk: Kara Hultgreen," Wikiwand, Wikipedia: The Free Encyclopedia, https://www.wikiwand.com/en/Talk:Kara_Hultgreen#/%22she_crashed%22.

169 **We humans love to be right:** Described as one of many logical flaws that prevent sound reasoning in chapter 3.

170 **promoting peace instead of war:** Eran Halperin et al., "Can Emotion Regulation Change Political Attitudes in Intractable Conflicts? From the Laboratory to the Field," *Psychological Science* 24, no. 2 (2013): 106–11.

CHAPTER 10: RAISING INSUBORDINATE KIDS

173 **high school sophomore Hannah Watters:** Madeline Holcombe, "Georgia Student Who Posted Photo of a Crowded School Hallway and Called It 'Good and Necessary Trouble' Is No Longer Suspended, Her Mom Says," CNN, August 7, 2020, https://www.cnn.com/2020/08/07/us/georgia-teen-photo-crowded-school-hallway-trnd/index.html.

173 **The school had "ignorantly opened back up":** Lauren Strapagiel, "Two Students Say They Were Suspended from Their Georgia High School for Posting Photos of Crowded Hallways," *Buzzfeed News*, August 6, 2020, https://www.buzzfeednews.com/article/laurenstrapagiel/north-paulding-high-school-suspensions-for-hallway-photos.

174 **"I was concerned for the safety of everyone":** Holcombe, "Georgia Student."

174 **the superintendent acknowledged:** Holcombe, "Georgia Student."

174 **train youth to disagree, defy, and deviate:** On the parenting wish list, we want kids to be happy, intelligent, physically healthy, and functionally independent, with a wide range of virtues. I want to add the oft-forgotten member of the list: staying strong and committed when in a minority position. We want kids to be motivated to make their lives—and the lives of those around them—better. Conformity has its place when groups and society are working well. There is a time and place, however, for the spirit of dissent.

175 **Setting high standards and regularly affirming students' potential:** For a review, see Geoffrey L. Cohen and David K. Sherman, "The Psychology of Change: Self-Affirmation and Social Psychological Intervention," *Annual Review of Psychology* 65 (2014): 333–71. For a conceptual model, see Gregory M. Walton and Timothy

D. Wilson, "Wise Interventions: Psychological Remedies for Social and Personal Problems," *Psychological Review* 125, no. 5 (2018): 617–55. For an example of an effective performance-enhancing intervention, see David Scott Yeager et al., "Breaking the Cycle of Mistrust: Wise Interventions to Provide Critical Feedback across the Racial Divide," *Journal of Experimental Psychology: General* 143, no. 2 (2014): 804–24.

176 **"belonging uncertainty":** Gregory M. Walton and Geoffrey L. Cohen, "A Question of Belonging: Race, Social Fit, and Achievement," *Journal of Personality and Social Psychology* 92, no. 1 (2007): 82–96.

176 **Constantly gauging whether you fit in:** Mark R. Leary and Katrina P. Jongman-Sereno, "Social Anxiety as an Early Warning System: A Refinement and Extension of the Self-Presentation Theory of Social Anxiety," in *From Social Anxiety to Social Phobia: Multiple Perspectives*, ed. Stefan G. Hofmann and Patricia Marten DiBartolo (Boston: Allyn & Bacon, 2001), 579–97; Mark R. Leary, "Sociometer Theory," in *Handbook of Theories of Social Psychology*, ed. Paul A. Van Lange, Arie M. Kruglanski, and E. Tory Higgins (Thousand Oaks, CA: Sage, 2012), 141–59.

177 **let them hear from kids:** Gregory M. Walton and Shane T. Brady, "The Social-Belonging Intervention," in *Handbook of Wise Interventions: How Social Psychology Can Help People Change*, ed. Gregory M. Walton and Alia J. Crum (New York: Guilford Press, 2020).

177 **Lowering standards:** Roy F. Baumeister et al., "Does High Self-Esteem Cause Better Performance, Interpersonal Success, Happiness, or Healthier Lifestyles?," *Psychological Science in the Public Interest* 4, no. 1 (2003): 1–44.

177 **"I am not in control":** From the author's multiple interviews with Mark Murphy in 2019–2020 while working with him as a research coordinator for GripTape.

177 **an invitation to start a learning journey:** Because some youth are stumped trying to articulate their thoughts in writing, there is an option to submit videos as an alternative. Interviews with prior youth in the program (not adults) allow applicants another opportunity to express themselves in the most optimal manner.

178 **GripTape is agnostic toward content:** Judith M. Harackiewicz, Jessi L. Smith, and Stacy J. Priniski, "Interest Matters: The Importance of Promoting Interest in Education," *Policy Insights from the Behavioral and Brain Sciences* 3, no. 2 (2016): 220–27; Chris S. Hulleman et al., "Task Values, Achievement Goals, and Interest: An Integrative Analysis,"

Journal of Educational Psychology 100, no. 2 (2008): 398–416; Jennifer Teramoto Pedrotti, Lisa M. Edwards, and Shane J. Lopez, "Promoting Hope: Suggestions for School Counselors," *Professional School Counseling* 12, no. 2 (2008): 100–107.

178 **GripTape's methodology is extremely effective:** Maria Avetria et al., "In the Driver's Seat: Learning Report," GripTape, Youth Driving Learning, December 2018, New York, NY, https://griptape.org/wp-content/uploads/2018/12/2018-Learning-Report.pdf. The report is based on surveys and interviews with 450 youth (and their parents) from thirty states:

- 91 percent of youth said, "the experience changed the way they will approach learning in the future."
- 89 percent of youth strongly agreed that, "participating in the GripTape Challenge helped me discover a sense of purpose or direction in my life."
- Youth with low grades (Cs and Ds) and from socially disadvantaged environments were just as likely to complete the ten-week Learning Challenge as youth with high grades (As and Bs).
- 98 percent of youth strongly said they "know more about their own areas of strength and where they need to keep learning or improving."
- 97 percent of youth "were more confident they could get better at challenging things if they work hard."
- 81 percent recruited friends and peers to apply to the Learning Challenge.
- A single intervention offers teenagers greater awareness of their strengths, a mindset of curiosity and intellectual humility, and a lifelong learning mentality, while also helping them to discover a sense of purpose in life. Based on interviews six months to two years after the Learning Challenge ended, 91 percent always or frequently assessed the quality of their work and made improvements if needed, and 89 percent always or frequently adjusted their plans or goals based on their learnings or experiences. The teenagers gained agency and showed evidence of responding to feedback and setbacks with open-mindedness. The changes are not short term.

178 **when others let us feel safe to be ourselves:** Andrew J. Elliot and Harry T. Reis, "Attachment and Exploration in Adulthood," *Journal of Personality and Social Psychology* 85, no. 2 (2003): 317–31; Jeffrey D. Green and W. Keith Campbell, "Attachment and Exploration in Adults: Chronic and Contextual Accessibility," *Personality and Social*

Psychology Bulletin 26, no. 4 (2000): 452–61; Mario Mikulincer, "Adult Attachment Style and Information Processing: Individual Differences in Curiosity and Cognitive Closure," *Journal of Personality and Social Psychology* 72, no. 5 (1997): 1217–30.

179 **what we share becomes more interesting and meaningful:** Evan M. Kleiman et al., "Perceived Responsiveness during an Initial Social Interaction with a Stranger Predicts a Positive Memory Bias One Week Later," *Cognition and Emotion* 29, no. 2 (2015): 332–41; Samuel S. Monfort et al., "Capitalizing on the Success of Romantic Partners: A Laboratory Investigation on Subjective, Facial, and Physiological Emotional Processing," *Personality and Individual Differences* 68 (2014): 149–53.

179 **more curious and want to take more risks:** Brooke C. Feeney and Nancy L. Collins, "A New Look at Social Support: A Theoretical Perspective on Thriving through Relationships," *Personality and Social Psychology Review* 19, no. 2 (2015): 113–47; Shelly L. Gable and Harry T. Reis, "Good News! Capitalizing on Positive Events in an Interpersonal Context," in *Advances in Experimental Social Psychology*, vol. 42, ed. Mark Zanna (Cambridge, UK: Academic Press, 2010), 195–257; Harry T. Reis, "The Interpersonal Process Model of Intimacy: Maintaining Intimacy Through Self-Disclosure and Responsiveness" in *Foundations for Couples' Therapy: Research for the Real World*, ed. J. Fitzgerald (New York: Routledge, 2017), 216–25.

179 **If they feel uncomfortable:** Excerpted from my prior writings on this topic: Todd B. Kashdan, "Six Ways for Parents to Cultivate Strong, Curious, Creative Children," *Huffington Post*, September 3, 2009, https://www.huffpost.com/entry/six-ways-for-parents-to-c_b_249031.

179 **active engagement and an experience of joy:** Deena Skolnick Weisberg, Kathy Hirsh-Pasek, and Roberta Michnick Golinkoff, "Guided Play: Where Curricular Goals Meet a Playful Pedagogy," *Mind, Brain, and Education* 7, no. 2 (2013): 104–12.

179 **youth explore and discover best when they are in control:** Consider an example of what happens when learning is free of constraints such as adult directions and expectations: Aiyana K. Willard et al., "Explain This, Explore That: A Study of Parent–Child Interaction in a Children's Museum," *Child Development* 90, no. 5 (2019): e598—e617. Parents of four- to six-year-olds received minimal instructions on how to guide their child's learning through a gear machine exhibit at a local museum. Fifteen gears of different sizes sat disassembled on a table.

Participants had to attach the gears to a machine in different ways so that different functions would start up. Some parents received a single index card with instructions for controlling the learning experience, such as "Try asking them to explain how the gears work," "Ask them to tell you about the gears or to describe what happens when they interact with the gears in different ways." Other parents received a single index card with instructions for encouraging curious exploration, such as "Ask them to try new things with the gears. Urge them to interact with the gears in different ways. Suggest that they figure out how the gears work, or what will happen when a gear moves. Encourage them to experiment with how the gears work." Researchers surreptitiously observed the kids and parents, documenting behavior and conversation. When exploration was encouraged, children spent more time asking questions, connecting gears to the machines, and troubleshooting when gears would not spin or drifted apart, and parents offered more encouragement and spent less time telling them what to do. When parent control was encouraged, in contrast, kids spent six times as much time talking about machines and parents spent four times as much time troubleshooting ways to get the machine to operate. Essentially, parents took over the discovery and problem-solving portion of the exhibit. Most important, overbearing parental behavior did not translate into discernible educational gains: kids in both conditions did equally well in remembering what they had learned and in generalizing their understanding of how gears work when re-creating a brand-new machine in another room. See Claire Cook, Noah D. Goodman, and Laura E. Schulz, "Where Science Starts: Spontaneous Experiments in Preschoolers' Exploratory Play," *Cognition* 120, no. 3 (2011): 341–49; Daniel L. Schwartz et al., "Practicing versus Inventing with Contrasting Cases: The Effects of Telling First on Learning and Transfer," *Journal of Educational Psychology* 103, no. 4 (2011): 759–75; David Sobel and Jessica Sommerville, "The Importance of Discovery in Children's Causal Learning from Interventions," *Frontiers in Psychology* 1 (2010): 176. For a review, see Tamara Spiewak Toub et al., "Guided Play: A Solution to the Play versus Discovery Learning Dichotomy," in *Evolutionary Perspectives on Education and Child Development*, ed. David C. Geary and Daniel B. Berch (New York: Springer, 2016), 117–41.

180 **explain it to a peer:** David Duran, "Learning-by-Teaching: Evidence and Implications as a Pedagogical Mechanism," *Innovations in Education and Teaching International* 54, no. 5 (2017): 476–84; Logan

Fiorella and Richard E. Mayer, "Eight Ways to Promote Generative Learning," *Educational Psychology Review* 28, no. 4 (2016): 717–41; Logan Fiorella and Richard E. Mayer, "The Relative Benefits of Learning by Teaching and Teaching Expectancy," *Contemporary Educational Psychology* 38, no. 4 (2013): 281–88.

180 **What Adults Can Say and Do:** Researchers found that the adult behaviors on this list are the most strongly associated with children and adolescents feeling autonomous during a learning activity. These behaviors also produced youth who are more curious, attentive, and persistent during a learning activity, and who devote more effort, enjoy themselves, and boost performance. See Johnmarshall Reeve and Hyungshim Jang, "What Teachers Say and Do to Support Students' Autonomy during a Learning Activity," *Journal of Educational Psychology* 98, no. 1 (2006): 209–18. Adults can be effectively trained to drop their control agenda and support independent thinkers and doers. See Johnmarshall Reeve, "Autonomy Support as an Interpersonal Motivating Style: Is It Teachable?," *Contemporary Educational Psychology* 23, no. 3 (1998): 312–30.

182 **Six Questions That Encourage Kids:** The questions are modified, developmentally appropriate variants of the nine "tools for skeptical thinking" in chapter 12 "The Fine Art of Baloney Detection" of Carl Sagan and Ann Druyan, *The Demon-Haunted World: Science as a Candle in the Dark* (New York: Random House, 1995).

182 **Be wary when people start with the conclusion they want:** Steven J. Frenda et al., "False Memories of Fabricated Political Events," *Journal of Experimental Social Psychology* 49, no. 2 (2013): 280–86.

184 **the process of scientific discovery:** Yannis Hadzigeorgiou and Vassilios Garganourakis, "Using Nikola Tesla's Story and His Experiments as Presented in the Film 'The Prestige' to Promote Scientific Inquiry: A Report of an Action Research Project," *Interchange* 41 no. 4 (2010): 363–78; Yannis Hadzigeorgiou, Stephen Klassen, and Cathrine Froese Klassen, "Encouraging a 'Romantic Understanding' of Science: The Effect of the Nikola Tesla Story," *Science & Education* 21 no. 8 (2012): 1111–38.

184 **Both girls and boys showed a greater appreciation:** Hadzigeorgiou, Klassen, and Klassen, "Encouraging a 'Romantic Understanding' of Science."

185 **promoted psychological strengths:** Katherine Perrotta, "Pedagogical Conditions That Promote Historical Empathy with 'the

Elizabeth Jennings Project,'" *Social Studies Research and Practice* 13, no. 2 (2018): 129–46.

186 **it isn't just physical bravery:** Shane J. Lopez et al., "Folk Conceptualizations of Courage," in *Psychology of Courage: Modern Research on an Ancient Virtue*, ed. Cynthia L. S. Pury and Shane J. Lopez (Washington, DC: APA Press, 2010), 23–45; Christopher R. Rate, "Implicit Theories of Courage," *Journal of Positive Psychology* 2, no. 2 (2007): 80–98.

186 **they display *personal courage*:** Cynthia L. S. Pury, Robin M. Kowalski, and Jana Spearman, "Distinctions between General and Personal Courage," *Journal of Positive Psychology* 2, no. 2 (2007): 99–114.

187 **The defining quality of courage:** Stanley J. Rachman, "Fear and Courage," *Behavior Therapy* 15, no. 1 (1984): 109–20; Cooper R. Woodard and Cynthia L. S. Pury, "The Construct of Courage: Categorization and Measurement," *Consulting Psychology Journal: Practice and Research* 59, no. 2 (2007): 135–47.

187 **there are two ways of being courageous:** The formula listed along with other insights can be found in this underappreciated gem: Robert Biswas-Diener, *The Courage Quotient: How Science Can Make You Braver* (New York: John Wiley, 2012). As for the denominator, fear is only one mental obstacle that inhibits us from speaking out or standing up for a worthwhile reason. Other mental obstacles include depleted mental or physical energy, a sense of doubt, a lack of awareness, self-centeredness, and insufficient concern about others. This incomplete list of mental obstacles influences our perception of risk and danger. Addressing them can empower us to take deliberate action despite high perceived risk and fearful feelings.

187 **a fear of retaliation:** James A. Dungan, Liane Young, and Adam Waytz, "The Power of Moral Concerns in Predicting Whistleblowing Decisions," *Journal of Experimental Social Psychology* 85 (2019): 103848.

187 **why youth do not report bullying:** Wanda Cassidy, Margaret Jackson, and Karen N. Brown, "Sticks and Stones Can Break My Bones, but How Can Pixels Hurt Me? Students' Experiences with Cyber-Bullying," *School Psychology International* 30, no. 4 (2009): 383–402.

187 **series of small choices:** Harris, *ACT Made Simple.*

188 **think of themselves as heroes in waiting:** Elisabeth K. Heiner, "Fostering Heroism in Fourth- and Fifth-Grade Students," *Journal of Humanistic Psychology* 59, no. 4 (2019): 596–616.

188 **five factors that increase the odds of taking action:** Peter Fischer et al., "The Bystander-Effect: A Meta-Analytic Review on Bystander Intervention in Dangerous and Non-Dangerous Emergencies," *Psychological Bulletin* 137, no. 4 (2011): 517–37.

188 **break down conquering fears:** Stephane Bouchard et al., "Considerations in the Use of Exposure with Children," *Cognitive and Behavioral Practice* 11, no. 1 (2004): 56–65.

EPILOGUE

194 **it often takes about six to eight weeks:** Kate Cavanagh et al., "Can Mindfulness and Acceptance Be Learnt by Self-Help?: A Systematic Review and Meta-Analysis of Mindfulness and Acceptance-Based Self-Help Interventions," *Clinical Psychology Review* 34, no. 2 (2014): 118–29; Thomas Haug et al., "Self-Help Treatment of Anxiety Disorders: A Meta-Analysis and Meta-Regression of Effects and Potential Moderators," *Clinical Psychology Review* 32, no. 5 (2012): 425–45.

Index

Page numbers in *italics* refer to figures and tables.